Garden of Life

Sue Denney

CrossBooks™
A Division of LifeWay
1663 Liberty Drive
Bloomington, IN 47403
www.crossbooks.com
Phone: 1-866-879-0502

©2011 Sue Denney. All rights reserved.

No part of this book may be reproduced, stored in a retrieval system, or transmitted by any means without the written permission of the author.

First published by CrossBooks 6/2/2011

ISBN: 978-1-6150-7901-8 (sc)

Printed in the United States of America

This book is printed on acid-free paper.

Any people depicted in stock imagery provided by Thinkstock are models, and such images are being used for illustrative purposes only.

Certain stock imagery © Thinkstock.

Because of the dynamic nature of the Internet, any web addresses or links contained in this book may have changed since publication and may no longer be valid. The views expressed in this work are solely those of the author and do not necessarily reflect the views of the publisher, and the publisher hereby disclaims any responsibility for them.

Contents

Introduction	2
Garden of Life	4
Recognizing weeds in the Garden of Life	6
Problems weeds cause	8
Removing the weeds	10
Results of a weeded garden	12
God's Garden	14

Introduction

A couple of years ago my family decided to grow a vegetable garden. I got my children involved preparing the soil, removing all the rock and weeds. We bought the necessary tools and plant food. We went shopping for the seeds and plants. The day came when we planted our garden.

Every few days we would look for signs of growth. The day we saw our little plants coming up through the soil, we were so excited.

As the plants started growing, we begin to see a few weeds. It was easy to pull the weeds up and destroy them. We talked about the day we could pick our vegetables and eat them. As our garden grew so did the weeds. What started as a few weeds became many weeds that had to be removed and destroyed as quickly as possible. When the garden was at its peak, I had to have surgery and couldn't take care of the garden for several weeks. When I was able to see our garden again, weeds were everywhere. You could barely see the vegetables. Our garden was overtaken with weeds.

Garden of Life

Life is like a garden. You have to keep the weeds out for you to grow physically, emotionally, and spiritually. Weeds are those lies that are planted during childhood or during a traumatic experience. Weeds of childhood abuse, emotional abuse, neglect, victims of bullying and name calling leave very little space for healthy growth in life's garden. Weeds in your adult garden of life could be from domestic violence, rape, or a traumatic experience.

As children, teenagers, and adults, you experience weeds that have to be recognized and removed from your garden of life. You can be aware of the weeds or they can be totally hiden among your everyday life. Many times you try to remove the weeds by using drugs or alcohol. You have bad relationships and sexual problems. The weeds stay gone for a short time only to come back. The weeds have to be dug up at the roots and destroyed.

Recognizing weeds in the Garden of Life

There are some weeds that are pleasant to look at but they are still weeds. In your life's garden, weeds hide themselves in your daily life. These weeds can trigger panic attacks, physical pain and melt downs. Weeds that hide in certain smells, locations, or pieces of clothing can cause havoc in everyday life.

Problems weeds cause

Weeds or lies can cause many problems in your life's garden. Physical weeds may cause high blood pressure, eating disorders, sleep disorders, or stomach problems. Emotional weeds may cause depression, low self-esteem, loneliness, insecurity, and thoughts of suicide.

Weeds from traumatic experiences such as rape may cause poor relationship with sexual partners and fear of not being believed you were raped.

Weeds from domestic violence may cause lack of self confidence, loneliness, and isolation.

Removing the weeds

Each year thousands of dollars are spent on weed killers. You see people in their gardens working hard trying to destroy the weeds.

In your garden of life you may spend money and time covering up the weeds or ignoring them.

Removing weeds is a process that must take place for there to be a healthy beautiful garden of life.

1. Recognize you have weeds or lies in your garden
2. Have a desire to remove the weeds or lies
3. Find the proper tool: A counselor, pastor, or support group
4. Digging down to the roots

Some weeds can be pulled up easily but some weeds have to be dug up. Sometimes you have to experience physical pain to get to the root.

Reliving the memories can be hard and scary. You may want to quit before you get to the roots but to have a beautiful garden, you have to remove the weeds at the roots.

Results of a weeded garden

When you remove the weeds of life you get a beautiful productive garden of love, joy, peace, patience, kindness, and goodness. You can have a faithful, gentle, and self-control life.

When you do not remove the weeds of life you may get a life full of sadness, hatred, full of jealousy, and fits of anger. Many times you become victims over and over again because of poor choices of weed killing.

What choice of weed killer are you going to use today?

God's Garden

God wants you to have a healthy and happy life. You can have a personal relationship with Him by:

Admitting to God that you are a sinner

Repent turning away from your sins

Believe by faith that Jesus is God's Son and accept Jesus gift of forgiveness from sin

Confess your faith in Jesus Christ as Savior and Lord

If you are choosing to believe Jesus died for your sins and to receive new life through Him, pray a prayer asking Jesus to forgive you of your sins and to live in your heart.

CPSIA information can be obtained
at www.ICGtesting.com
232166LV00002BC

9 781615 079018

WAVERLEY STEAM NAVIGATION COMPANY

WAVERLEY STEAM NAVIGATION COMPANY

COMPILED BY ALISTAIR DEAYTON AND IAIN QUINN

AMBERLEY

We dedicate this book to the WSN Co. Ltd directors who have given so much time and effort to keep Waverley in steam, some no longer with us and many retired. We acknowledge them all.

First published 2014

Amberley Publishing
The Hill, Stroud
Gloucestershire, GL5 4EP

www.amberley-books.com

Copyright © Alistair Deayton and Iain Quinn 2014

The right of Alistair Deayton and Iain Quinn to be identified as the Authors of this work has been asserted in accordance with the Copyrights, Designs and Patents Act 1988.

All rights reserved. No part of this book may be reprinted or reproduced or utilised in any form or by any electronic, mechanical or other means, now known or hereafter invented, including photocopying and recording, or in any information storage or retrieval system, without the permission in writing from the Publishers.

British Library Cataloguing in Publication Data.
A catalogue record for this book is available from the British Library.

ISBN (print) 978 1 4456 4155 3
ISBN (ebook) 978 1 4456 4169 0

Typeset in 10pt on 12pt Sabon.
Typesetting and Origination by Amberley Publishing.
Printed in the UK.

Contents

Introduction – Iain Quinn	7
The Scottish Transport Group Years – John Whittle	11
Reflections – Douglas McGowan	13
Forty Years of *Waverley* Preservation – Peter Reid	19
A Pleasure Steamer Business – Terry Sylvester	26
What is a Timetable? – Terry Sylvester	44
Ports, Piers and Harbours Called at by *Waverley*, 1947–2014 – Terry Sylvester, Iain Quinn and Alistair Deayton	48
Events & Opportunities – Terry Sylvester	57
A Captain's Memories: Part 1 In the Beginning 1974/75	60
A Captain's Memories: Part 2 The Formative Years 1976–78	69
A Captain's Memories: Part 3 Building the Business 1979–89	80
A Captain's Memories: Part 4 Other Ships and Projects	109
A Captain's Memories: Part 5 The Slow Decline 1990–98	128
A Captain's Memories: Part 6 A New Beginning 1999 Onwards	137
Forty Years of Waverley Steam Navigation Company: A Purser's Eye View of the Early Years – Cameron Marshall	139
Waverley Connections – Captain Murray Paterson	155
Prince Ivanhoe Memories – Jim Buchanan	165
Waverley Shop – Peter Brackenridge	168
The *Waverley* Triple Expansion Engine Model – Robert McLuckie	170
Waverley's Preservation: An Enthusiast's View – Alistair Deayton	173
Crew Photos	176
Timetables and Publicity	181
Further Reading	188
Final Thoughts	190
Photographic Credits and Acknowledgments	191
Who Owns *Waverley* and *Balmoral*?	192
Business Principles – Terry Sylvester	192

An aerial view of Dungeness, showing a full crowd of passengers on board.

Introduction

From Evanships to Waverley Steam Navigation Co. Ltd and a celebration of forty years of owning *Waverley*, the last sea-going paddle steamer in the world. This is the compelling story of it all: the searching, powerful and sheer determination of the men who did it. Getting *Waverley* to steam again in 1975 was the result of the will to do it, enthusiasm and the nerve to withstand hard knocks and major criticism and face them all square on. That they did and we all hope you enjoy the journey of the men who got it all started and took *Waverley* into a new and challenging life.

By way of setting the scene I go back to 1974. Why preserve a paddle steamer? Well, why not? This part of the world called the Firth of Clyde is by far the finest cruising area in which to operate her, with lochs, the Kyles and a river journey into the city of Glasgow. In 1974 Caledonian MacBrayne Ltd was only operating *Queen Mary II*, *King George V* and *Maid of the Loch*, but on the Clyde the *Mary*'s operation was poor, with only the Kyles of Bute as a possible destination. Not since 1812 and Henry Bell's *Comet* had there been a summer with no paddle steamer in service on the Clyde. All that was to change quickly, thanks to the WSN Co. Ltd and its founding fathers. Bear in mind that through all of this, WSN had no office, staff, crew or cash, just PS *Waverley*. From day one in November 1973 through to the handover in August 1974, to sailing time with VIPs on that Thursday in May 1975, so much had turned into reality. Operation had now arrived. There was excitement, I'm sure, but filled with some fear and trepidation, only natural for those who got it to 22 May 1975 and a new life of cruising.

John, Douglas, Terry, Peter and the other contributors have put it into print. However, WSN owes so much to the many friends, enthusiasts and councils I can't name them all, but here are a few with the rider that if you aren't named please accept our apology and thanks:

Western Ferries (for crew)
Weir's Pumps
Glasgow Corporation (1974–5), City of Glasgow District Council (1975–96), Glasgow City Council (1996 to date): Sir William Gray and councillors from 1974 to date
Successive Lord Provosts since Sir William

Councillors within City Chambers, Glasgow and similar bodies UK-wide who have contributed

The old Strathclyde Regional Council

Pier masters, harbour authorities and staff UK-wide, in particular those manned piers voluntarily

PSPS, for much financial support down the years, and other like-minded groups for donations over the years

Mr and Mrs Weir (lottery winners from Largs), for considerable funds to help *Waverley* continue

All directors of WSN down the years – what a contribution

Chairmen: Mr J. T. Sylvester, Mr I. M. MacLeod, Dr N. J. James. Yes, only three since 1974. Very credible

The list is endless but everyone deserves huge credit and all involved with this story acknowledge with grateful thanks those who have and continue to support WSN, a registered charity in Scotland, No. SC005832.

Waverley did sail again in 1975 and busked through those days and weeks and difficult winters until the business had some funds.

It never fails to impress me that within five years, re-boilering was complete and a second ship purchased, all on the back of the Gantocks grounding in 1977 – that alone would see attitudes today of 'it's finished'. 1981, 82 and 83 were monumental seasons with Round Britain. 1984 saw the tenth year, 1994 the twentieth year, 2004 the thirtieth year and look, now *Waverley* brings herself another birthday. I am very proud of WSN Co. Ltd and the 'fight we must' attitudes of its directors; *Waverley* is a prized gem with unrivalled competition anywhere in the UK. WSN must fight on and I am sure they will. Waverley Excursions Ltd is another story. That company came about in 1980 from the baby, Waverley (Cruises) Ltd, which never got started. Excursions is not a charity; they operate the business and the story of the operator is not told in this publication.

Waverley Steam's success continues thanks to you, the passengers, enthusiasts, the many who donate individually and councils, etc.

Can *Waverley* go on? Yes is the answer, as in 1975 – with will, determination and enthusiasm, passengers and those donations, *Waverley* can go on. Crew and sympathetic regulatory bodies have been vital and they all deserve acknowledgement.

Waverley is steel and wood brought to life by human hand.

History through *Waverley* is told daily and those owning and operating must remember that you can't rewrite history. This publication is a factual account of their story.

Captains 1975–2000

D. L. Neill
J. Addison
J. M. Paterson

S. P. Michel
G. Gellatly
S. P. Colledge
P. C. Tambling
E. C. Davies
K. C. Fraser

The captains are included only up to 2000 for the continuity of the publication. We acknowledge the others who have continued the good work and those who have given more of their time than the call of duty warrants to WSN. Post-2000 we leave to another time and perhaps a follow-up volume.

To countless Chief Officers, pursers, engineers and crew, chief stewards and catering managers, huge thanks.

As for myself, I was an avid follower of WSN's life from 1974/5 and admired the growth of the business from nothing to its peak in the 1980s; I was then active in the heart of it as *Waverley*'s announcer from 1989 to 2009 inclusive, then quartermaster from 1993 to 2009 inclusive; until 2007 I was on a voluntary/certificated basis, and then on a retainer from 2007 to 2009. It was a huge privilege to serve in both positions with the company with all who allowed it to happen. In all my time, it was super fun in among the serious 'must-do' parts. I made special speeches for great contributors to WSN, and those great days with 7–800 passengers aboard made giving the commentary very memorable.

Life moves on and I sail the same now as I did in 1975, with an annual season ticket. Nothing has changed there and I love it as I did then. Sadly, the atmosphere has changed and that too must be noted. The passenger numbers aren't as high, yes, and a general decline is happening, but we keep smiling.

To WSN at forty! You all deserve our sincere thanks for some very special occasions aboard the magnificent *Waverley*, last of her kind in the world – the last surviving Clyde paddle steamer.

Iain Quinn

Waverley in CalMac livery in 1973, at Gourock.

The Scottish Transport Group Years

Moving to Gourock in 1969 to take over the management of the Caledonian Steam Packet Company (later to merge with David MacBrayne Ltd to form Caledonian MacBrayne) was a significant turning point in my career. It was the start of both an enduring affection for the ships and the sobering realisation that all was far from well financially.

The fleet included five vessels devoted to excursion sailings: three paddle steamers and two turbine steamers. These were magnificent vessels which, with others like them, had given excellent service on the Clyde and Loch Lomond, but, the ever-increasing demands of vehicle traffic having rendered them no longer adequate for the regular ferry services, they now incurred the punishing costs of a lengthy winter lay-up. Moreover, being more suited to an earlier age, when fuel and labour were less expensive, the revenue was inadequate to support them all.

Some contraction was inevitable so the paddle steamer *Caledonia* and the turbine steamer *Duchess of Hamilton* were early casualties. Plans by her new owners to use the *Duchess* as a floating restaurant on the Clyde collapsed and, sadly, she was sold on for scrap. *Caledonia*, however, was more successful in a similar capacity on the Thames until she was, unfortunately, destroyed by fire. More happily, her engine has been preserved in a steam museum in Surrey, where it is occasionally steamed using a portable boiler.

This left the Clyde excursion sailings in the hands of the paddle steamer *Waverley* and the turbine steamer *Queen Mary II*, while the paddle steamer *Maid of the Loch* continued on Loch Lomond.

Here, I gladly acknowledge the support our efforts to retain these vessels received from the various enthusiast groups. Revenue benefited from their frequent charters and few sailings failed to attract the patronage of their members.

The Paddle Steamer Preservation Society (PSPS), understandably, concentrated their support on the two paddle steamers and a Waverley Study Group, led by Douglas McGowan and Terry Sylvester, was established to assist in broadening the appeal of the ship. I had regular meetings with Douglas and Terry to discuss progress and their suggestions.

In his excellent book *Waverley: Paddler for a Pound*, Douglas comments, perhaps with some surprise, that despite the heavy demands on my time, I 'chose to listen willingly to a "couple of steamer nutters" [his description, not mine] at various meetings over four years'. The reason is simple. Like most enthusiasts, they took a keen interest and were genuinely anxious to help. Moreover, I had learnt long before that nobody, including me, has a monopoly of original thought and problems are more readily overcome by encouraging others to help seek solutions.

I also had the advantage of a very positive contribution from the efficient and enthusiastic management team. We were, however, plagued by two difficult problems. Rampant inflation during the early 1970s escalated operating costs faster than revenue could grow with acceptable fare increases. Added to that, the vagaries of the Scottish climate all too often meant that dismal weather deterred potential custom.

At the end of the 1973 season, we had to 'bite the bullet' for it was clear that one ship had to go. The choice was inevitable. *Waverley* had lost several days off service due to boiler problems in both 1972 and 1973 and the engineers were concerned that without substantial (and costly) re-tubing, the problem would worsen. Moreover, *Queen Mary* had recently been extensively refurbished and had the larger passenger capacity.

In discussion with Moris Little, the Caledonian MacBrayne chairman, it was agreed that the commercial case for withdrawing *Waverley* was undeniable. But she was the last of her kind, historically important, and selling her for scrap was unappealing. Becoming another floating restaurant wasn't attractive, so how could her survival be secured? Having discussed the contribution the PSPS had made, it was agreed to offer *Waverley* to the Paddle Steamer Preservation Society. This was, of course, subject to approval by Caledonian MacBrayne's parent company, Scottish Transport Group. To Moris Little's credit, he quickly secured approval and in November 1973 I made the offer at a memorable meeting with Douglas McGowan.

At another memorable event, on 8 August 1974, Colonel Thomas, chairman of Scottish Transport Group, and I met Douglas and Terry to formally hand over the vessel in return for the princely sum of £1. Incidentally, Colonel Thomas donated that sum to the PSPS, thus making *Waverley* an outright gift.

It was my impression that the Scottish Transport Group Board believed *Waverley* would be tied up somewhere or 'embedded in a concrete base' to serve as the society headquarters and museum. I was very much aware, however, that the society had already preserved and was in the course of restoring the paddle steamer *Kingswear Castle* and surmised they could access funds and resources unavailable to Caledonian MacBrayne which could enable them to return *Waverley* to service. Consequently, the transfer agreement included a clause forbidding operation of *Waverley* in direct competition with any Caledonian MacBrayne activity! That clause was never invoked to prevent Clyde excursions by *Waverley* but enabled both of us to avoid treading on each other's toes.

My expectation proved correct for, thanks to the dedication and determination of the society members, sufficient funds were raised to enable *Waverley* to inaugurate operation in preservation on 22 May 1975, the start of an illustrious second career. Few could have anticipated that she would still be sailing forty years after the formal handover. Every tribute is due to those whose hard work, perseverance and sheer 'cussedness' has made this possible. I am glad to have this opportunity to express my gratitude to them for vindicating the decision to hand *Waverley* to them for preservation and to wish them every success in maintaining their efforts to keep *Waverley* sailing for many more years to come.

N. J. D. Whittle,
Former General Manager, Caledonian MacBrayne

Reflections

It is important to remember that without a Scottish Branch of the Paddle Steamer Preservation Society (PSPS), it is unlikely that Caledonian MacBrayne would have proceeded with their famous 'gift'. So how and when was the Scottish Branch launched?

I joined the PSPS in 1966. I was already a member of the Clyde River Steamer Club but their objectives did not extend to preservation. At that time, the PSPS had branches in London, Wessex and the Bristol Channel, but no representation north of the border. I viewed this as a very significant omission and as the DEPV *Talisman* was being withdrawn from service and sent to Arnott Young's breakers yard at Dalmuir, I decided that I could simply not stand aside and witness the similar destruction of our two remaining Clyde paddlers, *Caledonia* and *Waverley*. Furthermore, the Clyde was the birthplace of the passenger steamship, made famous by Henry Bell's *Comet* in 1812!

By October 1969, the Denny paddler *Caledonia* was subsequently taken out of service and laid up and so, encouraged by PSPS colleagues in the south and in particular by my good friend Chris Phillips, at that time National Secretary, a meeting was called of existing PSPS members resident in Scotland to launch a Scottish Branch. This meeting was held in the Christian Institute building in Glasgow's Bath Street and was attended by twenty-five brave souls! Maybe you were one of them? These days, the branch boasts a membership of over 700 and vies with the London Branch for having the most members.

Only a few months later, in May 1970, the PSPS started a relationship with the Caledonian Steam Packet Co. (forerunner of Caledonian MacBrayne) by chartering the *Waverley*. Further charter sailings followed over the next three years, including the *Maid of the Loch* on Loch Lomond. During this period, Terry Sylvester and I started to have meetings with John Whittle, General Manager of CSP/CalMac to encourage the company to market the *Waverley* differently to other members of their fleet. These positive discussions and the good relationship which was established, led to that magnificent gesture of the 'paddler for a pound'.

It is difficult to believe that *Waverley* is now in her fortieth season as a preserved steamer. Why is it difficult to believe? Because she survived her first season in 1975 despite boiler problems, paddle problems, crew problems and a huge amount of inexperience on the part of the ship's officers and crew and the brand new board of directors who had always enjoyed the pleasures of sailing on a paddle steamer, but had simply no track record in either owning one or indeed operating one.

It is also difficult to believe because many enthusiasts of the day forty years ago, including some very notable ones, had written us off before we had turned a paddle! Even after we had been in service for a few weeks, only the most optimistic supporter wearing rose-tinted spectacles would have given us more than one season. It's hard to admit, even now, but I might even have fallen into the latter category myself as we came up against obstacle after obstacle. Captain David Neill and Second Engineer Ken Blacklock must take a huge amount of credit for keeping the show on the road as we faced countless challenges. David in particular had an amazing determination to succeed, with a tremendous commitment that infected us all. There was simply no way we were going to fail: such a huge effort had been invested in setting up the business and preparing the ship that I can honestly say that failure was never an option and was never at any time discussed.

We were a good team in those early formative years, all focussed on the same task, all headed in the same direction. No politics, no external interference: we simply got on with the job in hand. We all had passion in abundance.

On that sunny afternoon in May 1975 when *Waverley* left the James Watt Dock, Greenock, for compass adjustment and trials, it was a very tense Douglas McGowan who stood alongside David Neill as he edged the old girl out of the dock, a tricky manoeuvre at the best of times, but even more nerve-wracking when you've never handled a paddler before! I needn't have worried – David completed the manoeuvre as if he had done it a hundred times before! I think I was more nervous than he was!

That determination to succeed was highlighted on only our second day in public service, Sunday 25 May. The previous day, on charter to the Paddle Steamer Preservation Society, she famously returned to Glasgow at 0355 in the morning, following a major problem with the starboard paddle wheel in Loch Fyne. Standing on Largs pier at 1 p.m. with my wife the following day, I said to her, 'Don't hold your breath, it will be a miracle if she sails today, following last night's adventure.' And yet, the words were hardly out of my mouth when lo and behold, she appeared round the point on her approach to Largs, bang on time.

I have been asked many times why Caledonian MacBrayne gifted the steamer to the Paddle Steamer Preservation Society. Some commentators at the time thought it was a neat way of avoiding the inevitable bad press of sending a unique part of our maritime heritage to the knacker's yard. Me? I believe it was a genuine gesture on the part of the Scottish Transport Group (CalMac's parent) to give *Waverley* some kind of future in the ownership of an organisation with which they had not only built some kind of fledgling relationship but which they also trusted. Terry Sylvester and I, over quite a long period of time, had a number of friendly and constructive meetings with John Whittle, general manager of the Caledonian Steam Packet Company, which became Caledonian MacBrayne in 1973, *Waverley*'s last summer in public ownership.

There is no doubt (and this has since been confirmed to me by John Whittle in recent times) that the trust shown towards Terry and I during this period was a major ingredient in the magnanimous gesture which was to follow forty years later.

We must never forget that without this incredible 'Paddler for a Pound' moment, it is most unlikely that any kind of preservation move with *Waverley* could have got off the ground. It is also interesting to reflect on those heady days of 1974, when the sheer shock of the gesture immediately led to thoughts of static preservation. A static exhibit in a Glasgow dock, perhaps a floating museum of some kind that the PSPS could use for our monthly meetings: these were the initial thoughts going through both Terry's mind and my own. But not for long! Soon, the prospect of actually having a go at operating the ship became more appealing and realistic.

My own duties and responsibilities in 1975 were many and varied. Firstly, during 1974, my primary task was to seek sponsorship from about 100 different companies, either to donate labour and materials or supply at cost. The companies I approached were many and varied from Esso to Weir's Pumps to Armitage Shanks to Scott's Ship Repairers to White Horse Whisky etc., etc. White Horse was the first to respond. It helped that their PR manager was a steamer enthusiast! The responses were all supportive and without that support, it is dubious whether we could have realised our objective of returning the ship to service. I was responsible for the recruitment of the Purser's Department. Harold Jordan was our first Chief Purser. Harold had many years' experience as purser on the famous MacBrayne ships, most recently on the *King George V*. Assistant Pursers were Cameron Marshall, Derek Peters, Mark Beveridge and Graham Macleod.

I was responsible for the creation of a souvenir shop, stocking it and staffing it with volunteers. Previously (and rather curiously), the *Waverley* under CalMac did not boast a shop (unlike the turbine steamers). I was convinced that if we were successful as a business, there would be a market for 'Waverley Souvenirs'. And so a space between the aft gents toilet and the entrance to the dining saloon, previously used I think for storing deck chairs, was established as our new 'Retail Emporium'. While we were in the Garvel Dry-Dock at Greenock in February 1975, the Scott's sign writer created a very attractive 'Souvenir Shop' sign which was positioned above the shop. My next task was to source an attractive selection of souvenirs – postcards, books, mugs, pencils, rubbers, notebooks, hats, confectionery, etc., etc. And so a business and trading relationship was established with a myriad of suppliers, the majority willing to supply their goods at a specially discounted rate as they too wanted the *Waverley* to succeed. The confectionery aspect of stocking the shop was no problem – it was the one area in which I knew what I was talking about! To 'add value' to buying a souvenir postcard on board, I was able to persuade the Royal Mail to donate a Victorian post-box from Scone in Perthshire, which was positioned opposite the shop. I sourced a special rubber stamp reading: 'Posted on board paddle steamer Waverley, the last sea-going paddle steamer in the world.' Postcards posted on board were stamped by the purser and posted ashore. This tradition is maintained today. The shop was run in 1975 by three dedicated volunteers – Jean Teviotdale and Reg and Bunty Collinson. All worked tirelessly to make the shop a success and it proved to be a key source of income, as it is today. Reg painted stones from the seashore to sell in the shop as well as miniature models, which he made. Bits of old paddle float and sundry discarded items from the engine room were crafted into brass table lamps and ornaments, all proceeds to the preservation effort!

Flags were my next *bête noir*. Don't ask why I got involved with the procurement of flags as I have absolutely no idea! My trusty flag supplier was a small family firm based in

Glasgow's Admiral Street called McSymon & Potter. They were real craftsmen supplying good quality flags which invariably lasted a season or more. In 1975, a name pennant or house flag cost us £25. I would hazard a guess that today that would be at least £300! However, as *Waverley* does not seem able to fly either a name pennant or house flag these days, an immediate cost saving is evident! At the end of the season, we would auction off the old flags to raise money.

On-board entertainment was next on the list: I approached William Tennant, who had led the last Clyde steamer band on *Duchess of Hamilton*, and latterly on *Waverley* in 1972 and 1973. He agreed for his trio to perform aboard *Waverley* in 1975, subject to permission being granted to 'rattle his box' around the decks! I felt this was very much part of the traditional Clyde steamer experience. I also engaged numerous silver bands from all over Scotland and several from abroad, including Norway and Sweden, to entertain our passengers. They proved very popular although feeding them all proved something of a nightmare!

I was responsible for first point of contact and local liaison and meetings with local councils, tourist bodies and other potential funders. This was a key role and one which took up much of my time, especially during 1974 and 1975. At times, it seriously competed with my full time job in the world of chocolate!

And last, but by no means least, I was responsible for PR, media contacts, press releases and press conferences. Terry Sylvester was responsible for getting feet up gangways, advertising and creation of timetables and I was the local guy on the spot, endeavouring to keep the press on side. Again, this was very time consuming but it was rewarding over the years to observe a number of typically jaundiced, sceptical 'hacks' being gradually converted to fully blown '*Waverley* nutters'! Some of them are still supporters today, forty years later.

I suspect that when we started operations on 22 May 1975, there must have been an element of embarrassment at CalMac HQ. I don't think they believed for one minute we would actually operate the ship, but, to be fair, neither did we … to begin with!

Some forty-five years on from the day we first met, I am delighted that my 'partner in crime' Terry Sylvester and I remain very firm friends, perhaps not surprising given we both came from a commercial and sales background. We don't always agree on absolutely everything but always respect each other's point of view. I often describe us as 'blood brothers', with one of us knowing what the other is going to say before he says it! Sometimes, after a one-and-a-half-hour phone conversation with Terry, I do wish he would say it in a shorter time (sorry Terry!). Even today, he still has amazing drive and energy and served as a director of Waverley Steam Navigation Company until June 2014.

I am also delighted to say that John Whittle and I still keep in touch and we quite recently enjoyed a lovely meal together in Glasgow, reminiscing about the 1970s.

What has been achieved? I believe, forty years of giving a unique kind of pleasure and education to over 5 million people. We have not only preserved the world's last sea-going paddler: we have, importantly, preserved the only way to see Britain's coastline from a large excursion vessel. That should never be forgotten. We have also kept numerous piers open and been the reason for many others to be refurbished and reopened.

How do I feel when I step aboard these days? I feel a huge sense of pride. Pride that many moons ago, I played a part in preserving this maritime icon. Nothing gives me more pleasure than to see the ship full on a sunny summer's day (yes, they do still occasionally exist!), watching families on deck enjoying the ship, enjoying the scenery, enjoying the ambience and generally having a special and memorable day out. It makes me proud to see dads explain the mystery of the triple expansion engine to their offspring and watching the youngsters mesmerised by those polished crankshafts whirling round. And I always get a special tingle running down the back of my neck when I take any of our five grandchildren on board to experience the delights of yesteryear. That is really what we have preserved for future generations to experience and enjoy.

Despite all the pressures of starting up a brand-new business and appointing personnel, we did have lots of fun and there were many comical moments in 1975. For instance, the day old Alec McLeod, one of our ABs, lured a seagull into his clutches and carried it squawking and shrieking into a very packed dining saloon, passing all the bewildered diners and into the galley where, out of sight, he released the petrified bird into its natural habitat. Naturally, passengers assumed it was going to be the key ingredient in the following day's seagull curry. Unfortunately, and encouraged no doubt by his audience, Alec continued with this party trick until he had to be told to resist further temptation. Presumably, our catering sales were being affected.

Still in the dining saloon, there was the day in July when the old galley chimney became blocked during a very busy lunchtime. Bear in mind that up to 100 passengers per sitting had to be served from an ancient galley which had not really changed since 1947. There was no AC, no proper refrigeration and fresh supplies had to be loaded daily: a far cry from the relatively modern facilities we have today. All the cooking was done on a coal-fired range and the cook's ability to adjust the heat was extremely limited. So picture the scene on this particularly busy day when the galley chimney became blocked. It had probably not been swept since 1947 and it may have been overlooked during the February 1975 refit. Anyway, within seconds, the galley filled with thick black smoke which quickly spread into the dining saloon. We had no choice but to evacuate all passengers from the dining saloon, cancel catering for the rest of the day, quickly extinguish the fire and call in the chimney sweep that evening!

One of the funniest incidents that happened to me personally took place towards the end of our first season, in September 1975. The steamer had 1,000 passengers on board and there was a large party of about 300 from a social club based in Glasgow's east end. There was a good atmosphere on board and many members of the special party had been in the White Horse Whisky bar since Rothesay and were somewhat past their sell-by date. It had been a challenging season to put it mildly, full of trials and tribulations, and after a long day helping out in the souvenir shop, I descended to the bar with my very good friend Joe McKendrick (sadly no longer with us) to have a 'quiet' refreshment and ponder upon the season's positives and negatives. What greeted us was a packed, smoky bar (remember those days?) with an inebriated 'choir' screeching at the top of their voices a dubious melody which vaguely resembled 'I Belong to Glasgow'. A very large bearded chap was sitting in the corner, slumped over a battered accordion. As the late Eric Morecambe would have said, 'He was playing all the right notes, but not necessarily in the right order.'

Joe and I rather sheepishly sat beside what appeared to be the choirmaster, trying very hard not to get noticed.

'Are you all right there Jim?' he asked, looking straight at me. 'Yes, fine thank you', I replied, trying to avoid eye contact and his Tennent's Lager dragon breath. About ten minutes passed, by which time we had graduated to 'The Northern Lights of Old Aberdeen'. 'What's up Jim?' my friend enquired in somewhat aggressive tones. 'Nothing', I responded, sorely tempted to advise him that my name was not Jim. 'Yer nae singin', Jim.' By this time, there was a slightly threatening note in his voice. 'I'm not a very good singer actually', was my pathetic reply, hoping this might placate him. And that was the moment it happened. 'You know what you are, don't you Jim?' I thought, 'Oh my God, what's coming next?' 'You're just a stuck-up c---'. Immediately, my trusty friend Joe spoke up and leapt to my defence. 'You can't talk to my friend like that. Don't you know who he is?' 'Who the f--- is he then?' came the riposte. 'He is the man that bought this ship, the *Waverley*, for £1', Joe countered. There was a brief silence. 'Aye that'll be b------ right!' Joe then rushed upstairs, grabbed a souvenir booklet from the shop, returned to the bar and turned to the page of yours truly handing over the pound note. Another stunned silence. Our hairy friend looked at the picture, then looked at me, then looked again at the picture. 'Jesus Christ Jim, ah cannae believe it!' showing the booklet to all his friends. 'I'm really sorry Jim, put it there. Ah had no idea. Can ah get you a pint?'

So, what of the future? It is no secret that operating an elderly paddle steamer in the twenty-first century is becoming ever more challenging; more and more regulation, coupled with the challenge of sourcing experienced steam engineers and other officers; crumbling piers, the cost of fuel and the biggest challenge of all – the constant battle to match revenue with expenditure. What appears to be changing weather patterns in recent summers adds to the challenges.

I have always said that the longer we can keep this unique piece of maritime history sailing, the more special and unique she becomes. Nothing lasts forever and of course it will be a great shame when those two giant paddle wheels turn no more. Then it will be the right time to ponder what we originally considered forty years ago – some kind of static role for the ship. But we are certainly not there yet and every effort must go into maintaining this living museum. After all, stuffed and mounted ... not quite the same, is it?

Regrets? Only one, actually. On 8 August 1974, when Sir Patrick Thomas took that pristine Royal Bank of Scotland note from his wallet, gave it to me and said, 'We want this to be an outright gift, so here is the £1', of course, I then gave it back to him. But why on earth did I not have the presence of mind to ask for it back as a souvenir? I could have sold it years later on eBay! I might have become a millionaire!

Douglas McGowan
2 April 2014

Forty Years of *Waverley* Preservation

I had always been interested in Clyde steamers, having lived in Gourock from a baby and been taken down to Gourock Pier in my pram on almost a daily basis.

At the age of eleven I moved to Wishaw, in darkest Lanarkshire, as my dad became manager of the Clydesdale Bank branch in the neighbouring village of Newmains. We returned to Gourock, on holiday, and I was able to obtain an eight-day runabout ticket on the Clyde steamers.

I attended secondary school at Wishaw High School and on leaving there started a five-year apprenticeship as a chartered accountant with a firm in Glasgow. Once I qualified, I worked abroad for a few months (in Berwick-upon-Tweed) then became assistant accountant with W. Alexander & Sons (Midland) Ltd, a bus company that was part of the newly emerging Scottish Bus Group (part of the Scottish Transport Group) and was based in Camelon, Falkirk. I then moved to become the last chief accountant with David MacBrayne Ltd, being based at the Travel Centre at 302 Buchanan Street, Glasgow.

At this time David MacBrayne's cargo shipping service was being run down, with cargo being transferred to road, and MacBrayne Haulage Ltd was formed with custom-built premises at Blochaim Road, Glasgow, and I moved there as its first company secretary. I did not remain in that position for very long and was moved to Caledonian MacBrayne Ltd at Gourock in mid-1974 but the position offered there did not really materialise and I left Caledonian MacBrayne Ltd in October 1974 and did assignment accounting thereafter.

Since the late 1960s I had been a member of the Paddle Steamer Preservation Society and had been present at the formation of the Scottish Branch at the Christian Institute, Bothwell Street, Glasgow, in 1969 and through that got to know Douglas McGowan; I was also on the Branch Committee, 1970–71, although I left for a while during STG days, but rejoined on leaving Caledonian MacBrayne Ltd.

Douglas and Terry Sylvester had been beavering away for some years to promote interest in PS *Waverley* and in 1973–74 things were hotting up; I was asked by them to become involved (someone had to hold the jackets), so while Douglas and Terry were the front men on the publicity side I was behind the scenes.

I had been in Edinburgh, on 15 April 1974, attending a MacBrayne Haulage Ltd monthly board meeting, and after that went to a company registration agent and purchased a £100 share capital ready-made company (using my own funds) called Evanships Ltd; subsequently, the name was changed to Waverley Steam Navigation Co. Ltd, with the three of us being shareholders at £10 each and also directors. In the spring of 1975 I had acquired a small group of clients and set up P. Morris Reid & Co. Chartered Accountants, with my office at Waterloo Chambers, 19 Waterloo Street, Glasgow, and WSN was registered there, so we were up and away in earnest.

When it came to write this chapter, I would have liked to refer to the original WSN cash book to see how the finances of those early days were being set up but after my removal as Finance Director of Waverley Excursions Ltd in 1996 I no longer had access to that book and sadly those who came after me did not appear to have kept the early records, so this article is now based on WSN board minutes and vague recollections that I have of these hectic early days.

The first WSN board meeting was on 16 April 1974, the day after I had formed Evanships, and I do not have details of that meeting but assume it would have been a formality to rename the company as WSN.

***

Thur. 8/8/74. 69 Stanmore Rd, Glasgow [Douglas's home]. 7.30–11.15 p.m.
Douglas resigned as chairman and Terry appointed chairman. Bank account opened with Clydesdale Bank, Gourock.
George C. Train invited to and accepted becoming a director.
[No mention in Minutes of the historic hand-over of *Waverley* that day]

Sun. 8/9/74. On board 'Wav.' in James Watt Dock, Greenock. Ended 8 p.m.

Financial Position	Ex. PSPS	1,000.00
	Sundry Donations	6.00
Share Issue (JTS, DWMcG, PMR, GCT.)		31.00
Total		1,037.00
Less:	DOTI Survey Fee	281.15
	Register of Shipping fee	3.25
Clyde Ships Stores & Services		131.62
Total expenditure		416.02
Net assets		£620.98

Sat. 26/10/74. On board 'Wav.' in James Watt Dock. 11.30 a.m.–12.45 p.m.

Cash in Bank	407.48
Cash in Hand	2.00
	£409.48

Insurance premium £1,425. Funds would be needed to be transferred from PSPS to cover this.
Public appeal had been launched the previous day on board 'Wav.' for £50,000 with STV personality Bill Tennant launching the appeal.

Sat. 14/12/74. 69 Stanmore Rd. 2.30 p.m.–5.30 p.m.
Funds appeal. £2,000 to be made by Clyde Tourist Association and a further £5,000 to come from Glasgow Corporation.

Sat. 15/2/75. Central Station Hotel, Glasgow. 11 a.m.–5.45 p.m. [Nearly 7 hours]
Financial Position	Cash in bank and in hand	234.50
	Estimated capital commitments	10,100.00
	Appeal fund held by PSPS	33,463.00

David Muir engaged as handyman/watchman at £20 a week plus travelling expenses.
Account received from Caledonian MacBrayne for £1,100 for watchmen's wages at James Watt Dock.
Suggestion to form another company Waverley (Cruises) Ltd to operate the vessel and if that fails then asset of *Waverley* separate from creditors as vessel owned by WSN.
Scottish Tourist Board would give £25,000 capital grant if Strathclyde Region would provide subsidy.

Sat. 8/3/75. On board Waverley in Scott's Garvel Graving Dock, Greenock. 2.30 p.m.–5.45 p.m.
Strathclyde Regional Council had met WSN directors the previous day and the Leisure & Recreation Committee had recommended a £30,000 operating subsidy for 1975 season and also a similar amount to Cal. Mac. for them to operate *Queen Mary II*. This meant that Cal Mac would not operate *Waverley* on our behalf and we would not be able to use Gourock Pier. Later that day WSN directors met with Ian Harrison & Ian Burrows [directors of Harrisons (Clyde) Ltd – operators of Western Ferries] and they agreed to operate *Waverley* at no management fee.
They suggested appointing a ship manager at £200 a month.
George Train suggested an operating schedule based on Ayr Monday to Thursday, Friday lay up for maintenance and Saturday and Sunday out of Anderston Quay, Glasgow.
100,000 advance timetables to be printed.
Captain D. L. Neill to be appointed master from 1/4/75

25/3/75. At Harrisons (Clyde) Ltd office, Woodside Cresc., Glasgow. 7.30 p.m.–10.15 p.m.
Wage rates to be based on NMU rates plus 10 per cent which would give an able seaman a rate of £56.58 for a seventy-three-hour week, plus leave at one day a week or £8 paid for a day of leave worked.
Twenty companies had been contacted to undertake catering and only 1 had replied then changed their mind.
PSPS were building a float to take part in the Glasgow 800 procession and WSN agreed to purchase a trailer for £200 and it would be used for future publicity.

Sun. 13/4/75. Central Station Hotel. 2 p.m.–6.45 p.m.
Ship's Officers appointed: Skipper: Captain D. L. Neill
Chief Officer: Ian Dunderdale
Chief Engineer: William Miller

Second Engineer: Kenneth Blacklock
Purser: Harold Jordan
Manager: Robert Wilson

Directors' Responsibilities:
J. T. Sylvester and D. W. McGowan – Commercial and marketing
I. E. Burrows – Operations and preparation of vessel [Ian had been appointed a director at the 25/3/75 Board meeting]
G. C. Train – Scheduling, sailing timetable and fare structure
P. M. Reid – Accounting, finance, secretarial.

The bank account had been transferred from Clydesdale Bank, Gourock branch, to Head Office, Glasgow. [The Head Office manager at that time was a well-known steamer enthusiast, Donald Robertson. Donald was an imposing figure and I would be standing in the queue at the bank counter when Donald would issue forth from his office, spot me, and come over. 'Well now, Peter, how's things with *Waverley*?' You don't get service like that from banks now.]

Sun. 27/4/75. Harrisons (Clyde) Ltd. office, Woodside Cres., Glasgow. 10 a.m.–1.15 p.m.
Verbal agreement from Commercial Catering (Scotland) Ltd to operate our catering on a 50/50 profit basis. Until they were fully operational, officers would be paid £1.50 a day subsistence and crew £3.50 a day lodging and food.

Wed. 7/5/75. 69 Stanmore Rd. 8 p.m.–11.15 p.m.
Esso fuel supply. They wanted Esso emblem on funnel for full season and three-year contract and Terry calculated this would save £4,000 a season.
Ayr pier dues were reduced from £76 a call to £36.
Almex ticket machine purchased for £120. Harold Jordan had designed tickets and blank ticket books for agents.

Thu. 22/5/75. On board 'Wav.' at Anderston Quay. 9 a.m.–10.15 a.m.
[No mention that this was the day of the inaugural cruise for councillors and guests] Scottish Tourist Board had agreed to pay 50 per cent of repairs up to £30,000.

Fri. 23/5/75. Harrisons (Clyde) Ltd office, Woodside Cresc., Glasgow. 7 p.m.–10.45 p.m.
If Class III certificate of 571 ex Ayr were to be increased a further six liferafts would be needed at cost of £3,000.
Esso suggested a fuelling agreement of first 75 tons fuel free plus a gallon rebate plus 1p a gallon duty rebate.
At the start of the inaugural cruise Phillip Taylor [Chief Executive of Scottish Tourist Board] handed over a cheque for £12,500.
£10,000 to be paid to account of Scott's shipyard account and this would leave £15,000 due on first instalment of refit.
Suggested that Robert Wilson [Manager] move into Waterloo Chambers [my offices] and a full time typist/clerkess be engaged at £1,700 – £1,800 a year.

Wed. 11/6/75. Harrisons (Clyde) Ltd office, Woodside Cresc., Glasgow. 6.30 p.m.–10.45 p.m.
Assistant Pursers to be paid £10 a week until 28 June and £7.50 thereafter. Secretarial/ Accounting fee to me at £2.50 an hour.

Thu. 21/8/75. Harrisons (Clyde) Ltd, Glasgow. 6.30 p.m.–10.45 p.m.
Still no sign of Strathclyde Region Council £30,000 subsidy.
Officers' bonuses for season   D. L. Neill   £100
    K. C. Blacklock   £75
    H. Jordan   £50
    J. MacAllum   £50
[John MacAllum was the retired Chief Officer of *King George V* and had been drafted in as Chief Officer following the departure of Ian Dunderdale]

Sun. 12/10/75. 69 Stanmore Road, Glasgow. 2.15 p.m.–7.30 p.m.
Officers' bonuses increased by £25 due to disquiet among officers.
J. M. Wallace [development director of Scottish Tourist Board] appointed to WSN Board.
Financial position [at end of first season] Operating deficit: £36,957 plus additional pre-season deficit of £5,454. Scott's refit full account totalled £ 57,265.
Lease granted for premises at Anderston Quay, Glasgow, at £1 a month

Sun. 29/11/75. 69 Stanmore Road, Glasgow. 2 p.m.–6.30 p.m.
£20,000 received from Strathclyde Regional Council and grant of up to £30,000 from Scottish Tourist Board.
Financial position still bleak. Creditors' money to be used to pay wages and salaries. Small creditors to be paid in full and larger ones to account.
If Strathclyde Regional Council did not guarantee an operating subsidy by the end of the year then no alternative but to liquidate the company.
Offices to be transferred from Waterloo Chambers to Anderston Quay from May 1976 and £50 allocated for desks, carpets etc. [Last of the big spenders]

Thu. 11/12/75. 10 Thom Rd, Bearsden (J. M. Wallace's house). 7 p.m.–10.30 p.m.
Strathclyde Leisure & Recreation Committee of the opinion that their budget could not cover cruising.
£10,000 received from Strathclyde Regional Council for balance of 1975 subsidy.

* * *

This summary of WSN board minutes takes us from the start of the company to the end of the first calendar year of operational preservation of PS *Waverley*.

There are volumes of WSN and Waverley Excursions Ltd minutes to cover subsequent years up to date, enough to fill a book, but it has taken me ages to research and record the above.

As well as the official WSN board meetings, there were innumerable behind the scenes meetings and interminable telephone calls. At that time I still lived in Wishaw with my parents and inevitably Terry would be on the phone late at night and we would still be on the phone when my parents went to bed. The phone was in the hall outside their bedroom and inevitably there would be a yell from their bedroom for me to get off the phone so they could get to sleep.

Another recollection was with Terry. He lived in Barry, South Glamorgan, and would travel up by train for board meetings and back down by overnight train. It wouldn't be the first time we would be running up Platform 1 at Glasgow Central to push him onto the train, with him hanging out the window, still talking. As well as the meetings, some of us were also attending work parties on board *Waverley* in our spare time.

I hope all that hard work has been worth it to keep *Waverley* sailing over the past forty years has been worth it.

Waverley Financial Statistics

REVENUE	1975	1984	1996
Excursion	77,203	551,409	929,103
Charter	15,870	58,427	130,377
Fruit Machines	—	1,440	—
Waverley Times	—	2,315	—
Totals	93,073	613,591	1,059,480
CATERING			
Turnover	—	179,742	392,035
Wages and Salaries	—	34,677	83,810
Supplies	—	93,544	163,942
Overheads	—	14,120	34,143
Total expenditure	—	142.341	281,895
Surplus	2,000	37,401	110,140
SOUVENIR SHOP			
Turnover	8,819	61,308	91,239
Supplies	7,541	35,000	62,456
Overheads	243	1,512	1,999
Wages	—	278	1,552
Total expenditure	7,784	36,790	66,007
Surplus	1,035	24,518	25,232
Miscellaneous Revenue	177	3,365	744
Sundry Donations	—	28,841	5,230
Operating Subsidy	30,000	20,860	33,210
Interest Received	632	4,833	—
Miscellaneous total	30,809	57,899	39,184
TOTAL REVENUE	126,917	733,409	1,234,036

| Passenger Carryings | 121,847 | 221,328 | 174,276 |

Expenditure

	1975	1984	1996
SHIP ADMIN			
Berth & Pilotage Dues	13,016	55,840	69,822
Insurance	2,975	36,611	54,435
Sundry Admin	2,049	2,966	9,020
	18,040	95,417	133,277
SHIP OPERATING			
Officers and Crew			
Salaries and Wages	43,370	170,766	279,231
Fuel	40,061	169,188	135,068
Running Repairs and Stores	15,144	13,679	38,101
	98,575	353,633	452,400
VESSEL REFIT EXPENSES	—	68,854	262,247
Ticket Agents Commission	639	13,963	37,555
Coach Hires and Shore Excursions	367	7,257	44,866
Ship Entertainment	499	2,067	13,293
	1,505	23,287	95,714
ADMIN AND OFFICE			
Salaries & Professional Fees	2,802	21,067	62,284
Telephone & Postages	—	4,797	11,577
Travelling Expenses	625	7,639	10,028
Stationery & Printing	401	1,344	—
Advertising	9,651	40,547	92,951
Office Upkeep	—	4,635	8,322
General Expenses	656	5,160	2,064
Rent and Rates	275	7,934	5,795
Professional Fees (Wav. Excursions)	—	—	48,462
Computer Expenses	—	—	3,355
Other Expenses	—	—	15,865
	14,410	93,123	260,683
TOTAL EXPENDITURE	132,530	634,314	1,204,321
OPERATING SURPLUS (LOSS)	(5,613)	99,095	29,715

P. M. Reid
30/1/2014

A Pleasure Steamer Business

> The two essentials for a preservation business – Love It – Make a Profit.
> Michael Draper, Severn Valley Railway

Through the benefits of charitable status, financial donations and voluntary contributions by so many and the exceptional efforts of some key personnel, the '*Waverley* Story' became possible. Everyone who has played any part over the past forty years can be very proud. We have achieved what, by the late 1960s, when the pleasure steamers of Britain appeared to be in terminal decline, would have seemed then to have been an impossible dream. However, the essential element was that the *Waverley* had to be run, as far as possible, as a business. All the wonderful contributions and efforts contributed to making that business succeed.

This is just my contribution to this wonderful fortieth anniversary book. It is almost entirely written from memory. I was too focused on gaining passengers for the next day, next week, next month, next season to be able to spend time on recording events of previous days. I may well have made mistakes and certainly omissions in what follows, but as Cameron Somerville wrote in his foreword to his beautiful booklet *Colour on the Clyde*: 'Please write and tell me about them'. Although I have recalled my own personal experiences and contributions, what follows is a tribute to so many who I hope will be reading and enjoying this book.

In our great world the *Waverley* story is just one trivial happening, but in the world of the pleasure steamer it has rewritten the history books of every area where the pleasure steamers of Britain ever sailed.

***

My story really began in 1946 when I was taken, on two consecutive days, by my great aunt and the following day by my parents, on cruises from Barry Pier to 'off Weston': on Saturday on *Ravenswood* (which Clifton Smith-Cox, managing director of P. & A. Campbell in their final years, told me was the first paddle steamer he sailed on), and on the Sunday on *Glen Usk*. I, and my family, sailed on all six paddle steamers of the post-war White Funnel Fleet.

In 1966, I was standing by the funnels of the paddle steamer *Bristol Queen* on a late evening cruise up the River Avon. Standing beside me was a young man of some seventeen years of age and we got into conversation. He told me he had come from the Clyde to experience the last of the Bristol Channel paddle steamers, in which he was rather disappointed. 'You should see the *Hamilton* steaming out of Rothesay', he told me. In the formal way of those days, he told me his name was Mr Marshall (thirty-six years later, I was in *Waverley*'s Glasgow office and Ian McMillan said, 'There is someone here who wants to see you' – it was Mr Marshall. Bob was once again influencing the *Waverley*'s future as he was working as a volunteer to design the new funnels for *Waverley*'s rebuild) and if I gave him two shillings and six pence he would send me a booklet on the Clyde steamers. I hesitated: should I trust this unknown with all that money? Well, fate decreed that I did, and I duly received *Steamers of the Clyde* by MacArthur, McCrorie, and MacHaffie. This introduced me to the wonderful Clyde steamer fleet and in 1968, after the withdrawal of *Bristol Queen*, we came on holiday to the Clyde. After seeing the Clyde, I said there was not a finer place in the world to run a pleasure steamer, but certainly never thought I would ever be involved in doing so. On holiday in 1969, I was invited to Douglas McGowan's twenty-first birthday at Dunoon and from this came the (very!) informal Waverley Study Group, which culminated in the sheer nerve of presenting to John Whittle, General Manager of the Caledonian Steam Packet Company, a report on the Clyde steamer operation. We certainly weren't a modest group! I said that our aim must be to make the *Waverley* so famous on the Clyde that her withdrawal would become unthinkable. I wrote the first publicity leaflet, *Britain's Last Sea-Going Paddle Steamer*, and included in this a membership form to join the Paddle Steamer Preservation Society. I produced large, full-colour posters to promote *Waverley*'s sailings from all Clyde departure points, sent them out to all tourist offices and everyone else I could think of and gave a supply to Caledonian Steam Packet Company.

On a November night in 1973, Douglas McGowan telephoned me to say that on one of his regular visits to the *Waverley*, in winter in the James Watt Dock, Greenock, he found the ship 'like the *Marie Celeste*' – a half-drunk cup of tea and a half-eaten biscuit on the table. The ship was obviously not going to be recommissioned for 1974 and we were invited to a meeting with John Whittle at Gourock – would I come to Scotland for the meeting? My response to Douglas was to say, 'We are going to be thanked for meddling over the past four years and be presented with the ship's bell – you go and collect the bell.' After the meeting, Douglas telephoned to say we had been offered the bell but also the rest of the ship as well! The central committee of the Paddle Steamer Preservation Society simply could not believe this and the true facts are it was not the society that took ownership of the *Waverley* – it was Douglas McGowan, Peter Reid and Terry Sylvester, who formed Waverley Steam Navigation for this to be able to happen. However, the Scottish Transport Group began to realise that giving away a publically owned asset to this new company, owned by 'the three', could result in them simply selling it and pocketing the money. Things started to get rather complicated and I decided on a simple solution – I would sign a personal guarantee to Caledonian for £25,000, this being the notional scrap value of the ship, so that if in any way *Waverley* was disposed of, Caledonian would receive the scrap value from me. To make sure that I didn't run away to Australia, Peter Reid was asked to be a second signatory and Douglas bravely accepted to be the third in the event that I defaulted.

On 8 August 1974, we took ownership of the *Waverley*. There was no money in the Paddle Steamer Preservation Society, but so that we would have at least some working capital I deposited £10,000 in our new bank account and we were underway.

An appeal letter was urgently sent to all members of the Paddle Steamer Preservation Society. It began: 'Have you cherished a dream – a dream that just one great paddle steamer could sail on far into the future. This dream can now come true – we own the *Waverley*.' The letter was signed by our then dear chairman, Bill Prynne, but I wrote it!

Although it was Douglas, Peter and I who were the initial owners of the *Waverley*, we always made it clear that we were acting on behalf of the Paddle Steamer Preservation Society. We held an open day on board *Waverley* on the Sunday following our taking ownership and at this event David Neill came forward to offer to be 'Ship's Husband' and Ian Burrows volunteered to be Engineering Director. We were underway. The original plan was that we would be the owners but Caledonian would operate *Waverley*, but when Strathclyde Regional Council announced that they would give a grant to keep the *Queen Mary II* sailing on the Clyde, the *Waverley* plan was withdrawn. We were left with deciding whether to give up or to carry on and operate *Waverley* ourselves. A key issue in this was that we needed a captain. David Neill shyly offered to consider being this. I never had any worries about the commercial aspect of running Waverley – I was quite used to running businesses – but I did have concern as to whether we could be confident of carrying up to some 1,000 passengers in reasonable safety. I had to get to know David and so on a winter's night I travelled to where he then lived, at Sandbank near Dunoon, and in front of the fire grilled him mercilessly. He came through that hard interview with flying colours and I left Sandbank that night in complete confidence that I could trust *Waverley* to David's command. The board of directors was soon strengthened by the addition of Ian Burrows and George Train, soon joined at the boardroom table by Captain David Neill.

Establishing the Business

It was now late in the year of 1974 and the vital need was to generate business to operate *Waverley* in 1975. The key to successful operational preservation was income and that income could best be raised by sailing the ship. The history books were all telling us that the operation of paddle steamers was now economically impossible. However, in a long telephone conversation with Peter Reid, who had some inside knowledge, having worked for MacBraynes, I was able to obtain from Peter some figures on crewing costs, fuel, etc, etc. Armed with this information, it took very little time to produce approximate calculations that if we could use *Waverley*'s passenger capacity and then sell those tickets, *Waverley* was perfectly viable – the key was writing the right timetable, setting the right fare structures, and selling the tickets! All this was assuming, of course, that the ship was in good reliable operating condition and manned with fully capable officers in the key departments of the bridge and engine room. The Clyde timetable for 1975 was compiled by George Train, some of which remains unchanged to this day. The Clyde with its many piers, able to be used at any state of the tide, is the easiest main operating area in Britain to timetable, but George taught me the vital principle of taking the ship to the people and not to expect the majority of passengers to travel significant distances to join the trips.

In November 1974, I produced the first publicity leaflet to seek private hire (charter) and group bookings. The leaflet featured every reason I could think of as to why a customer may wish to take advantage of *Waverley*. I sent several thousands of these out to every potential customer I could think of. Don Rose, who had lost a great deal of money in his attempt to sail *Queen of the South* (*Jeanie Deans*) on the Thames, sent me a telegram – I think the only telegram I ever received in my life – which said, 'Congratulations, if everything else is to this standard you will surely succeed.' How kind of Don, who I found to be a lovely person. In later years, after Don had lost his family wholesale grocer's business in London, he took over a pub in Rochester, acquired a former naval patrol craft and renamed her *Queen of Kent*. Some years later, the boat was laid up with engine trouble and Don wrote to me, offering the boat to us for 10p. He said that as we paid £1 for the *Waverley* he thought 10p was about all *Queen of Kent* was worth. I considered the possibilities in taking *Queen of Kent* into our 'fleet' but decided that the work and time that would be involved could not be justified against the potential income and had to decline. Don died not long afterwards and I think that he had made this kind gesture knowing that his time was running out. John Whittle was said to have waved our first leaflet around the Caledonian offices at Gourock, saying, 'Why couldn't we produce something like this?' Paul Clegg, who wrote 'Short Sea Survey' in the magazine *Sea Breezes*, wrote, 'The *Waverley* Organisation has issued its first publicity leaflet obviously written by someone who knows how to capture the public imagination.' I mention these points not as self-praise but because they are clear illustrations of what you have to do to succeed with the business. I always tried to remember Paul Clegg's point about 'capturing the public imagination' in all publicity material I produced. I am sure I did not succeed, but it was always my aim.

In addition to all the other challenges, there was the rather important element of on-board catering. We had no director with catering experience and knew of no one, so I decided that we must offer the opportunity of providing catering and bars on board to an outside caterer. I sent out letters to all the outside caterers that I could find in the local telephone directory, inviting them to come to an open day on board *Waverley* at Greenock to tender for this great business opportunity. I sat waiting all day and just one caterer, who lived in Greenock, turned up. He said, 'I have only come to offer you advice, don't even attempt full catering just sell cakes and pre-packed sandwiches.' There were now only weeks before our first sailing – what should we do? I was given information that a company, Commercial Catering, provided outside catering and I set off to their premises in Stirling to persuade them that this was a great business opportunity, not in any way suggesting they were our last hope. They accepted, and for 1975 they fed the passengers. In 1976, John Tetsill, who had managed the catering in 1975, took over the operation on his own account.

After great efforts, and contributions, from so many people, the great day finally arrived and *Waverley* sailed 'under the banner of the Paddle Steamer Preservation Society' for the first time, with invited guests from Glasgow in May 1975. The guest list included many who had contributed, including representatives from companies who my family business had dealt with that I had persuaded to donate anything from carpet and lino to cover some of the well-worn floor coverings in the saloons, to many gallons of paint, and even flock wallpaper for the dining saloon – which someone described as looking like a Chinese restaurant! But it was all to give the *Waverley* a brighter image. Realising that many of these invited guests and contributors – some of whom I hoped might contribute again in the future – had never seen *Waverley* before, and if they boarded at Glasgow on a low tide, went on a cruise and came back they would never really see the ship in operation, I arranged with Captain David Neill that we would all go ashore at Dunoon for a short period and that *Waverley* would do a steam-past to give our many guests the chance to see the ship in all its glory steaming at speed past Dunoon Pier. This was a great success and many cameras were clicking. At the end of this first cruise, Captain David Neill invited us to the lower bar and opened the evening by raising a glass and proposing a toast to me as 'the man who made it all possible'. That was David using exactly the right words; I certainly did not do it all – not by any means – but probably by my financial contribution, and obtaining bookings and charters before the ship had ever sailed, made the beginning of the business possible. However, that was only one part of making it possible, as I was surrounded and supported by so many wonderful people – I was very fortunate.

I had discovered that the great Clyde fleet under Caledonian was operating with virtually no newspaper advertising and indeed in the Bristol Channel P. & A. Campbell, while they advertised in the press regularly, had adverts that were little more than a timetable of destinations – there was no desire created to encourage people who did not sail on the ships to want to do so. I realised that to draw the numbers of passengers we needed, we had to communicate with large numbers of the public, so, starting with blank sheets of paper, I designed press advertisements for every relevant newspaper in the west of Scotland together with Scotland's national daily newspapers, and Douglas McGowan engineered publicity opportunities to gain extensive editorial coverage. I produced local leaflets for every Clyde departure point. I had realised, in my early years of sailing on the Clyde before we owned *Waverley*, that Caledonian had no system for booking tickets in advance for individual passengers. The same was the case in the Bristol Channel with P. & A. Campbell. You could make a group booking in advance and, if you visited the Caledonian offices at Gourock or the Campbell offices in Bristol and insisted that you wanted to buy a ticket, they would probably sell you one, but, as I wrote in the Waverley Study Group Report, the ships arrived at piers hoping that 'the sun would be shining and the passengers would be waiting'. We also needed the ability to buy tickets in advance from every possible town, village and seaside resort that *Waverley* sailed from and the network of agents was rapidly developed.

After operating the 1975 season, I realised that we needed a daily report from the purser and this led to the design of the purser's return. This provides essential information every day: it gives the number of passengers embarking and disembarking at every pier, the value of tickets sold from each booking point and agent, the value of sales in catering, the bars and the souvenir shop. Every purser was told to post copies to the offices at Glasgow and Barry every day; envelopes were often given to regular passengers to put in post boxes on their home from the ship. Now these are sent by fax.

With many booking points, it is essential to keep control of the number of tickets being sold in advance. For many years this function for all areas of Britain, except the Clyde, was carried out from Barry. At one of the meetings I led after I had left Waverley Excursions Limited, I posed the question, 'Why do we count the number of passengers booked in advance?' Up went the hands to answer, 'To prevent being over booked.' No, I told them, 'To ensure that the ship is fully booked!' A rather good example of the difference between administration and business.

Tourist information centres were expanding in many towns and seaside resorts and we appointed many of these as ticket agents. We were fortunate that in the west of Scotland there was a travel agent with many branches; our newspaper advertisements were able to say, 'Be sure of your tickets – book now at any branch of A. T. Mays or your local Tourist Information Centre – or buy your tickets on board *Waverley* when you sail.' Advance booking meant that substantial numbers of people who would read a newspaper advertisement would immediately book. This was vital insurance against rain and poor weather. It was very noticeable that if the sun was shining the day after newspapers were published, advance bookings by telephone would immediately rise, even though the customer was often planning to sail on some future date – sunshine increased the desire.

Local leaflets were produced for every departure point we ever sailed from, and by 1977 I realised we needed a national timetable for mass distribution to PSPS members and other enthusiast organisations together with our ever-increasing customer base. Mailing to all customers whose addresses we had was relatively expensive but it was target marketing and the customer address list expanded enormously once we began taking bookings by credit card in 1986. A number of members of the *Waverley* board at that time were completely against us taking bookings by credit card and it took David Neill and I to insist that we had to do this. Booking by credit card became an ever-increasing percentage of advanced ticket sales.

By 1976 our rather famous purser, Harold Jordan, had educated me that we needed advertising cards for almost every departure point and from this developed what came to be called 'hanging cards' for every departure point on the Clyde, Bristol Channel, Solent, Thames, North Wales coast, etc. Countless thousands of these were mailed out direct to every hotel, guest house, tourist information centre, steam railway, museum, etc., and by far the greatest number of these envelopes – many, many thousands – were packed by my mother, Mrs Violet Sylvester, working from her home in Barry.

Against the predictions of some 'enthusiasts' that the *Waverley* story would 'last a fortnight', through the sheer determination of Captain David Neill and his great supporter (then) second engineer Kenneth Blacklock, *Waverley* completed the 1975 season. We fully expected the grant support we had received from Strathclyde Regional Council in 1975 would be repeated in 1976; it was a severe blow when the council decided to give the full Clyde Cruising subsidy to Caledonian MacBrayne. We had so little capital at that time that without the Strathclyde contribution we could not see that we could continue, but through a personal visit by Harold Jordon to the offices of the *Sunday Mail*, the newspaper ran a campaign: '10 days to save the *Waverley*.' Donations poured in and spirits were lifted again and *Waverley* sailed for a second season.

In the winter of 1976/77, we were approached by Conwy Council for a charter for *Waverley* to sail from Llandudno for the Centenary Celebration of Llandudno Pier.

Planning went ahead, but with just weeks to go, the Tourism Officer telephoned me to say that the council were not going to proceed. What should we do? We decided to go it alone and take *Waverley* to Llandudno, Liverpool and North Wales on our own account and the visit proved a success and gave great experience in operating *Waverley* outside the Clyde. Why did the council pull out at the eleventh hour? Well, I discovered that the tourism officer had once been in that position in a seaside town in south Devon. The famous locomotive *Flying Scotsman* was passing through en route and he tried to take advantage of this by getting the *Scotsman* to make a brief stop at his town's station. With the mayor and the town band and many local people lined up on the platform, the *Scotsman* came into view and steamed straight through without stopping. I had a sneaking feeling that he thought the same thing might happen with the *Waverley*. I produced press advertising and press releases to announce *Waverley* sailing from Llandudno and soon had a telephone call from the tourism officer. 'Delighted you are coming after all', he said, 'we would like to bring the mayor to welcome you.' My reply was, 'How dare you think you can take advantage after you have let us, a small preservation charity, down so badly. However, if you pay the pier dues you can bring the mayor' – they paid them! Crowds lined the pier as *Waverley* arrived and the mayor, wearing a plastic boater, welcomed every passenger going ashore with a handshake and, 'Croeso Y Llandudno.' It was a charming welcome but made us rather late.

After *Waverley*'s grounding on the Gantocks Rocks off Dunoon in 1977, the ship was out of revenue-earning operation for most of July and the whole of August. With the information that the former Scarborough pleasure boat *Coronia*, now renamed *Queen of Scots*, was surplus to the requirements of McAlpine and was anchored at Ardyne, I was soon on the train to Glasgow and with Captain David Neill went to inspect *Queen of Scots*. It was thought that she would at least allow us to retain key officers and staff and provide some income during *Waverley*'s absence. However, after a couple of weeks it was obvious that *Queen of Scots* was not earning enough to pay the running costs and pay a charter fee to McAlpine's. What should we do? Well, I telephoned the McAlpine office in Berners Street in London and asked if I could come to meet Sir William McAlpine. Permission was immediately granted and when I met Bill I simply said, 'We can't afford to pay you' – the charter fee was waived!

After the loss of *Waverley*'s July and August income, we were in desperate straits that winter and sterling work by Peter Reid obtained a moratorium from our creditors that they would wait for payment until we earned money the following summer. Realising completely that the essential way to earn money was to operate *Waverley* for the longest possible season, Captain Neill set out to plan a most ambitious programme in some of the areas that had once had their own pleasure steamers, on the south coast of England, London and the Thames. We sailed from Newhaven in mid-April and although all this unknown territory left me with a daunting task to effectively promote and advertise *Waverley*'s sailings, this was achieved and the programme was an outstanding success. That year we succeeded in paying off all the creditors – simply by using the *Waverley* for the longest possible season for the purpose for which she was built. The springtime programme in England was guaranteed financially by the late Professor John Leech but such was the financial success of *Waverley*'s visit that it was not necessary for John to provide any actual financial support, but without his personal guarantee the programme could not have gone ahead.

Around this time, I was approached by John Easton, who had covered the *Waverley* story in the early years for the *Glasgow Herald*. John said, 'Now that I have got to know some of you, I think you are a genuine bunch – I would like to help, what can I do?' 'Publish a ship's newspaper,' I said and from this came *Waverley Times*, produced by John, who obtained the advertisers, articles and photographs, arranged the printing and delivered, each year, a substantial quantity to be sold around the decks – a splendid contribution by John.

In 1979 we planned to restore the historic link between a paddle steamer named *Waverley*, from the Clyde, and the Bristol Channel. The first steamer to come from Scotland, in 1887, to begin the famous P. & A. Campbell White Funnel Fleet was named *Waverley*! P. & A. Campbell, now owned by the ferry company Townsend Thoresen, were still operating *Balmoral* in the Bristol Channel, led by their long-serving managing director Sydney Clifton Smith-Cox. Clifton's friend, Colonel Christopher Jennings, who often joined with him to sail their model paddle steamers in Clevedon and Kidwelly, was a supporter of PSPS. He had bought the Clyde paddle tug *Flying Scotsman* in 1946; he told me he sailed her around the Western Isles until he ran out of coal and ran out of stokers! Christopher was wise; he realised that while Clifton could not prevent us bringing *Waverley* to the Bristol Channel, he could perhaps be awkward as he could see it as competition to *Balmoral*, albeit for a very short period. I had never met Clifton so Christopher arranged for us to meet in the Park Hotel, Cardiff, of which Clifton was also managing director. Welcoming me warmly, Clifton said, 'You've all done a marvellous job but we continue to do it without any subsidy.' (Completely ignoring that Campbell's had been subsidised for years by Townsend Thoresen.) 'I hear', said Clifton, 'that you would like to bring *Waverley* to the Bristol Channel. If you would like to come for a few days we will give you all the help we can, but if you want to come for a few weeks Bugger Off!'

A real benefit from *Waverley*'s first visit to the Bristol Channel was meeting Commander Tom Foden. Tom lived just a few doors away from Clifton Smith-Cox and worked part-time for him to gain school and charter bookings. After Campbell's closed down, Tom joined us as our 'Bristol Area Agent' and made a great contribution through both school and charter bookings and practical assistance to our ships. Tom could tell some less than complimentary stories about Clifton, which included, 'He can't sail *Balmoral* from Bristol any longer as he has made enemies of everyone in the Port!' Tom, and his wife Joan, both great characters, are sorely missed.

P. & A. Campbell had, for many years, issued coupon books which gave the purchaser a 25 per cent discount when they bought tickets. I soon copied this scheme as it was a valuable means of bringing in income before the start of the operating season. Colin Crafer, a PSPS member, asked me if he could have a season ticket and this led to the Commodore Club, which offered tickets for one season from each principal area of Britain, or a Life Commodore, giving sailings aboard our ships for the holder's life. Many who bought a Life Commodore considered that they were supporting the future of our ships and this was certainly true. Colin Crafer bought a Life Commodore but emigrated to New Zealand after only a few years. Dear Sydney Robinson, from Penarth, bought his Life Commodore at the age of ninety-two!

The Second Ships

The experience of the Gantocks grounding and the loss of almost two months' peak earnings by *Waverley* proved how vulnerable the business was with only one ship. The first 'second ship' was therefore *Queen of Scots* and there was a realisation that a truly suitable second ship was essential for the long term future. At a Paddle Steamer Preservation Society dinner in London in late 1980, I was sat between David Neill and Kenneth Blacklock. 'The *Shanklin* is up for sale in Portsmouth,' said David. 'We are going down tomorrow to see it and you're coming!' The *Shanklin* was one of a trio of motor ships built by Denny of Dumbarton for sailing from Portsmouth to the Isle of Wight and *Shanklin*, as the newest ship, also undertook some cruises. Taken out by motor launch to the mooring in the middle of Portsmouth Harbour where *Shanklin* was laid up, out of service, it was immediately apparent that this was a superb passenger ship. Fitted with what were known as the 'Rolls-Royce of Diesel engines – Sulzer', Shanklin was in beautiful condition except that there was a crack in the cylinder block of the main port engine. Returning to Barry, I tracked down the senior marine engineer in British Rail Portsmouth and asked him if the cracked block could be repaired? 'Of course', he said. 'British Rail simply don't need the ship and want to dispose of it.' Given confidence by what seemed a most knowledgeable man, I telephoned British Rail in London. 'You are too late', said the man on the end of the telephone line, 'she is being sold to be a Chinese restaurant – but they haven't paid any money yet! If you can come up with £25,000 by Wednesday [this was Monday!] it's yours.' I telephoned Ian Harrison of Harrison's Clyde and Jim Buchanan, in business as an estate agent at Dumbarton, and said, 'I will put £10,000 towards it, will you contribute the rest?' Trusting what I had to say completely and without any further complications, both Ian and Jim agreed immediately in a single telephone call. The British Rail man came from London to my office at Barry; we took a three-minute walk to a café for a light lunch, I handed him the cheque and he handed me the documents – the *Shanklin* was ours. The plan was that we would make the ship available to the *Waverley* companies at no cost, but that Waverley Excursions would be financially responsible for returning the ship to passenger certificate. I thought the name *Ivanhoe* would fit together well with *Waverley* and she should be owned separately under a new company, which would be named Firth of the Clyde Steam Packet Company – after the owners of the original Clyde paddle steamer *Ivanhoe* – but the name was not available on the British register of shipping and this was why she became *Prince Ivanhoe*. A small new board of directors was formed to oversee the return of the ship to passenger certification, and under the leadership of Ian McMillan and Ken Angel the crack in the block was Metalocked and *Prince Ivanhoe* was made ready for operation.

Meanwhile, the big question was what we were going to do with the ship? My original plan was based on the fact that Strathclyde Regional Council were providing a significant subsidy to Caledonian MacBrayne for operating the car ferry *Glen Sannox* on passenger sailings on the Clyde. My logic was that if we took *Prince Ivanhoe* to Glasgow and presented her to the regional councillors, they would see what a superior passenger ship she was and that we could obtain the full subsidy. Strathclyde Council soon put an end to this theory by announcing that they were not giving any subsidy to anyone for 1981 and the future, so what was to be done? Ken Angel had been second engineer on *Balmoral* for P. & A. Campbell. Ken had grown up in the next road to me, living just two doors away from Ian McMillan's grandfather, who was a customer of ours in our decorating shop. It was Ian's grandfather who, in 1969, had said to my mother that he had a young grandson interested in paddle steamers. Ian lived in Bridgend but came on Saturdays to visit his grandparents. It was suggested to my mother that Ian come up and visit me one Saturday afternoon and it was on one of those visits that he introduced me to the Paddle Steamer Preservation Society, of which at the age of fourteen he was already a member. So all those who have not been too pleased at my involvement over the years have Ian to blame for it!

Ken Angel telephoned me to suggest that we should offer *Prince Ivanhoe* to P. & A. Campbell as *Balmoral* required some significant expenditure to repair bottom damage suffered at Clovelly. *Ivanhoe* could be put into service at a significantly lower cost. Accordingly, I telephoned Clifton Smith-Cox, managing director of P. & A. Campbell, who said, 'Come with me to London to meet John Smith.' John Smith was head of the Landmark Trust, who run Lundy Island, and who in 1980 had formed a new company, White Funnel Steamers Limited, with Smith-Cox to keep *Balmoral* operating after Townsend Thoresen – the real owners of P. & A. Campbell – had intended to close down the operation. *Balmoral* was made available to White Funnel Steamers Limited for 1980. Her timetable was appalling, constantly running from Swansea to Ilfracombe to Lundy, and with only some four sailings in the entire season from Penarth, which became the busiest passenger pier in Britain under our operations, and only some six sailings from Bristol. It was a financial disaster. Arriving at the Landmark Trust offices, Smith-Cox spread before Sir John Smith some papers and said, 'We have a ship here we can commission for much lower cost than *Balmoral* for 1981.' John Smith stood up and said, 'Ships – I want nothing more to do with ships,' as it was Sir John who had paid off the debts of 1980. He opened the door and showed us out. As we stepped out into Dean's Yard, Westminster, two days before Christmas, the snow was falling. Smith-Cox turned to me and said, 'That's me finished – it's over to you now.'

This meant that the Bristol Channel was fully available to us and was now the obvious place to principally operate *Prince Ivanhoe*. However, Smith-Cox offered to act as agent, through P. & A. Campbell Limited, which still existed as a company. I thought it was a good idea to accept this as I believed Campbell's must have considerable business contacts with group organizers, hoteliers in Ilfracombe, etc., but I soon found that they had virtually no business left at all! Smith-Cox had already written the full timetable for *Balmoral* to operate in 1981 and, although I had grown up on the Bristol Channel, I certainly did not fully understand it. Smith-Cox was proposing that the timetable be a repeat of the disastrous 1980 and with my then limited knowledge, and with the season fast approaching, I made efforts to improve the commercial value of the timetable, but I did not have enough knowledge or enough time to make the best of it – it took several years to develop the Bristol Channel's full potential. Sailing up the River Avon, to Bristol, to begin the season, *Ivanhoe* tore a gash in her hull and took in water. The excuse was that *Ivanhoe*, with her broad beam, was unsuitable for the River Avon. The urgent task was to get the ship to dry-dock in Barry for repair; the captain had been relieved of his command

and we had no one available to be master for the voyage to Barry. What could I do? Living in Penarth, and now retired, was Captain Philip Power, who had been master of the paddle steamers *Cardiff Queen* and *Bristol Queen*. I telephoned him and asked would he bring the ship to Barry? It was an immediate yes from Philip, I drove him to Bristol, he stepped aboard, quickly took in the detail on the bridge and said, 'Let go!' I drove downriver to the infamous horseshoe bend and watched *Ivanhoe* behave perfectly with a competent man in command. *Ivanhoe* was not too broad in the beam for the River Avon! Philip would accept no payment for his contribution and several years later, as a guest speaker at the PSPS Bristol Channel Branch Annual Dinner, instead of expecting any fee, he gave a donation – a lovely man. Just as there were strong signs that we were succeeding in effectively marketing *Prince Ivanhoe*, the sad events of 3 August 1981 resulted in the ship being a total loss after striking an underwater object off the Gower coast. The search for a second ship had to begin again.

There are a number of essential and logical financial reasons for the second ship. The first is the need to maintain income in the event that *Waverley* was out of action. The second is that shore costs, management, staff, offices, publicity, can be shared between two operating ships. Publicity benefits of a two-ship programme include the willingness of tourist authorities to include free of any charge photographs and editorial in their publications, which they will often only do for a significant number of sailings from their area. On the Thames in particular, press advertising for *Balmoral*'s programme in June could include, at minimal cost, *Waverley*'s autumn sailings and always brought significant advance bookings. The third and most important reason is the availability of ports and piers. Only by making a significant number of calls at piers could we achieve restoration, reopening and on-going maintenance of many of Britain's piers. Also, a motorship is more economical to operate than a paddle steamer, and with her narrower beam giving access to ports and harbours that a paddle steamer could not use, there was the opportunity of adding a number of new ports of call and bringing in increased revenue, which will certainly have led to increased membership of the Paddle Steamer Preservation Society. The fourth reason is that captains are able to qualify for pilotage exemption certificates through being able to make sufficient trips each year within various pilotage districts, saving many thousands of pounds in pilotage costs.

This all led to 1985 and the rescue of *Balmoral* off the mud at Dundee, where the ship had spent some three years – a few months as a failed floating pub and the rest of the time abandoned and almost derelict. *Balmoral* was in the hands of the bank, as mortgagees, who were undoubtedly delighted beyond words to receive an offer for what could hardly be viewed as an asset. Supported financially by Mrs Jennifer Leech, *Balmoral* was purchased and Kenneth Blacklock and Ken Angel soon had the engines running again. The ship was sailed to Glasgow, under her own power, to be rebuilt in the winter of 1985/86. One essential was to increase *Balmoral*'s passenger accommodation and I asked David Neill to arrange the conversion of the open former car deck at the stern into a new dining saloon. My contribution to this was just a few words: David got the job done!

There was the potentially disastrous possibility of a fourth 'second ship'. In 1987, a small group entered discussions with British Rail at Portsmouth with a view to some kind of financial arrangement to take over the motorship *Southsea*, which was an earlier version of *Shanklin* (*Prince Ivanhoe*). The plan appeared to be that the Waverley Organisation would carry the costs of overhauling *Southsea* and would operate it with some kind of financial return to her owners, Sealink. This plan, if correctly reported, was sheer madness. We were struggling to understand how to operate the second ship (*Balmoral*) in a financially viable way. There was no area in Britain that had room for the full operation of a third pleasure steamer. Verbal reports said that the *Southsea* had her main deck windows boarded up and was being made ready to leave Portsmouth for Glasgow when the main board of Sealink squashed the plan. It was said that the Sealink manager at Portsmouth lost his job over the scheme. I cannot say whether all this information is true, but what is true is that any idea that we in the Waverley Organisation had the capacity and the financial backing to operate a third ship or that there is any viable area in Britain for that third ship to fully operate showed a breath-taking ignorance of the pleasure steamer business that we were involved in. I could not convince almost all my fellow directors on the Waverley Excursions board that getting involved with the *Southsea* was something we simply should not do under any circumstances. I could not as Chairman of the Board carry my fellow directors with me and accordingly I had no choice but to resign as chairman and a director.

In a revealing example that proved that very few of the directors of that time had any real understanding of the volume of work carried out at Barry and by myself, they made no attempt whatsoever to make any other arrangements or to replace me. I therefore simply carried on as before but as I now no longer had the authority to sign cheques, I paid for almost all the newspaper advertising for the rest of that year. I was finally repaid some 50 per cent of this expenditure. While I continued working exactly as before, and continued to attend Waverley Excursions board meetings, it was some two years before I returned as a director of Waverley Excursions Limited.

Meanwhile, our understanding of how to timetable and operate the second ship continued to improve and with Captain Stephen Michel in command of *Balmoral*, the number of ports and piers visited rapidly expanded. More than 50 per cent of the offices of my family business were being used for the *Waverley* and *Balmoral* work. The building had been built as the Barry Goods Depot for the Barry Railway Company *c*. 1890 and renamed, by me, Gwalia Buildings after the beautiful paddle steamer *Gwalia* built for the Barry Railway Company by John Brown in Clydebank in 1905. At Barry we had a full-time staff of two employed directly by Waverley Excursions Limited, summer booking clerks to take the constant credit card bookings and enquiries for six full days a week, and at certain peak times on Sunday mornings, also myself, who was certainly working very full-time for *Waverley* for some seven months of the year, and never really 'off-duty', and from 1982, when she joined our family business as a secretary, *Waverley* benefitted enormously from the work of Susan Koops. Sue became solely responsible for typing all of what became thousands of newspaper advertisements, similar quantities of editorial press releases, copy for advertising cards, magazine adverts and articles etc., but also played a major role in the development of our membership of the Group Travel Organisers' Association. This had begun as a small voluntary body but developed to have a full-time employee and many thousands of members throughout Great Britain. The membership varied from a Mothers' Union in the village hall to the national Civil Service Retirement Fellowship. For the most modest membership of some £240, we were able to have an advertisement in their magazine, which was mailed to all their members; a full list of all members to whom we mailed, every year; relevant area leaflets promoting charters and group bookings; and attend and have a display stand at the Annual Conference – the morning was a sales campaign with our own display stand, the afternoon the Annual General Meeting and the evening the Annual Dinner. At all of these there was extensive networking and literally hundreds of bookings were achieved from group organisers and several full charters of the ships. It was estimated in one year that Sue's work via the Group Travel Organisers' Association brought in some £400,000 worth of business.

In my years with Waverley Steam and Waverley Excursions from 1974 to 1999 there were three general managers based in the Glasgow office. Bob Wilson, for the first two years, was no general manager but was a great man in a crisis. Then there was Kyle MacKay, who was a *Waverley* enthusiast and who as a young boy had featured in a film aboard the Clyde steamers named *Kyle's Clyde*. Kyle only stayed for some two years and I then had to interview for a new general manager. The person I chose from the interviews turned the job down and the late David Duncanson was my second choice. I am sure my first choice was wrong and that the person would not have displayed the tenacity, indeed stickability, that David did. A number of people thought that David Duncanson did everything, others thought he did nothing, but the truth was that David never wrote a timetable, set very few fares and created only a minimal amount of publicity, but made a valuable contribution by leading the administration, purser's department and catering, and presented a smart appearance in the Glasgow office for some seventeen years.

Ports & Piers

> Piers need Pleasure Steamers and Pleasure Steamers need Piers
> Terry Sylvester

It is essential that we are involved in the retention, or restoration, of piers. Every pier that can be retained in use or be restored to use in Britain adds thousands of pounds to most days that we are able to call there. Without the use of certain piers, the Thames, Bristol Channel and Solent would become areas where it was not financially viable to operate. Piers and their landing stages that would not have been restored without our two-ship programme include Clevedon, where an outstanding effort by the Clevedon Pier Trust achieved the rebuilding of the main promenade pier, but ran out of money to install the decking. David Neill and I met with Clevedon Pier Trust and persuaded them that they should borrow the money to re-deck the pier and they would then be able to earn income from the sailings by *Waverley* and *Balmoral*. We promised to pay the trust a slightly higher fee for our use of the pier in addition to what they would earn in pier tolls from every passenger and promenader. This allowed the pier to reopen. A few years later, when some of the trustees had retired or even passed away, I became a director of Clevedon Pier Trust and spent some five years supporting the tremendous effort of the pier managers, Ivor and Maggie Ashford, to complete the restoration of the landing stage. We also provided *Waverley* for fund raising cruises for the pier, charging only for fuel and crew overtime.

The restoration of Penarth Pier landing stage would also never have happened without two ships sailing from the pier, but this work was to be carried out by closing the pier for one year. Without Penarth the Bristol Channel is not viable, as Penarth, with our two ships in full operation, provided the greatest number of passengers each year of any port or pier in Britain. The Vale of Glamorgan Council, the pier's owners, called me to a meeting to advise that the pier would be closed for one year for the landing stage to be rebuilt. I advised them that if this happened we would have to lay-up the second ship – *Balmoral* – and that we would have no funds to retain *Balmoral* for the following year. Faced with this hard fact, the council wrote into the contract that the pier had to be kept open for passenger use and with a superhuman effort by the contractors (who did try to be released from this obligation in the contract) we did not lose a single sailing while an extensive programme of rebuilding was carried out.

At Ilfracombe, we were advised that the pier had become unsafe for passengers owing to steel work rusting inside the concrete, with the risk of lumps falling off. Again, without Ilfracombe, the Bristol Channel is simply not viable and I arranged a meeting with the chief executive and the consultants, which was attended by Ian McMillan and myself. I proposed that they wrap polypropylene netting around the horizontal members of the pier that were considered at risk of crumbling and Ian provided the method to chain the wooden fenders to prevent any risk of them coming adrift. The pier was kept open! North Devon District Council then set out to obtain grant funding to build a completely new pier and I provided for this application a report on the use of the pier by the pleasure steamers and the fact that as substantial grants had already been given to Clevedon and Penarth, this was a pointless use of public money if Ilfracombe was not to be retained. I would not have used this information before the restoration of Clevedon and Penarth!

On the South Coast, Swanage Pier, completely unusable, was brought back into use by the then-owner, who was inspired by Captain David Neill. A few years later, when the pier had to be closed, I organised boat landing and embarkation by Marshes Motor Boats to retain the income from Swanage and when the Swanage Pier Trust wonderfully achieved full restoration, I supported this by arranging to provide them with evening cruises by *Waverley* to raise additional funds by simply paying for the fuel and crew overtime of the ship.

Sailing aboard *Waverley* from Ipswich, I was amazed to see the condition of Walton-on-the-Naze Pier and it appeared from the view as we steamed past that the landing stage could be put back into use. Tim Wardley and Ken Adams paved the way for David Neill to meet the owners and as a result of us carrying the cost of installing just a few wooden fenders, Walton became available for steamer calls.

At Margate, I saw a photograph in one of the books published by Bernard McCall and realised that if coasters could use it, why not *Waverley* and *Balmoral*? Again, the London branch team, together with David Neill, arranged for us to bring back steamer sailings to and from Margate. Much successful work was done at other ports and piers around Britain, the latest being the complete restoration of the landing stage at Llandudno, but, excluding the Clyde, all pier landing stages will only be maintained if they receive the amount of use every season that can only be achieved by a two-ship operation.

Advertising and Publicity

All advertising should seek to conform to AIDA, that is: command Attention, develop Interest, create Desire, and ensure an Action.

My experience of newspaper advertising began when I was fourteen years of age, in our local newspapers for our family business. My first paid advertisement for *Waverley* was to raise funds, an advert for principal Scottish newspapers illustrating a thermometer, showing at the top the target, with the thermometer filled in up to the amount we had then raised. Newspaper advertising for the first sailings of 1975 began in early May. I researched the newspapers, including all relevant local papers that covered the catchment areas for each departure point. I then negotiated prices with every newspaper, which included checking their standard rates in the Bible of British newspapers – *BRAD*, telephoned each newspaper and negotiated the best price I could obtain for a series of advertisements, then asked what reduction they would give to a charity, and finally, whether they would give a cash discount for us sending the cheque in payment with the order – most newspapers gave this. This all combined to achieve the lowest possible costs. I then started with blank sheets of paper to write the copy as I had no examples from previous pleasure steamer operators of any similar style of advertising.

As *Waverley* and the 'Second Ship' expanded our programme to almost every coastal area of Britain the same pattern of work was required. Every advertisement was in a portrait – vertical – format as all the experts tell us that newspapers are read in columns from top to bottom, not landscape from left to right! Over all the years literally thousands of newspaper advertisements were produced, almost all typed and administered from the offices of my family business at Barry. Press releases, for editorial columns, were produced in their thousands and these all had to conform to what the then-editor of the *South Wales Echo* said to me when I met him at a function: 'I will always print your press releases – as long as they contain news!' In truth, our press releases aimed to be an advertisement but they had to begin the opening paragraph, in every case, with something that was news worthy. Press releases – editorial – are of course printed in newspapers free of any charge.

Advertising cards, which became known as hanging cards, were also developed for all departure points in Britain that had any significant number of sailings. At times I created television adverts and radio adverts, although these produced a significantly lower response than newspapers and were quite costly. Radio and television do not have the benefit of newspapers and leaflets – they cannot be retained.

By the late 1970s, with *Waverley*'s programme expanding to other areas of Britain than the Clyde, I realised that there were a number of keen enthusiasts who were willing to travel to different areas to take part in *Waverley*'s programme. This led to the introduction of the national timetable, sent out to all members of the Paddle Steamer Preservation Society and eventually to our ever-growing customer mailing list. This was an expensive exercise but it did follow the long-understood principle of advertising, namely that those who have already been your customers are potentially the 'hottest prospects' for repeat business. Advertisements were also placed in many tourism magazines and shipping and steam railway magazines, and individual leaflets promoting charters and group bookings were produced for all the main areas of operation.

In 1992 I began the production of four-page, full colour tabloid programmes, for the Clyde, Bristol Channel West area, Bristol Channel Wales area, Thames and Solent. It appeared that some enthusiasts did not understand the reason for this style, and size, of publicity. I came to realise that publicity leaflets for our ships had to conform to the 'Command Attention' principle and that they would only do this if they were seen very prominently in tourist information centres, steam railway stations, museums, etc., etc. To command attention, the last place we wanted our leaflets to be was to be in leaflet racks with a host of other competing attractions. We needed our material to be seen and picked up, by every person entering any of these premises. The way to do this was to produce programmes that would not fit into standard tourist information centre racks, as to gain maximum attention they needed to be displayed on their own. To achieve this, I purchased wire baskets that were produced for tabloid newspapers and these were provided to every possible distribution point with a header card that said 'Free Programme'. From observation, I could observe that in many places very few people passed by the basket without picking up a copy. In later years we were able to place the baskets in some major supermarkets and this was achieved at no real cost, simply by giving the store manager complimentary tickets to distribute to their staff. Using the wire baskets in these busy supermarkets could achieve a take-up of over 5,000 copies in a full season, from some supermarkets in the Bristol Channel area.

The production of the first full colour tabloids was the subject of a letter to the editor in the PSPS magazine *Paddle Wheels* late in 1992, written by the late Patrick Taylor, an enthusiast who was one of the early pioneers to travel to sail on a number of the paddle steamers in Europe. This was Patrick's letter:

Better Publicity Material
The new Style timetables issued this year by Waverley Excursions Limited, covering all of the cruises operated by Waverley and Balmoral from various locations in the UK are the best of their kind that I have seen anywhere in this country and overseas. The layout is first class and the coloured illustrations of the ships and places visited really 'sell' the cruises advertised. In future years these are going to be much sought after collectors items. The charter promotion leaflet is also a masterpiece in its presentation.

C. P. G. Taylor

The main distribution of the colour tabloids, and baskets, was achieved by 'Grand Tours' of major operating areas, around the Bristol Channel from the Gower Coast, near Swansea, as far as Bideford in Devon; the Solent from Portland to Southsea; and North Wales. Each year would see two cars leave our offices at Barry, loaded down to the springs with huge quantities of material. Personal calls were then made at every possible tourist information centre, holiday camp, steam railway centre, etc., etc. to present the baskets and place them in strategic positions filled with the programmes, and to put on display hanging cards, 'Book Here' advertising cards and copies of full-colour picture posters from John Nicholson original paintings. All this was to achieve maximum impact in all the key departure points and we always travelled with substantial quantities of drawing pins, blu-tak and sellotape. Individual leaflets for group bookings were mailed to hundreds of members of the Group Travel Organisers' Association who were based in areas that were reasonably accessible to the ships' departure points.

All newspaper advertisements, leaflets and advertising cards were headed with artwork principally by the late John Nicholson, and some by Joe Marshallsay, and it was only in later years, with the improvements in the reproduction of colour photographs, that these replaced some of the artwork. Dear John and Joe always produced everything I ever asked for, always trying to meet my specifications for maximum impact, and they never made any charge for all their wonderful work.

Souvenirs

The excellent work of designing, sourcing and organising the highly successful souvenir shops on board the ships was begun by Douglas McGowan, continued by Jim Buchanan and then for so many years by the late Dr Joe McKendrick. In the early years I provided some items, in particular reproductions of some of the paintings by John Nicholson and Ian Orchardson. These were extremely profitable as they could be produced in quantity at very low cost per unit; again, John and Ian provided all their beautiful work completely free of any charge. In the early years I produced leaflets for sales by mail order of an extensive range of steamer books and postcards.

The Past and the Future

I have told just some of the story of the work required to produce the essential income to sail the ships. So many wonderful people have contributed to the story and I thank you all. *Waverley* and *Balmoral* are in far superior condition to when we originally acquired them and, given, like the everlasting carpenter's hammer, a new head and a new handle, they could sail on 'for ever'.

To sail on into the future, our ships need people who are prepared to learn from the experience of the past, to operate a two-ship business to ensure the maintenance of pier landing stages, the retention of pilotage certificates and the sharing of fixed shore costs; chairmen and directors who understand the pleasure steamer business; and marketing that understands how to create desire among younger generations. Any business that costs money for twelve months needs to be earning for the longest possible period each year, therefore it needs the longest possible operating season. *Waverley* and *Balmoral* will not survive by seeking donations and grants to cover their operating costs in 'normal' seasons – appeals are only sustainable to cover exceptional circumstances or really major work, for example a new boiler.

While it is true that all businesses need to evolve, the pleasure steamer business has not fundamentally changed for over 100 years. Passengers' desire is still to have a 'Great Day Out', enjoy an afternoon cruise, an evening 'showboat' or sail to and take part in a great event.

I would like to thank Alistair Deayton and Iain Quinn for the opportunity to contribute to this book. It has been my privilege to play a part in the *Waverley* Story for forty-five years and to have been so fortunate as to have had, for many of those years, people working with me who were cleverer than I was.

Terry Sylvester

The family that allowed it to happen. The first day of sailing in preservation by *Waverley*, 22 May 1975. Waverley Steam Navigation Company chairman Terry Sylvester, his wife Anne and daughters Victoria and Sharon. The children are wearing their promotional jumpers, knitted by Anne.

What is a Timetable?

The headline of a newspaper advertisement in 1897 for P. & A. Campbell's famous White Funnel Fleet was 'Pleasure Steamer Sailings'. The Campbell brothers knew what their business was – the headline did not say 'Steamer Services'. It is the same business today: *Waverley*'s timetable is a programme designed for our customers' pleasure and not an advertisement for a ferry service. The timetable must be planned to take those customers to places that they cannot easily reach by road, to take them across water, to visit islands, to view magnificent scenery or to take part in great occasions that are best seen, and enjoyed, from the decks of a pleasure steamer. Adding a visit to a steam railway, steam fair, theme park or stately home now brings significant numbers of extra passengers – but perhaps with pleasure steamers it always was so: the paddle tug *Fiery Cross*, sailing on the Firth of Forth 100 years ago, included in her timetable encouragement to 'See the bowling match at Aberdour'!

While the magnificent *Waverley* is a great attraction, most customers select that part of the timetable which appeals to them. Consider the ship to be the chocolate box and the timetable the chocolates! Each individual chooses the excursions which appeal to them and capture their imagination.

The timetable also plays the major role in controlling the business: it is substantially, in modern parlance, the business plan. It is also a constant reference work and a driving force for staff, both on board the ships and ashore. It controls a host of costs – or cost-savings. It determines the number of hours the ship will run and therefore the amount of fuel consumed and the wage costs. The cost of using a port or pier can be anything from free of charge to £1,000; the cost of newspaper advertising for one day could be £300 or £1,500. The timetable determines the cost of pilotage – free if our captain holds the necessary pilotage certificates, perhaps £1,000 for a day if he does not. The income earned from catering can also be greatly increased, or decreased, according to the timetable.

Passengers disembarking from a day trip before 12.30 p.m. are least likely to purchase lunch on board; passengers on short crossings may spend no money at all in the catering department; while those on a full cruise who spend all day aboard the ship purchase two meals during the day.

Must we employ rope handlers at the port or pier at additional cost? What is the cost of fresh water? Will the ship incur additional costs by sailing to another port for fuel? Do the local agents for ticket sales give their services free, or at nominal cost? What will coaches cost to take customers home if the ship cannot make a return sailing in the time available – or if the tide will be out at the necessary return time? Where will the ship spend the night or begin the next day's sailing? All these aspects, and more, have to be considered when creating each day of a timetable.

Each year the work of compiling the timetable can be compared to making a jigsaw puzzle. Firstly, the pieces have to be collected. What special events are taking place in Britain at suitable times and suitable locations? What enquiries have there been for private hire and will they result in a booking? Are they just a possibility or unrealistic, the enquiries of dreamers who will not proceed? What has been learned from the results of the previous year? Have 'new' ports or piers been identified that may be used? Have any become unavailable? What ideas are there to consider from people who have written or just made a casual comment? Will they, as many such ideas have done, lead to the addition of successful elements to the timetable?

The real work to create the following year's timetable begins in late October. *Waverley* has sailed on her last trips of the season by mid-October and although there are a host of other things demanding attention – and the human beings involved may desperately need a holiday – the work of preparing for the following season begins immediately. The major role in planning the practical and marine elements of the timetable falls to the marine superintendent, a master with unrivalled experience of Britain's coast and estuaries. Having collected the first pieces of the jigsaw puzzle, the commercial director meets with the marine superintendent to prepare an outline timetable plan. If new ports of call are a possibility, or perhaps if pier repairs are needed, one of the masters would often travel many hundreds of miles to investigate, as we never entered a port or pier without paying a visit to study the navigational and practical aspects of a call.

Then it was time for detailed planning to begin. For the Clyde and the Solent, this was very easy: piers can be used at any state of the tide and much is well proven – the periods of the season for operating there and even most of the times and destinations – so year by year there is very little change in these areas. Indeed, some of the Clyde timetables have not changed significantly since *Waverley* became the first operating member of the 'PSPS Fleet' in 1975. If change or improvement seems to be needed, this is easy: calculate the ship's speed, ensure that the timings after sunset comply with the appropriate passenger certificates, and you can almost do whatever you think will produce the best results.

What a different picture in the Bristol Channel! Here we have the second highest rise and fall of tide in the world, and with no pleasure steamers operating in Nova Scotia, the Bristol Channel must be the most complex place in the world to plan a pleasure steamer timetable. Many other areas of Britain are also significantly affected by tide. This means that for all areas in which our ships operate, apart from the Clyde and Solent, timetable planning begins with a blank sheet of paper.

As an example, let us compare what happened on the Clyde on 2 August 1996 and what happened on the Bristol Channel.

Every Friday, 21 June to 30 August		Friday 2 August only	
Glasgow	1000	Penarth	0830
Kilcreggan	1155	Weston arr.	0920
Dunoon	1220	Cheddar Gorge & Caves Tour	
Rothesay	1305/1415	Weston dep.	0930
Dunoon	1515	via Flat Holm Island	
Kilcreggan	1535	Penarth	1100
Glasgow	1730	Steam Railway & Welsh Mountains Tour	
		Clevedon	1215
'Country & Western' Cruise		Cruise to New Severn Bridge	
(2 August only)		Clevedon	1515
		Weston arr.	1630 c
Glasgow	1900	Weston dep.	1745 c
River Clyde Cruise		Clevedon	1900
Glasgow	2230	Penarth	2015
		Weston	2115/2215
		via Weston Bay & Holm Islands	
C = by coach		Penarth	2330

Both these timetables have been designed to show the highest possible earnings against the lowest running costs. The Friday schedule for the Clyde has been unchanged for many years, while the Bristol Channel's was created for one day only, to take the best advantages of the tide times of that one day. The Clyde requires no coach connections. In the Bristol Channel special coach connections were sometimes essential to operate a timetable with the highest possible earnings and to overcome the problem that the tide does not allow calls by the ship at certain piers at essential times of the day. There are also coaches to Cheddar Caves and to the Welsh Mountains, for the steam railway: all are included to increase the revenue earned on this day.

By the Christmas season, a first draft timetable would be available for study. There may be changes in customers' requirements for private hire and these can occur daily. More information may not be available about special events – but much information will still not be available. Those who organise such events did not plan them to suit our requirements, or to the tides! With the first draft, the intense and detailed work to achieve the best possible commercial results would now begin. Every day would be studied carefully to see if the potential earnings can be improved. Can operating costs which are not justified against the potential revenue be eliminated? Can operating hours be reduced? Can advertising costs be made more effective by changes to the timetable? Great efforts would now be made to ensure that the timetable offers all possible options to attract different customers. For example, if the Thames tides allowed sailings from London to Whitstable on three consecutive days, this may be an easy option – but there will not be enough customers for three consecutive days for the same destination. It is essential that the timetable includes all possible variety so that different customers are constantly attracted. The ideal was that every day included a day trip and an afternoon cruise – with an evening cruise every Friday and Saturday – from almost every port we sail from! This of course was impossible to achieve, but these options are what our customers really desired.

Changes to the first draft of the timetable based on commercial judgement and customers' requirements had to be practical and meet all the marine requirements. Many faxes and phone calls passed between the marine superintendent and the vommercial director in an intense effort to ensure that every detail would be right. As our timetable developed, we now had to check other people's timetables since many of our days included trips on steam railways, visits to steam fairs, tall ships parades, cruises to meet other famous ships. Could we use all the ports and piers at the times that we wanted to? Many telephone calls and letters were exchanged, for we had to communicate effectively and successfully with people in many parts of Britain. We cannot miss the opportunity for all the extra passengers that these additions to our timetable could bring, but we had to get every detail right. Just imagine the results if we arrived at a pier in time to miss the steam train, or sailed to meet the Royal Yacht *Britannia* and arrived just five minutes after the great ship had passed by.

Final details were often being changed in the last hours before printing of the timetable began. No effort could be spared in making sure that our timetable was as correct as it could possibly be. There is only one timetable that we should publish – and that was the right one. In 1975, our first year, we issued an advance timetable at Easter and one day in July passengers who had consulted it were waiting at Troon harbour. *Waverley*, though, sailed past – for we had changed the timetable and our call at Troon was to be a day later. If we had continued to do this, passengers would be waiting all over Britain at the wrong piers on the wrong days – and on the days we did call, many passengers would not have been there.

Every year, the race is on to complete the timetable by early March and sometimes it was late March before we won the race. Twenty-five years of experience showed the commercial director that there was only one thing worse than a late timetable and that was a wrong timetable. If we got it right, the summer ahead would be full of happy days and happy passengers – and we would earn the vital income that made it possible for *Waverley* to sail on and avoid an annual financial crisis.

As examples of the extensive programmes operated by *Waverley* and *Balmoral* during some of the peak seasons: in 1992 *Waverley*'s timetable was 126 days of public sailings, *Balmoral* 143 days, and in 1997 *Waverley*'s timetable was 135 days of public sailings, *Balmoral* 131 days.

Terry Sylvester

Ports, Piers and Harbours Called at by *Waverley*, 1947–2014

Firth of Clyde
Glasgow (Anderston Quay)
Glasgow (Lancefield Quay)
Glasgow (Windmillcroft Quay) (To load launch *Westward Ho* in 1987)
Glasgow (Stobcross Quay)
Glasgow (Yorkhill Quay)
Glasgow (Science Centre)
Glasgow (Fairfield Basin)
Glasgow (Merklands Wharf)
Clydebank (Rothesay Dock)
Clydebank (UIE yard, formerly John Brown's)
Dalmuir (Sewage Works) (Emergency call after boiler tube problems)
Dunglass (Oil Jetty) *
Old Kilpatrick (Oil Jetty) (To transfer to *Queen Mary* in 1976 after paddle failure and for decommissioning of berth with RFA *Pearleaf*, 1980)
Bowling (Frisky Wharf)
Greenock (Customhouse Quay)
Greenock (Bristol Berth)
Greenock (Container Terminal)
Gourock
Helensburgh
Kilcreggan
Largs
Wemyss Bay
Millport
Millport (Keppel Pier) – 2014
Fairlie (Admiralty Pier)
Portencross
Ardrossan
Irvine

Ports, Piers and Harbours Called at by Waverley, 1947–2014

Troon
Ayr
Girvan
Cairnryan
Stranraer
Garlieston
Dunoon (Old Pier)
Dunoon (Argyll Breakwater)
Dunoon (Coal Pier)
Ardnadam
Kilmun
Strone
Blairmore
Succoth Admiralty Pier (Loch Long)
Rothesay
Ormidale (By tender)
Tighnabruaich
Tarbert
Ardrishaig
Otter Ferry
Inveraray
Lochranza
Brodick
Lamlash (By tender)
Campbeltown
Carradale

West Highlands
Port Ellen
Crinan
Colonsay
Oban (North Pier)
Oban (Railway Pier)
Oban (Lighthouse Pier) (Lay-over only)
Fort William (Until 2013)
Craignure
Tobermory
Tobermory (By tender)
Staffa (By tender)
Iona (By tender)
Coll
Tiree
Rum (By tender)

Mallaig (Steamer Pier)
Mallaig (Inner Harbour)
Armadale
Kyle of Lochalsh (Railway Pier)
Kyle of Lochalsh (Fish Quay)
Broadford
Portree
Uig
Dunvegan
Raasay (Old Pier)
Raasay (New Pier)
Gairloch

Western Isles
Stornoway (Loch Seaforth Pier)
Stornoway (Admiralty Pier)
Tarbert (Harris)
Lochmaddy
Lochboisdale (South Uist)
Castlebay (Barra)

North-West England
Liverpool
Fleetwood
Heysham *
Workington
Whitehaven

North Wales
Llandudno
Holyhead

Isle of Man
Douglas (Victoria Pier)
Douglas (Edward Pier)
Peel
Port St Mary

Northern Ireland
Belfast
Donaghadee
Warrenpoint

Republic of Ireland
Dundalk
Dublin
Dun Laoghaire (Car Ferry Berth)
Dun Laoghaire (Mail Pier)
Wicklow
Arklow
Rosslare
New Ross
Waterford
Youghal
Cork
Cobh
Kinsale

Bristol Channel
Fishguard
Milford Haven
Tenby
Swansea (Ferryport)
Mumbles
Briton Ferry
Porthcawl
Barry (No. 1 Dock)
Barry (Lock Entrance)
Barry Island Harbour
Penarth
Cardiff (Welsh Assembly Berth)
Cardiff (Outer Dock)
Steep Holm Island (By tender)
Flat Holm Island (By tender)
Newport (Dock)
Newport (River Usk berth)
Sharpness
Bristol (Cumberland Basin)
Bristol (Arnolfini)
Avonmouth (Inside docks)

Avonmouth (Lock entrance)
Portishead
Clevedon
Weston-super-Mare
Minehead
Porlock Weir (By tender)
Lynmouth (By tender)
Ilfracombe
Clovelly (By tender)
Lundy Island (by tender)
Lundy Island Pier
Bideford
Padstow

Devon and Cornwall
St Ives *
Mevagissey
Falmouth
St Mawes (By tender)
Plymouth (Millbay Dock)
Salcombe (On a buoy, passengers landed by small craft)
Kingswear
Torquay (Haldon Pier)

Dorset
Weymouth (Pleasure Pier)
Weymouth (Ferry Berth) *
Swanage
Poole
Bournemouth

Solent
Southsea (Clarence Pier)
Portsmouth Harbour Pier
Southampton (Town Quay)
Southampton (Royal Pier)
Southampton (Eastern Docks) Berth 49
Southampton (Western Docks, berth 101)
Southampton (Western Docks, berth 104)
Yarmouth (IOW) (Inner Harbour)
Yarmouth (Pier)

West Cowes Pontoon
Ryde
Sandown

Sussex Coast
Worthing
Brighton Marina
Newhaven
Eastbourne
Hastings

Kent Coast
Folkestone Harbour (Outside Berth)
Folkestone Harbour (Inside Berth)
Dover (Prince of Wales Pier)
Dover (Admiralty Pier)
Dover (Western Docks)
Deal
Ramsgate
Margate (Old Harbour)
Whitstable
Chatham Dockyard
Gillingham

Thames Estuary
London (Tower Pier)
Greenwich
Masthouse Terrace Pier
Victoria Deep Water Terminal*
Woolwich
Gravesend (Railway Pier)
Gravesend (Town Pier)
Tilbury (* and passengers)
Gravesend
Swanscombe *
Southend
Clacton
Walton-on-the-Naze

East Anglia
Harwich (Halfpenny Pier)
Ipswich
Southwold
Great Yarmouth (Britannia Pier)

River Humber
Hull
New Holland
Goole

North-East England
Scarborough
Middlesbrough
Hartlepool
Newcastle (Quayside)
South Shields
North Shields
Blyth

Firth of Forth
Grangemouth
Granton
Inchcolm (By tender)
Burntisland

East Coast of Scotland
Dundee
Montrose
Aberdeen *

* Calls for fuel only

Winter Refits
Govan Dry-Dock
Greenock (James Watt Dock)
Greenock (Garvel Dry-Dock)
Lamonts Pier (Port Glasgow) (CSP and CalMac only)
Birkenhead (Cammell Laird)

Milford Haven
Swansea
Cardiff
Southampton (Husband's Slipway)
Great Yarmouth (Prior's Yard)

Additional calls 1947–73 which had closed by the WSN era:
Glasgow (Bridge Wharf) (Until 1969)
Glasgow (Princes Dock) (1970–73)
Glasgow (Plantation Quay) (1973) (Now current berth)
Govan Pier (1961, for a launch)
Greenock (Princes Pier) (Tender to *Empress of Scotland*, 10 October 1951)
Craigendoran (Until 1972)
Fairlie (Until 1971)
Arrochar (Until 1972)
Lochgoilhead (Until 1965)
Hunter's Quay (Until 1964)
Kirn (Until 1964)
Innellan (Until 1972)
Auchenlochan (1947–1949)
Kilchattan Bay (One call, 1952)
Millport (Keppel) (Until 1971)
Whiting Bay (Until 1961)

Pre-preservation refit and winter lay-up locations
Glasgow (Queens Dock) (Winter lay-up, 1967/68)
Glasgow (Princes Dock) (Winter lay-up, 1971/72)
Glasgow (Govan Dry-Dock) (1963/64)
A. & J. Inglis, Pointhouse (Refit, 1947–62)
Clydebank (Rothesay Dock) (Winter lay-up, 1969/70)
Bowling Harbour (Winter lay-up, 1947–52)
Lamont's Slipway, Port Glasgow (Refit, 1965/66)
Greenock (Victoria Harbour) (For engine fitting, 1947)
Greenock (Albert Harbour) (Winter lay-ups, 1954–67)

It is worth noting that a number of these piers, etc. are no longer available for various reasons: commercial, health and safety, or their poor condition.

Total numbers of piers and harbours called at:

Clyde Coast	54
West Highlands	27
Western Isles	6
North-east England	5
North Wales	2
Isle of Man	4
Northern Ireland	3
Republic of Ireland	13
Bristol Channel	34
Devon and Cornwall	8
Dorset Coast	5
Solent	12
Sussex Coast	5
Kent Coast	11
Thames Estuary	13
East Anglia	4
Humber	3
North East England	7
Firth of Forth	4
East Scotland	3
Refit locations	10
Pre-preservation	16
Pre-preservation refits and lay-up locations	9
Total	**258**
Total (in WSN Ownership)	**233**

These totals include five calls purely for fuelling purposes. At some of the ports and piers fuel has also been taken before embarking passengers.

Terry Sylvester
Iain Quinn
Alistain Deayton

Events & Opportunities

The late Jon Holyoak said to me, 'You have turned the timetable into a programme of events.' This was because I read in the book *Steamers of the Forth* by Ian Brodie that the paddle tug *Fiery Cross*, sailing from Granton, advertised, 'See the Bowling Match at Aberdour.' This inspired me to seek out every opportunity to take advantage of any event, in a suitable location, even if it was comparatively unrelated to our ships, or to add an additional attraction to the timetable. These days brought countless extra passengers, many days were sold out and all events were able to achieve higher fares than ordinary days – I believe the record was £95 for the Tall Ships Parade of Sail from Newcastle. There follows a list of all those that I can remember that were researched, marketed and managed by myself and staff at Barry:

Steam Railways

Everywhere around Britain that our sailings could link in with a steam railway would bring extra passengers.

West Somerset Railway
East Somerset Railway
Lynton & Barnstaple Railway
Brecon Mountain Railway
Barry Island Railway (including inclusive ticket for rides on the Barry Island Funfair)
Jacobite Steam Train (Fort William to Mallaig)
Isle of Man (Three railways – electric, horse-drawn and steam)
Lakeside & Haverthwaite Railway
Ravenglass & Eskdale Railway
Swanage Railway
Isle of Wight Steam Railway
Romney, Hythe & Dymchurch Railway
North Yorkshire Moors Railway
Bo'ness & Kinneil Railway

Events & Opportunities (including connecting bus trips)

Tall Ships and Parades of Sail (Falmouth, Newcastle, Milford Haven, Clyde, Firth of Forth, Solent)
Tower Bridge Centenary
View Millennium Dome
Paddle Steamer Parades with *Kingswear Castle*
Two paddle steamers at Whitstable and Southend
Heritage Afloat (Thames)
Annual Church Service at Lundy Island (For over thirty years)
Garden Festivals (Ebbw Vale and Glasgow)
Dunkirk Fortieth and Fiftieth Anniversaries
Blackpool Tower visit
Inclusive Holidays (North Wales, Padstow, Milford – for the Tall Ships)
Escort HMS *Cardiff* leaving Cardiff
Escort Royal Yacht *Britannia* on Farewell departure from Cardiff
Millport Illuminations and Rothesay Revels
Escort Cunard liner *QE2* on the Clyde and 'Meet the Liners' at several other ports, most notably Southampton
Welcome liner *Norway* (former transatlantic liner *France*) to the Clyde
Service in Iona Abbey
Visit Mount Stuart via Rothesay
Liner *Canberra* Farewell
Welcome HMS *Invincible* home from the Falklands
Two Ships Days with *Waverley* and *Balmoral* (Bristol Channel, Campbeltown, Millport)
Steamer Anniversaries (Commemorating fiftieth anniversaries and centenaries of famous pleasure steamers)
WSN Tenth Anniversary celebrations
White Funnel Fleet former officers and crew days
Special welcome to those evacuated by paddle steamer from the Thames in the Second World War (the following year the Evacuees Association chartered *Waverley* for a day)
Second World War reunion days
Southend Fun-fair
Battle of the Atlantic (From Liverpool and Llandudno)
Centenary of Llandudno Pier
Celebrate Reopenings of Piers (Clevedon, Penarth, Ilfracombe, Blairmore and Lochranza)
Penarth Pier Centenary
Cardiff Bay visits and bay cruises
Penarth Festival Fireworks cruises
Opening of New Severn Bridge
Coney Island Funfair via Porthcawl
Inclusive tickets to Sea Life at Weston
Ilfracombe Victorian weeks
'Children Free' Days on suitable short cruises

Teddy Bear Parties
Junior Pirates Days
Senior Citizen 'Bring a Friend Free' days on quieter weekdays
Inclusive tickets to Butlins, Minehead
Inclusive tickets to Watermouth Castle family fun days via Ilfracombe
Three Ships Festivals at Lundy Island
West Somerset Railway transport rallies and steam galas
County cricket at Weston-Super-Mare
Three Castles tours via Penarth Pier
Cabot 500 (Escort sailing ship *Matthew* from Bristol)
New book launches on board with authors autographing copies
River Dart Cruise to Totnes
Southend Air Show
'Parades of Steam' on the Medway with *Kingswear Castle*
D-Day Fleet Review
Thames Sailing Barge races
Round-the-World Yacht Race
Visits to Clevedon Court and Tyntesfield (National Trust properties)
Round Arran and North Arran coach tours
Macrihanish tour to the Shores of the Atlantic
Welsh Mountain Tour
Cowal Games at Dunoon
Songs of Praise/Dunoon Pier Centenary
Ships Model Day
Cricket matches on Lundy Island
Cheddar Caves
Marconi Centenary of first radio transmission across water
Paddle Steamer Preservation Society open days, evening charters, day charters and nominated outings UK-wide
Clyde River Steamer Club nominated excursions and charters
Scottish Railway Preservation Society charters
David & Charles (publishers) charter

The programmes operated by *Waverley* and *Balmoral* during some of the peak seasons were extensive:

In 1992	*Waverley*'s timetable was 126 days of public sailings
	Balmoral's timetable was 143 days of public sailings
In 1997	*Waverley*'s timetable was 135 days of public sailings
	Balmoral's timetable was 131 days of public sailings

Terry Sylvester

A Captain's Memories: Part 1
In the Beginning 1974/75

The tale of the *Waverley*'s operational preservation is of huge historical significance. Our railway heritage has been looked after in an exemplary way but shipping hasn't fared so well. You can travel in historic carriages and behind steam engines dating back over 100 years, get on and off at magnificently presented and preserved period stations, and as a result be transported back in time in the most authentic of ways. In shipping it is difficult to find examples of ships that you can travel on in service, living ships doing the job that they were built to do, and the Paddle Steamer Preservation Society have three of them, each transporting you back to a bygone age of coastal and river transport in their own particular way. Apart from these three ships, and perhaps the SS *Shieldhall*, based in Southampton, you have to go abroad to see working examples of steam ships today. This is the story of one of them and the effort that went in to save her as a living memorial to cherish and admire.

There was a boy, just an ordinary boy, who fell in love with the sea and in particular the coastal cruising scene in the early 1950s. Coastal day excursions provided enormous pleasure to hosts of holidaymakers at that time and because of relatives in the south, he was to experience days out on the Thames, the South Coast and the Solent as well as in his home area of the Clyde and its glorious firth. One of his sets of grandparents lived in Ayr and the other in Eastbourne, and so he was to benefit enormously as a result, cruising all round the Firth of Clyde and along the South Coast between the Isle of Wight and the Thames estuary in his summer holidays. His interest in ships and the sea was encouraged, but it was the arrival of the paddle steamer *Caledonia* in Ayr in 1954 as Ayr excursion steamer which had the greatest impact and started a love affair with that particular ship which lasted right up to her destruction by fire in 1980. It also developed a lasting affinity with paddle steamers that continues to this very day. To quote that ship's last master in an article for the *Glasgow Herald*, just before she retired from active service in 1969: 'You could go to sea in this ship,' meaning that he would have been happy in her on a real seagoing voyage. Most of the twentieth-century paddle steamers were built for estuarial waters, which included short voyages out to sea, and were not seagoing ships in the true sense of the word. These sentiments were shared entirely by the writer; she was a wonderful vessel with a crowd of officers and crew to match throughout the 50s, and being down at Ayr you really did feel as if you were proceeding to sea each and every day that you went out of the harbour. This enthusiasm for the sea and the ship was cultivated in every way, and her master in the late 1950s taught this young lad many tricks of the trade regarding ship handling, steering and coastal navigation, in the days when no electronic gadgetry existed, not even radar before 1959. He was definitely his mentor and as a result this same boy was delighted to be able to welcome him back on board the *Waverley* when this very young man became the first master of that vessel in the preservation era.

That was the beginning of the story and it all started when I worked for a short period assisting in the cafeteria of the *Caledonia* in August 1959 and then full time in May 1960, first in the steamers and then into foreign-going ships later that year. I returned to coastal ships for a couple of months, working in General Steam's *Royal Daffodil* on the Thames in the summer of 1965, and then permanently from March 1966, when I joined MacBraynes with a brand new second mate's certificate in my hand. I had obtained my master's certificate by 1969 and spent most of my time as mate of various ships until moving to Western Ferries in 1973 as master of the *Sound of Islay*. I had done two very brief periods as master before that, my first command being the cargo ship *Loch Ard* in September 1969. My career continued in Western Ferries and I moved my home and family to Dunoon in 1973 to become a permanent master on the Clyde/Argyll service, my main ships being *Sound of Scarba* (1) and *Sound of Sanda* (1) with occasional spells of relief duty on *Sound of Islay* and *Sound of Shuna* (1). I brought the *Sound of Sanda* up from the Solent under her own power early in 1974, when she was still named *Lymington* following thirty-five years' service on the Lymington–Yarmouth (IOW) service. It was a great privilege to bring her home – she was built by Denny's in 1938, a great little ship. It was while master of *Sound of Sanda* in August 1974 that I found myself on board *Waverley*, volunteering my services as one of the work party leaders at a meeting chaired by the chairman of the newly formed Waverley Steam Navigation Company Ltd, which had just taken ownership of the vessel. These duties continued throughout the ensuing winter when time permitted, as Western Ferries were now ultra-busy servicing the oil production platform site at Ardyne Point. The ships were all busy, with lots of overtime being worked to keep the supplies to the yard coming as required while also keeping the regular service running between McInroy's Point and Hunters Quay. In February 1975 I found the chairman of the new Waverley Company at my door, wondering whether or not I might be interested in operating the *Waverley* for the summer season! It had been a boyhood dream of mine to one day drive a paddle steamer and now I was being asked if I'd like to do it for real!

After much deliberation and also considerable negotiation with Western Ferries, who were being asked to lose one of their masters when trade was so busy, I agreed to face my fears and live my dreams by accepting the challenge that lay ahead. Fortunately Western Ferries, part of Harrisons Clyde group at that time, were asked to and agreed to provide technical back-up for the operation so that certainly made the transition much easier. They were also willing to second me to the *Waverley* for the 1975 season and, unknown to me at the time, they continued to pay my salary. With a degree of trepidation, therefore, I joined

WAVERLEY
the world's last seagoing paddle steamer

WAVERLEY STEAM NAVIGATION Co. LTD.

TELEPHONE: 04462-78167 (Day)   04462-70252 (Night)   PLEASE REPLY TO   Gwalia Buildings, Powell Duffryn Way, Barry, Glamorgan.

CHARTER CHARGES FOR ADVERTISING CAMPAIGNS: COMPANY CLUB OR SOCIETY OUTINGS: SPECIAL PROMOTIONS: EDUCATIONAL CRUISES: CLUB OR SOCIETY FUND RAISING SCHEMES: CONFERENCES.

1975 SEASON — VESSEL COMPLETE WITH CREW & FUEL

		Weekdays	Sat & Sun
FULL DAY CHARTER	- AROUND 12 HOURS for	£1,750	£1,750
DAY CHARTER	- AROUND 9 HOURS for	£1,500	£1,750
HALF DAY CHARTER	- AROUND 6 HOURS for	£1,250	£1,500
EVENING CRUISES	- AROUND 3 HOURS for	£ 575	£ 575

PERIOD CHARTER   - ANY NUMBER OF DAYS @ £1,750 PER DAY
(SPECIAL REDUCTIONS CAN BE NEGOTIATED DEPENDING ON DISTANCES STEAMED)

WAVERLEY CAN CARRY UP TO 1,350 PASSENGERS - YOUR COSTS, THEREFORE, EVEN FOR A FULL DAY CRUISE COULD BE UNDER £2. PER HEAD

SPONSORSHIP DURING THE WAVERLEY'S PUBLIC SAILINGS

THESE ARE FULL DAY SAILINGS DURING THE PEAK TOURIST AND HOLIDAY MONTHS.

The total cost of WAVERLEY'S operation during tourist months is £1,950 per day and the Sponsor would guarantee the difference between the WAVERLEY'S operating cost for the day and the passenger fares received.

On Tourist Sailings, WAVERLEY will call at no less than 15 seaside resorts, cities, towns and villages to collect passengers and there will, therefore, be substantial passenger receipts.

WAVERLEY can carry up to 1,350 passengers on public sailings. The average price for cruise tickets will be around £2.95, therefore, the cost to the Sponsor could be minimal. On many days there may not be any cost incurred at all.

A FULL LIST OF WAVERLEY 1975 TOURIST SAILINGS WILL BE SUPPLIED ON REQUEST.

All offers or implied offers subject to alteration without notice.
All sailings under the terms and conditions of the operating company.

REG IN SCOTLAND
REG No 50789
REG OFFICE 45 RENFIELD ST GLASGOW G2 1JZ

CHAIRMAN J TERRY SYLVESTER
DIRECTORS DOUGLAS M GOWAN
P MORRIS REID SECRETARY
GEORGE TRAIN

IN ASSOCIATION WITH THE PADDLE STEAMER PRESERVATION SOCIETY — FOUNDED 1959
PATRON SIR JOHN BETJEMAN CBE   PRESIDENT PROF A R ROBINSON BA PhD

Charter rates for the 1975 season.

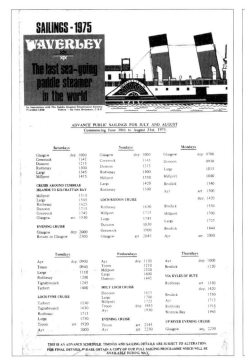

Above left: The advance timetable for *Waverley*'s 1975 season. The funnels and paddle box drawing was by Mrs June Bushell.

Above right: The actual timetable for the 1975 season.

the *Waverley* in the James Watt Dock, Greenock, in early May 1975 and I think that the twenty-three years that followed can best be described in Mother Teresa's words:

> If you are kind, people will accuse you of selfish motives; be kind anyway. If you're successful, you'll win both false friends and true enemies; succeed anyway. What you spend years building, someone may destroy overnight; build anyway. The good you do today most people will forget; do good anyway. Give the best you have and it may never be enough; give your best anyway.

How true those words were to become as the years progressed. The advance timetable had already been produced but some adjustments had to be made to it and the public timetable from 30 June 30 to 31 August was finalised. A list of charter rates had also been produced and the first month was to be spent on special sailings, excursions for schools, day and evening charters, and also some short public excursions. A few long day excursions were also planned just prior to commencement of the main season of sailings.

By 5 May final items of life saving appliances were returned on board and the ship's boiler inspected and passed by the then Department of Trade. On 9 May fires were lit and steam was slowly raised until full pressure was reached and the safety valves tested on

12 May. On this day also, two of the lifeboats were lowered, fire hoses rigged and pumps tested. The engine was also turned ahead and astern all, with satisfactory results. On 13 May the engine was thoroughly warmed through and the catering operation commenced using outside caterers; we were almost ready to go and an aura of excitement permeated throughout the ship. I brought a model of the ship on board and demonstrated various manoeuvring techniques using thread to simulate the ropes, all spread out on one of the dining saloon tables, as only one of the crew that we had engaged had had any experience whatsoever of sailing in an operational paddle steamer previously! On 14 and 15 May full lifeboat and fire drills were carried out in the presence of the DTI surveyor and the fire alarms were tested. Later on the 15th, the vessel departed for Tail of the Bank for compass adjusting, and thence to Gourock to land the compass adjuster and to uplift gangways. We sailed via Dunoon (where my wife and two kids joined us) to off Fairlie, before returning to Glasgow's Anderston Quay with a call at Greenock on route. The vessel was canted at Glasgow and my time with the crew at the dining saloon table two days previously had paid off: all the pier calls and the canting manoeuvre at Glasgow had gone off without a hitch. Canting is the manoeuvre whereby the ship is turned short round in a confined space. We were up and running; we could operate the *Waverley*. I slept well that night!

We had to return to the dock in Greenock on 20 May for some further minor repairs and adjustments before returning to Glasgow on my thirty-first birthday, 21 May. We were ready for service; I was pleased with the result and it was a fabulous birthday present, a dream come true. Perhaps the worst feature was the fact that the ship was to undertake the most ambitious schedule ever undertaken by a Clyde steamer since the Second World War, perhaps ever, based at a port never frequently used by this particular ship and in waters that she had never been intended to sail in, other than for the odd excursion. This was a daunting prospect for a young master who had two young children to support and so very much to lose if it all went wrong. It was also all going to have to be done in the glare of the media who, at the time, all thought us to be a bunch of incompetent, sentimental amateurs who would fail in just a few weeks. There was an article entitled entitled 'Awash with Sentiment' in the *Glasgow Herald* at the time which illustrates this view. I had spent a great deal of time in the weeks prior to starting on board going round a number of the Clyde masters who had previous experience of the ship. People who had spent a lifetime in the steamers on the Clyde knew nothing of bow thrusters, Voith Schneider propellers, Azi pods and all the latest electronic gadgetry which has been developed over the past fifty years. They were all vastly experienced people who did it with experienced crews and the back-up of all the facilities available to them at the Gourock office. I was to build the business virtually from scratch while also being my own marine superintendent, crew manager, pilot, radio officer and liaison officer for both on-board crew and passenger complaints alike. Attention from the media was regular and all the foregoing was coped with as well as the day-to-day running of the ship with all its problems in that first season. There were no mobile phones in those days, which had the benefit of allowing a little more freedom in what we were able to provide in the way of service, with small imperfections passing relatively unnoticed. These days the slightest thing out of the ordinary is immediately transmitted far and wide by people around the deck or ashore. The disadvantage of course was that to pass on information to our small office, or indeed anyone else, we had to use a

A newspaper cutting from the day of the VIP cruise, 22 May 1975.

radio link call or find a telephone kiosk ashore. In those early days, even the piers weren't keen to assist with passing on information on our behalf.

However, the information provided by these wonderful predecessors was invaluable and certainly helped me to accomplish much of what I achieved practically in that first season, and in fact a number of them became real friends over the years, not the least of whom was the ship's original chief engineer, who was to be an inspiration to us all. He had been involved since February 1975, supervising the overhaul work on the main engine and auxiliary machinery. To his dying day, he touched us all with his fantastic knowledge of the ship, his unwaning enthusiasm and his encouragement in times of trouble. He was an inspiration to us all and our new second engineer and he hit it off right away, with a great friendship resulting between them right up until his death in late 1977. He sailed with us frequently and was always at the other end of the phone if technical assistance was needed. On one occasion I had to take that up when one morning I awoke to the sound of the boiler safety valves lifting, and on checking around the ship I couldn't find a soul from the engine room department on board. The chief instructed me over the phone on how to shut the boiler down and was on board within forty-five minutes, at three in the morning. He also provided vital instruction on the need for rapid response to the telegraph orders in a paddle steamer and our second engineer at the time became so good at the manoeuvring that from the bridge, movements were so rapid that it was like being in a ship with bridge controls. He was eventually to become our chief engineer in 1977, a position that he held for some ten years, and of his wealth of knowledge, a lot of it, in so far as the *Waverley* was concerned, was gained from the original chief. It certainly ensured the mechanical reliability of the ship right through until the end of the 1980s, when the ship was not only sailing to the far corners of the Firth but also all the way round around the British coastline!

Being willing to be humble enough to listen to the experience gained from the past was a quality that we both were gifted to possess. One of her masters from pre-preservation days once said to me that if you have somebody in the engine room that can make the engine dance, you will make the boat dance. This was to prove very pertinent and vitally important as the years progressed. In all my deliberations to gain experience from the past, one thing shone out: we were bordering on madness taking the ship to Ayr! It was therefore going to be my greatest challenge operating the ship safely and reliably out of Ayr that first season. The other challenge was the one of the boiler, which had been very troublesome in her last season with Cal/Mac and had received very little attention prior to our operation, due to both a lack of time and a lack of finance. We had some wonderful officers and crew, many of whom provided dedication, commitment, enthusiasm and sheer tenacity well beyond the call of duty, and without this the ship would never have kept going. One such was an able seaman seen painting the silver fiddly deck around the funnels and he was to become the ship's bosun for the next twenty years, becoming a much loved character. The purser's department was absolutely outstanding, coping with all the enormous challenges that breakdowns and schedule alterations threw at them with skill and tact and also without complaint, a fantastic achievement, and in consequence lifting a huge burden from me. The chief purser could be moody and guilty of tantrums at times, which eventually led to his resignation, but his two young assistants were absolutely fantastic lads, joined by two others later in the season to strengthen the team and allow for some time off. The chief purser was later to return and play an incredible part in providing advance revenue and bookings for the 1976 season. The original mate moved on fairly quickly and was replaced by the famous former mate of *King George V*, and his comradeship and wonderful sense of humour were a tonic to us all, particularly when times were tough.

We were ready therefore to get going, and as I had already managed to navigate through the 70-foot-wide entrance to the James Watt Dock three times with both paddle boxes intact, I was beginning to gain some confidence with the ship! At 58 feet beam, it didn't leave a great deal of margin for error! Our first passengers boarded on Thursday 22 May 1975 for the inaugural cruise for invited guests and VIPs, which took us to Greenock and Dunoon, where we met *Queen Mary II* for the first time in WSN ownership, returning to Glasgow at 7.30 p.m.; the sailing operated without a hitch and all left suitably impressed. The proper maiden voyage took place on Saturday 24 May, from Glasgow to Tarbert and Ardrishaig, and it was clear that the timings were too tight for the ship, especially with the loads we were carrying. The passenger certificates issued were Class V (smooth waters) 1,225; Class IV (Partially Smooth Waters) 1,016; and Class III (seagoing) 571. Since building, the *Waverley* has always suffered from a weight problem and unfortunately ships always grow as they get older, a bit like most of us, with the result that the seagoing certificate had slowly reduced in numbers as the years progressed. The deeper the ship becomes, the slower she becomes, and if she develops a list, that reduces the speed even further. Similarly, the paddle wheels become under more and more stress the deeper they dig. On 24 May 1975, the ship was running with her Class IV complement on board all day. It was a combination of all these things which caused a paddle float to fail in Loch Fyne at around 7 p.m. In those days the ship carried no burning gear, with the result that it took much longer to remove the broken float than it normally does today and we didn't get under way again until 8.10 p.m. The catering had been very busy and the boiler in operational steaming condition for twelve hours, so when we reached Tarbert we had very little water left on board. There was a delay at Tarbert while further supplies were obtained and we set off at about 9.20 p.m. for Dunoon. I was to take many gambles in my years as master of the *Waverley*, but I was tired and not prepared to take the ship through the Kyles in the dark! We therefore didn't reach Dunoon until 12.10 a.m. the next morning and Gourock at 12.30. Caledonian MacBrayne's shore traffic manager had arranged a train to take the passengers home to Glasgow, another fantastic achievement and a kindness willingly extended to us in what had become a very stressful situation. Amazingly, some remained with us to the end despite being told that we were going to stop at Greenock to fill right up with water. We eventually reached Glasgow at 3.35 a.m. and, undeterred, were ready to sail at 10 a.m. on our scheduled public sailing the next day, which went off without a hitch.

On the Monday we were due to make an early start for a special cruise to Campbeltown but due to all the extra steaming and the delays on the previous Saturday, we didn't have enough fuel to make it, so frantic arrangements were made to rouse our friends at Esso in Bowling to see if we could get some on a bank holiday Monday. This was achieved, but not in time to meet our scheduled departure time, so the ship eventually left Glasgow fully an hour late. Our superintendent engineer from Harrison's (Clyde) sailed with us as chief engineer as our own engineers had been up all night replacing the paddle float broken the previous Saturday. All was going well and we were making up some of the time when between Largs and Millport the leading float (No. 1) failed, this time on the port paddle wheel. We couldn't continue and repairs undertaken by our own engineers involved removing the broken float, removing another float and repositioning it in the No.1 float position, no mean feat with the vessel tied up at Millport pier without the use of any shore-based facilities. The passengers had a day ashore in Millport instead of Campbeltown and the ship left on time, returning to Glasgow a few minutes ahead of schedule.

Our first weekend was over: lots of difficulties encountered, but we made it and it was just as well that we were a young team – it had been really hard work. It was clear that we were driving the ship too hard for the condition of the paddle wheels and the boiler, neither of which had received a great deal of attention prior to commencement of operations. Nevertheless, we had to stick with it – the timetables were printed. The ship performed reasonably well, including our first sailings out of Ayr on 30 and 31 May, until a boiler tube burst on Sunday 15 June and to avoid missing the scheduled sailing, the second engineer and the superintendent from Harrisons decided to put a plug in the tube without shutting down the boiler. The original boiler was double-ended, so the job entailed climbing in through one of the furnaces to the centre of the boiler, inserting the plug in the affected tube, which in turn was tightened into place from the stokehold end in the boiler room. This was a very dangerous thing to do but it was a thirty-six-hour operation to do this in the normal way with the original boiler, as once blown down and emptied, then refilled with cold water, it took twenty-four hours to raise steam again, which would have lost us the day's sailing. Unfortunately, our superintendent was badly burned exiting the boiler as large quantities of hot water had collected near the exit door from the leaky tube, so no such feats of bravery were attempted after that; the boiler was shut down while repairs were effected on each of the other occasions when tube trouble presented itself.

We continued on, starting our Ayr season on Friday 27 June and had a fabulous weekend of sailings, Round Arran to Campbeltown on the Saturday and a Girvan/Stranraer/Loch Ryan cruise on the Sunday, with the main season of sailings beginning from the Monday, which continued until 31 August. We met *Queen Mary II* every Sunday that season on our Loch Riddon cruise, which started the tradition of playing G. F. Handel's 'Arrival of the Queen of Sheba' as the vessel was passing through the narrows of the Kyles of Bute. The sailings continued with no major incidents apart from odd bits of boiler tube trouble and paddle float breakages, all by and large looked after by those on board. The deck officers together with the deck crew were regularly required to assist with paddle wheel repairs and maintenance and this included myself as we all tried to maintain as reliable a service as possible. We received a good degree of reliability and integrity of service until Sunday 27 July, when the ship only got as far as Dalmuir Sewage Works when the boiler lost most of its water. The ship had to be towed back to her berth and the ship only managed to make three sailings out of a potential seven between then and 8 August. Things looked pretty bleak, however, but we were then joined by a young and dynamic chief engineer from Australia and under his leadership she rallied and from then until she finished on 8 September she performed very reasonably except that the scheduled PSPS charter to Inveraray on Saturday 23 August had to be cancelled due to a further burst tube in the boiler. What an achievement – one that everyone involved can be truly proud of. The directors held their nerve and kept the operation going through the bleakest moments and for me my proudest moments were arriving at Girvan and leaving Ayr for the last time on 31 August – not a sailing cancelled due to weather, not a scratch on the ship. I was so proud of that and it confirmed my optimism that Ayr could be done on a regular basis with *Waverley*; for a large part of that first season, she was leaving with her Class III complement every day and often sizeable numbers were being left behind, unable to get on board because the ship was full. The ship was her own best advertisement coming in and out of the harbour, with large crowds turning up to watch and as a result seeking information about the sailings. It was clear that we were going to have to find a way of increasing the passenger certificate numbers. Much had been achieved but, alas, the financial result was not so good and much work was going to be needed to see her into another season – work that I was going to have all too little to do with due to a very busy winter in Western Ferries. I left *Waverley* on 13 September to return to *Sound of Sanda*. The first season of operation by the bunch of amateurs was over.

A Captain's Memories: Part 2
The Formative Years 1976–78

The WSN directors once again worked a wee miracle and work was put in hand to have the ship ready for another season, including the re-tubing of the boiler. The work was put in hand with the Stephen's repair facilities at Govan Dry-Docks, later to become Clyde Dock Engineering. Meanwhile, the purser from early 1975 had been engaged, working from the company's small offices at Lancefield Quay as commercial manager, 'selling' the ship with huge success. Charter and party bookings were flooding in, which together with schools and senior citizen business had the early season pre-booking situation looking very healthy indeed. I was asked if I would take the ship on again, which really put me on the spot. Western Ferries weren't going to be fairy godmother to me again; it was a clear choice this time, stay where I was or move to *Waverley* permanently. Eventually the call of *Waverley* was too much for me and despite much reservation expressed by my wife and two young children, I agreed to take it on permanently, provided that I was given a seat on the board. This was granted in early April and I took up my duties in early May as a permanent member of staff and director of WSN Co. Ltd. By this time the ship was in an advanced state of repair, thus I took little responsibility for the set-up in 1976. I considered the mechanical performance of the ship a disgrace. Wrong way and inconsistent engine movements were regular, slow response to telegraph orders frequent and breakdowns daily, making the handling of the ship extremely challenging. In fact, how we staggered from one Thursday to the next (Thursday was our off service day that year) I will never know. On four occasions I was forced to anchor in the main river channel while emergency repairs were carried out to the paddles, I personally joined the deck crew working all-night stints on the paddles each week, alternating with the mate, to keep the ship going. On Glasgow Fair Friday the steering gear failed completely, jamming hard a port, and miraculously we missed piling into a brand-new frigate, fitting out at Yarrows, by just a few feet. On the first Sunday in September the same thing happened while passing Dalmuir sewage works, but I managed to work the vessel safely alongside.

In those days there was no rudder indicator on the bridge to show you what the rudder was doing – you just turned the wheel and assumed the steering gear was responding. This was to be rectified after the grounding in 1977. In August, a complete paddle assembly fell off the port paddle wheel at Bowling and we had to crawl into Old Kilpatrick. Passengers were transferred to the *Queen Mary*, which was following us upriver, and she came alongside to pick them up. I was pictured talking to the captain and purser of *Queen Mary*, arranging for their onward transit to Anderston Quay. Temporary repairs were carried out by the ship's staff and we returned upriver later.

    The ship ran for weeks with either one paddle float or another off and became known as the golden paddler by Stephen's ship repairers, who were on board every week attending repair work of one sort or another, but mostly paddle wheel work. In all, fourteen paddle floats were changed during the season, almost all from the port paddle wheel. The deck crew maintained the starboard wheel so we seemed to do quite a good job! The cause of all these breakages was always put down to hitting something, which was the result of much discourse between me and our technical experts as I had experienced exactly the same scenario in the *Queen of the South* (ex *Jeanie Deans*) when I worked on her for a short period on the Thames in 1967. The real cause was clearly down to a lack of maintenance of the moving parts of the wheels and feathering gear. The catering was appalling; it was still in the hands of outside contractors, with the general standard of staff employed being mediocre. However, there were some exceptions, like the American Bicentenary celebrations on 4 July, when the dining saloon was decked out magnificently. White table cloths were back, each table with floral decorations, Stars and Stripes flags with memorabilia for the occasion: it was a sight to behold. This event was sponsored by the Scottish Tourist Board and the ship was packed, with gasps of awe from many of the passengers. However, the vast majority of the time the caterers were only interested in what they could make from the evening booze cruises. It was sad and led to much unrest among the officers and crew.

    The ship ran trials on 14 May and commenced service on the Spring Bank Holiday weekend, 22 May; despite all of the foregoing, no sailings were missed. The work on the boiler had certainly paid off and a long day's steaming was no bother to it, without any need for water replenishment; this was a huge benefit and gave peace of mind all round. At one stage our technical experts reduced us to 40 RPM maximum and the consequential late running caused huge unrest among our customers, which was borne mainly by the pursers, but also to an extent by the mate and myself. After about ten days of this, one breezy Saturday we arrived at Tighnabruaich about ten minutes before departure time for the return journey and so I announced that due to the late running of the vessel there would be no time ashore. This caused a near riot among the passengers, which was directed at the pursers and then at me. I managed to persuade the ring leaders to direct their tirade of abuse at the engine room and fortunately the technical expert responsible for this new speed rule was on board that day. He immediately came to me, demanding an explanation for this intrusion into his peaceful existence in the engine room by angry customers, who had paid for a visit ashore at Tighnabruaich. I responded that in future this is how we would direct such complaints unless more effort was made by his team to ensure that the timekeeping of the ship improved. I was at pains to explain to him that it was unfair to expect others to take the flak caused by a ruling from him with no authority from the board when all we were doing was trying to maintain the published schedule with the ship running around 2 knots slower than what was required. It was up to him to go to those who had provided the schedules and explain to them why, in his opinion, they couldn't be kept. This approach had the desired outcome and after a week or two the individual responsible resigned, obviously having failed to convince the other directors that it was right that the ship should run up to an hour late.

We did our best to honour what was printed in the schedules after that, although they were still a bit fast for the loads that she was carrying and the condition of the paddle wheels. Occasionally, when the tides were right, we would pass through the narrows via the crooked channel to save a few minutes and these occasional deviations from normal navigational practice were much appreciated by the passengers. Another thing to come from the technical experts at the time was that the ship couldn't be operated in waves greater than four feet high! For people that had known the ships all their lives and had sailed in them in all weathers, winter and summer, such information was just farcical. Before the advent of the first purpose-built ferries in 1953, it was ships like the *Waverley* that ran all the Clyde services all year round, quite safely and with a substantial record of reliability. Despite all this, however, 1976 must go down as a very successful season. We were blessed with fine summer weather and the passenger figures were absolutely outstanding: over 200,000 were carried in the season, with the ship packed to capacity out of Ayr almost every day despite having the Class III passenger certificate raised to 819 in mid-July. We frequently had to turn people away, resulting in the reproduced photograph from the *Ayrshire Post* entitled 'Just where is everyone going?' appearing, which only served to increase our popularity still further. It was electrifying for all of us and encouraged us all the more to keep the ship going, despite the problems. There was a fabulous team on board and we just faced each problem as it developed with courage and perseverance. The first off-service day after the bicentenary cruise was used to remove the aft port lifeboat and replace it with eight inflatable liferafts. This alteration saved about 4 tons in weight and we were able to demonstrate to the surveyor that after this work was completed the ship was about an inch lighter in the water than she was in May 1975. He allowed us as a result to have the full passenger numbers dictated by the Lifesaving Appliances (LSA), which equated to the 819 mentioned above, provided that for the remainder of that season we sailed with no more than 20 tons of fuel on board until a full lightweight survey could be carried out.

We had seen very little of the original chief engineer in 1976 due to ill health and the ship was definitely missing the influence of her young second engineer from 1975 but the engine room team kept her going in very difficult circumstances, as the loads on the paddle wheels were probably greater than the ship had ever experienced in her whole life, running in the outer Firth with over 800 passengers on board every day and regularly 1,000 or more on board in the upper Firth. Other than just keeping her going, little else could be done in terms of running maintenance and so she really was ready to finish when that season came to an end in mid-September. The original chief had a look round the engine room on the last day of the season and, shaking his head when he came out, he said to our chairman, 'I don't know whether or not you are a religious man, but if you are, you should get down on your knees and thank God that she finished the season.' 1976 was over and I went on leave, returning refreshed in early November to plan the winter refit.

1977

My first job prior to taking responsibility for the winter refit of the ship was to obtain agreement from my fellow directors for full autonomy over the ship – the way she was manned, the way overhaul and refurbishment work was carried out and how we were going to approach the task of putting her through her first five-year loadline survey under our ownership. I received their approval and set about preparing the ship for the biggest facelift that she had seen since her construction in 1947. A Government-sponsored job creation scheme existed at the time and with assistance from one of my fellow directors we successfully completed all the forms and administrative work required for us to join the scheme and obtain the grant associated with it, which effectively paid the wage bill to provide work for a given number of individuals. Interviews were carried out and twenty-two men were engaged of the various trades that were required. Work got under way: timber decks were repaired and renewed and wasted steelwork cut out and replaced, including the whole of the main deck port and starboard over the fuel tanks and boiler room. The wooden deck had first to be lifted, the wasted steel cut out and the blue asbestos insulation removed. This involved a whole tier of legislation, which had to be complied with to safeguard the personnel and also safeguard the disposal of the material, a very dangerous substance, especially when dry. New Rocksil insulation was installed and a new steel deck welded in. The dormitory-style crew accommodation was stripped out from forward and new, insulated light-weight partitions were installed to provide five two-berth cabins for the deck and engine room crews.

The public rooms were redecorated and refurbished, a new bar installed and the lower tea room remodelled in the hope of bringing this space back into use. We had decided to have a go at in-house catering to see whether or not we could manage it, rather than using outside contractors as in the previous two seasons. Every area of the ship received attention, from the bilges to the mastheads, and maximum effort went into reducing weight. The toilets were stripped, including 3-inch-thick concrete decks, and new lightweight fittings were provided, with the doors being scraped back to the bare wood and revarnished. The galley received similar attention, with the old coal range, coal bunker and sinks being removed and replaced with gas ranges and lightweight stainless steel sinks and worktops. The heavy linoleum was removed from the dining saloon deck and the original wooden deck sanded down for varnishing. It was a huge job. In the engine room big changes were underway too, with the original chief back directing operations. I managed to persuade an excellent steam engineer away from the security of a permanent position with a prominent coasting company to become the ship's first engineer. Interestingly, that company is no more and the *Waverley* still continues! Similarly, I also managed to entice the second engineer from 1975 away from deep sea trading, at great pecuniary sacrifice to himself, and he became the ship's chief engineer. After further persuasive tactics, my engineer from *Sound of Sanda*, who had been with the ship since we left Portsmouth together back in March 1974, also agreed to come as the ship's second engineer. What a fabulous team of engineer officers they were, as the years ahead would prove – nothing could stop her now.

The ship left for dry-dock on 9 March, where a huge overhaul of the paddle wheels was undertaken. Brand-new pitch pine paddle floats were fitted, together with a host of re-bushing to both paddle wheels, under the direction of the original chief. Pitch pine had been successfully used in the Humber paddlers as a successor to the original Canadian Rock Elm, which could no longer be obtained. A new steam alternator was also fitted to enhance the electrical supply on the ship and this was driven by an ex-Admiralty single cylinder Robey steam engine. Two of these were purchased absolutely brand new and still packed in their original wooden cases, complete with a full set of spares. She returned to Anderston Quay on 1 April, where all the new furnishings and carpets were installed, and trials were run on 18 April. Our new chief steward had led negotiations for sponsorship of the lower bar by White Horse whisky. What a transformation: the ship ran like a dream, smooth and very quiet in operation, with all the weight saving measures having paid off. We had managed to lighten the ship by some 32 tons, reducing her draught by 3 inches. The DOT marine survey office was happy and new loadline marks, CA and CB, were marked on the hull just forward of the paddle wheels. The passenger certificates were issued and numbers confirmed as Class V, 1,225; Class IV, 1,016; and Class III, 842; and these were to remain the same right up to the early 1990s, when new regulations were introduced regarding life saving apparatus, emergency escape routes, stability and seating requirements.

The ship entered service with a couple of Clyde cruises on 24 April before proceeding to Campbeltown the following Wednesday to undertake the Campbeltown to Ayr Agricultural Show excursion, via Brodick, the next day. This hadn't been done since 1973 with *Queen Mary II* but had been an annual event up until that time, to facilitate, in the main, the Kintyre and Arran farmers visiting the show, but many of their wives and families came along too for a day's shopping in Ayr, and so it was always very well supported. The next day the ship set off for her first voyage outwith Clyde waters on what was supposed to be a charter to Aberconwy District Council to celebrate the Year of the Pier (Llandudno pier centenary), but they unfortunately pulled out of this a couple of months before it was due to take place. This caused a terrible dilemma as a huge amount of time and effort had been put into the planning of these sailings and following a visit to the area by the writer, the chairman and the general manager of the time, it was decided to make the visit anyway on our own account. This gamble paid off as the ship was well received and ran full to capacity on the planned sailings over two weekends, except that one day had to be curtailed due to inclement weather, having to turn back in the region of the Crosby light float. It got so wild, in fact, that we had to retreat into the docks for the night, the motion alongside the landing stage being too much for us to remain there. Four of the intervening week days were filled with short river cruises for schools, senior citizens and the general public, with a charter to the Wirral Railway Circle one evening. On returning from her first visit to Llandudno at low tide, we discovered that there was no pier to lie against; instead, the pier appeared to be on stilts, with the facing piles about 8 feet above the water! The passengers on board were treated to an extra hour's cruise while we awaited the rising tide and despite leaving Llandudno seventy-five minutes late, with the engine running at an effortless 49/50 RPM, the ship duly arrived back in Liverpool only thirty minutes late. The visit ended on Monday 9 May, when she left Liverpool at 2.30 p.m. and made a record passage back to Ayr, arriving at 1.15 a.m. the following morning.

Following this, we settled into our early season programme of charters, party bookings and school parties until the main season of sailings started towards the end of June.

The Clyde early season at this time, and for many seasons thereafter, included unusual destinations and areas not visited before and in 1977 the ship made her first and only visit to Townsend Thoresen's ferry terminal at Cairnryan. Our own in-house catering operation was running well, with many compliments resulting from the improvements in the standard offered and the cleanliness of both the ship and the staff involved, and also the courteous way in which the service was provided. However, one day around the middle of June, I was confronted by one of the company accountants, accompanied by the company solicitor, instructing me to explain irregularities in the accounting and stock control in the catering operation, laying the responsibility for this at my door despite the fact that there were two accountants on the board and a manager in the office. I really took exception to this and was not able to add this responsibility to my duties, which brought me very close to handing in my resignation. With the events that were about to follow, it was a shame that I didn't take the opportunity to move on at this time.

Passenger numbers were reasonably good and the ship was running really well until disaster struck on Friday 15 July: when returning from a Loch Goil cruise, the ship ran aground on the Gantocks. This was later traced to a fault with the steering; however, the approach that I took that day had expected the ship to act in a very precise manner, something that I should have known not to do, so I decided to take full responsibility for the accident and fully expected to lose my job over it. The incident has been well documented over the years (see p. 153); suffice to say that the ship was very badly damaged as a result of being stranded on the rocks over a full range of the tide and no dry-dock was available to make permanent repairs until 7 August, some three weeks away. What a disaster: the ship was going to be out of action for all of the main part of the season. It was incredibly fortunate that she hadn't been declared a CTL (Constructive Total Loss) – she was a mere whisper away from it. The officers and crew had just proved themselves to be the finest bunch of professionals that any master could have wished for, a million miles away from the bunch of amateurs described in the media just two years earlier. The passenger evacuation was text-book, with no injuries, thanks to that very professionalism and the assistance of the *Juno* and the *Sound of Shuna*, with the *Sound of Sanda* standing by later. The ship was badly holed in one of the after spaces and the officers and crew dismantled one of the wooden gangways to shore up the bulkhead adjacent to this space, and with the help of the American navy, who supplied portable pumps, the ship refloated at around midnight and steamed into Dunoon East Bay coal pier, where she would dry out on each tide. This allowed us to make temporary repairs with cement boxes to plug the leaks so that she could proceed to Garvel Dry-Dock for a more permanent temporary repair. Unfortunately, the dry-dock was not available for long enough for permanent repairs to be carried out, so we had to settle for the installation of temporary girders to replace the strength lost by the ship's inner keel and a patchwork of doubling plates to seal the holes. The ship proceeded to Greenock under her own power at a speed of 16 knots on Tuesday 19 July, which established that the boiler and machinery were not affected by the incident. Some minor damage was done to a couple of paddle floats. She left Greenock on Wednesday 27 July to proceed to her berth in Glasgow, again under own power, but with a tug to assist with the steering, which had been damaged at the time of the grounding. She moved to a berth outside Clyde Dock Engineering's repair yard, formerly Stephen's ship repairers, where she was laid up until 7 August, when permanent repairs were begun. I was shattered by the whole episode but was encouraged to carry on and was engaged from 20 July in the charter of MV *Queen of Scots*, which ran a modified programme of sailings between 23 July and 31 August, while *Waverley* was under repair. More about this little vessel in A Captain's Memories: Part 4. Repairs were completed and *Waverley* ran trials on 31 August, with passenger certificates reissued. Stores were transferred from *Queen of Scots* at Millport and the ship proceeded lightship to Ayr to recommence service the following day. Thursday 1 September was a poor day, with a strong southerly wind blowing, and I wondered whether or not to sail. It was a case of damned if you do, and damned if you don't, with publicity surrounding our first day back in service running high. We set course for Brodick but it was clear that the swell was too great for reasonable comfort and so I decided to head up Firth and offer a cruise to Largs and the Holy Loch instead as we had an evening charter from Largs that evening anyway. Unfortunately, as we turned two windows were broken in the fore end by a large wave. My run of bad luck was not over because, as a result of bad media coverage, I was charged with taking the ship to sea in weather which was not 'Fine', as stated on the Class III passenger certificate, a charge, to my knowledge, never levied at any Clyde steamer master before; it was certainly clear that times were changing. On this occasion the charges were dropped by the procurator fiscal, which was a great relief.

A number of sailings were lost in September due to poor weather and to the fact, I think, that I was not at my best. All in all it was a successful month, with the ship packed at Millport Illuminations on Saturday 24 September. On the evening of 8 September a fault was discovered on the clutch mechanism in the steering flat which had probably been there for some time, but we now had a rudder indicator on the bridge, so we were able to see on the bridge that although the wheel was hard over up there, the steering gear and rudder were slowly slipping back to midships. I felt slightly vindicated but nevertheless very crestfallen that I was responsible for plunging the company into a serious debt crisis, threatening the very existence of the ship. I went off in a coaster, where I had time to reflect, gather my thoughts and see if there was anything that I could do to repay the money lost by missing thirty-eight potential sailing days, which at that time was reckoned to be a revenue loss of between £62,000 and £65,000. When I returned, the ship was in steam again for a shift to her new quarters at 54 Stobcross Quay while Anderston Quay was redeveloped, and this was to be her home until 1983. 1977 was over.

1978

During my spell on the coaster, I had put together an ambitious programme of sailings on the South Coast and had also enlisted the help of PSPS members and family in the South to assist me with the marketing of it, the idea being to obtain sufficient pre-booked business to cover the bare cost of the whole operation. This was to take place at a time when the ship would not normally be in service, early April until the Spring Bank Holiday weekend, and I set my target at £85,000 if I could manage it, so that the revenue loss from my navigational error in 1977 was fully recovered. The ship did not need further dry-docking and could proceed into service at any time once business was obtained. What a challenge, but I was a determined character. However, I didn't know that in my absence the company's bank accounts had been frozen, which meant that it had basically ceased trading until guaranteed business was obtained for it to trade at a surplus in order to pay back the many creditors outstanding as a result of the previous season's losses. The company accountant had skilfully managed to obtain a moratorium from all the major creditors, who were willing to wait until the next season's earnings produced some income to repay them from. This was an incredible achievement, without which the company would have been forced to liquidate, but it also meant that absolutely no money could be spent at all other than that which was necessary to protect the assets of both WSN and its creditors. Conversely, without the ship trading again, the creditors were only going to obtain a very small proportion of what they were owed, and so it was in their interests also to wait, and by so doing hopefully recover all that they were due. In those days, the *Waverley* had little value as nobody would have been interested in trading a thirty-year-old paddle steamer in the commercial world, and in any event a sum equal to her scrap value in 1974 would have been due to Caledonian MacBrayne in the first instance before anything would have been left for anyone else. We were therefore unable to proceed with any early season venture, let alone a speculative south coast one, without independent external backing. Along came one of our new directors, who offered to bareboat charter the ship at his own expense provided that (a) I obtained the pre-booked business mentioned above to cover the bare cost of the operation, and (b) that I became solely responsible for the use of his money to undertake all the costs involved for all services that the vessel would require, including wages and salaries, during the whole of the bareboat charter. My goodness, what faith and trust – it was an awesome responsibility to have to accept. However, we worked together, setting up various monthly accounts with a number of suppliers, not the least of which was for fuel, and what remained would have to be dealt with direct from the ship by cheque. I had to arrange for extra help on board by carrying a second mate, and for part of the trip two second mates, so that I could handle the extra administrative duties, leaving a lot of the navigational duties to my trusted team of officers and indeed what a team they were – nothing was a trouble to them. The other directors were not in favour of the venture and it caused much dissension around the boardroom table, which served only to undermine and unsettle me; however, our financial benefactor was unflinching in his support and once we had reached the stage of sufficient pre-booked business to proceed, there was nothing that could be said as any earnings were going to ease the situation with the creditors. Even thirty-six years on, I still cannot believe the huge effort and dedication that went in to assisting me with this venture – it was utterly fantastic; society members, harbour masters, port authorities, ships agents, coach companies – the list is endless and it was just an enormous team effort by so many people, many of whom are now deceased. For example, my mother and step-father (he was a former teacher) canvassed the schools in Sussex and filled the ship to capacity on schools sailings out of Eastbourne and Hastings. Grey-Green travel and A. T. Mays provided huge numbers of passengers in the Thames Estuary, with A. T. Mays chartering the ship completely for two days. The Wessex Branch of the society were particularly outstanding in provision and distribution of publicity for the sailings in the Weymouth, Bournemouth and Solent areas, with many of those involved also now deceased. I will never forget the dedication and enthusiasm of all these wonderful people, who supported the venture and turned it into the success that it was, because we were at least a week into the programme before any publicity material arrived from our own management sources, much to the dismay of huge numbers waiting to voluntarily distribute it on our behalf.

BBC's Radio One launched their Scottish week that year with a broadcast of the breakfast show from *Waverley*, with top disc jockeys Kid Jensen, Paul Burnett, Noel Edmonds and Tony Blackburn all taking part, and Kid Jensen was back on the Thames for further broadcasts from the ship later on; in fact, he sat with me in my cabin on one occasion while I attempted to make a link call to shore for him as his wife was expecting their first child. No mobile phones then! Steam was raised during the last week of March and the season commenced with a week's charter to the catering company Watson & Philip, starting in Glasgow on Friday 31 March, then taking the steamer to various Clyde resorts, promoting their products to very large numbers, testing our new AC electrical system to its very limits with all the various boilers and other appliances in use! A day sailing for the public was provided on Saturday 8 April before the ship was prepared for the voyage south. I had been down at Arnott Young's about three weeks previously, where some of the lads and I obtained spray-tight doors from a tanker being broken up there and these were for the fore and after end of the sponsons. We also obtained portholes with deadlights to replace the windows on the sponsons from the ex-Clyde Navigation Trust navigation buoy tender *Torch*, which was also being broken up at that time. All this was to improve the watertight integrity of the ship for the voyage south, a requirement laid down by the Department of Transport before a Loadline Exemption certificate for that voyage would be issued.

We also had to provide steel shutters to slide over the windows from outside, as previously the ship was only equipped with half-inch-thick plywood shutters applied on the inside, which were only sufficient to cover 25 per cent of the windows. In order to accommodate the steel shutters, steel angles had to be welded round the outside of each window, with great care being taken not to crack the glass as the original windows in the ship were only standard quarter-inch-thick plate glass, the same as many of the tenement houses had in Glasgow! All was completed between Monday 10 and Friday 14 April, with the loadline exemption certificate being issued on that day.

The forecast was favourable and so we set off from Glasgow early in the morning on Saturday 15 April, and after a fuel stop at Bowling the ship was on her way south by late morning and arrived at Milford Haven for more fuel at noon the next day. A bit of head scratching went on then as to how to connect this minute vessel to the terminal pipeline, normally accustomed to dealing with 250,000 ton tankers. She created quite a sensation among the terminal staff and cameras were clicking furiously, with the terminal's official photographer/reporter wasting no time in recording the event. She left Esso Milford Haven at 3.00 p.m. and rounded Land's End at 10.30 p.m. that evening, reaching Newhaven harbour at 6 p.m. on Monday 17 April. I went home for a few days as I had dental treatment to receive and the first sailing wasn't until Friday 21 April, an evening cruise with entertainment by the Shirley Western Showband. When I returned, the ship was transformed; the lads had been hard at it, the ship was painted all round, the brasses were gleaming and the engine room was a picture – what a fabulous team of lads and my bosom swelled with pride as we shifted down the harbour that afternoon ready for our first sailing. We left with a near full complement on board and all weekend at Newhaven numbers were about double what I had budgeted for. Thousands of passengers were carried during the whole visit, with capacity loadings frequent, and only two sailings had to be cancelled, the first a Deal–Clacton run due to rough weather and the other an evening cruise from Clacton when visibility was reduced to 50 yards. There were only two other incidents worthy of note, and that was losing the anchor while turning in the upper reaches of the Medway on 28 April due to a broken link in the cable. This was retrieved by the vessel *Medway Otter* and delivered back to us the next day at Southend. The crew of the *Medway Otter* would take nothing for this service other than half a dozen free tickets; it was a fantastic gesture and just epitomised the enormous goodwill that surrounded the vessel during that first visit. The other thing that happened was that on one of our mid-week arrivals at Tower Pier, there was no tug to swing us, but fortunately the tide was on the flood and so we were able to swing on the anchor, which had only been restored to its rightful position a couple of days earlier following the incident in the Medway! The ship sailed for thirty-six days and steamed 7,181 miles carrying 54,185 passengers, made 123 passenger carrying calls at piers or harbours and was in operation for 408 hours. Not a single minute was lost in this exhaustive programme through mechanical defect, a tribute to the efforts of a quite fabulous team of engineer officers and ratings. During the visit the ship earned £92,112 worth of ticket revenue, with a further £9,494 in the souvenir shop and £28,215 in the catering. The catering wasn't nearly good enough but that was a project for the future; my wildest dreams had been realised and the money lost through my accident the previous year returned to the company thanks to the trust and support given me by one of the directors, with all of this achieved at a time when the ship would otherwise have been laid up. The trip finished at Bournemouth on 17 May and the ship was back at her base at Stobcross Quay by 21 May, ready to commence her 1978 Clyde season. What an achievement – the company was back in business and able to resume normal trading, and also able to make a substantial payment to all the creditors. That was my thirty-fourth birthday so I celebrated it by going off for a week's leave!

The Clyde season went off extremely successfully, with a number of special sailings offered as well as the normal public timetable, scheduled to operate in part from 2 June to 2 July six days a week and then in full thereafter, increasing to seven days a week from 25 July. There were a number of special sailings offered. On Saturday 24 June we re-enacted the Royal Route to celebrate the centenary of PS *Columba*, which operated the route from her construction in 1878 to 1935. The scheduled departure time from Glasgow of 7.11 a.m. was honoured, with the ship arriving at Ardrishaig at 1.45 p.m. The return time allowed for *Columba* was forty minutes between Ardrishaig and Tarbert. Leaving Ardrishaig at 2.15 p.m., the *Waverley* managed to reach Tarbert by 2.52 p.m., three minutes ahead of schedule! We did cheat a little in that we were bow out at Ardrishaig, ready to depart! On Tuesday 22 August we visited Irvine, the first call by a Clyde steamer at that port since before the Second World War. It was once a winter retreat for ships of the Williamson-Buchanan fleet. The visit took place in the middle of the Marymass Festival and the ship became a floating Ceilidh, with bands, folk singers and artistes from the festival on board together with a near capacity crowd. ICI provided their tug *Garnock* free of charge to assist us out of the harbour; it was a great day and many accolades came from an appreciative crowd.

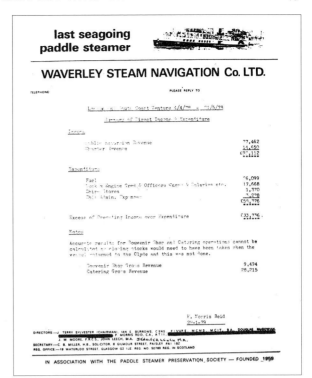

The financial results of the first South Coast venture, 1978.

Unfortunately, a crack appeared on the circumferential seam of the boiler around 7 July and the ship had to be taken out of service. This was a serious fault and was in fact the same sort of trouble that had finished the *Jeanie Deans* eleven years earlier on the Thames as *Queen of the South*. A careful repair was carried out but it was clear then that if the ship was going to have a long-term future, a new boiler would soon have to be installed. With repairs complete a week later, as steam was being raised a few rivets were found to be leaking also, this time on one of the riveted butt straps, so the boiler had to be shut down again, and it was the third week of July before the ship was back in service, having missed a potential twelve earning days as a result.

However, the ship performed in an exemplary way for the rest of the season until she finished following a well-filled September weekend of sailings on Monday 25 September. At the very last pier on the last day of the season, when approaching Dunoon in the evening, she broke a paddle float, the only paddle trouble of the entire season, embracing nearly 1,500 running hours. The creditors were all paid off and there was sufficient money left to dry-dock the ship too before lay-up for the winter and so the ship proceeded directly into dry-dock as soon as she was de-stored. A month's extension to the passenger certificates was obtained at the end of August to allow her to finish the season because she hadn't been dry-docked since the end of the Gantocks grounding repairs, which were completed towards the end of August 1977. Dry-docking and underwater repairs were carried out, trials were run and the ship then laid up at Stobcross Quay towards the end of November, ready for 1979. We were now truly ready to build the business and had some alterations planned to assist us in carrying this out. We also had an additional task on our hands to seek funding in order to replace the original boiler.

A Captain's Memories: Part 3
Building the Business 1979–89

1979

We all entered 1979 with a new determination to build the business into something which had a long-term future and could provide more security for those that worked in it. Into my life came two lads who were to make their own massive contribution to the cause, one becoming full-time master and manager of the *Kingswear Castle* from 1985 and the other taking on the *Balmoral* just a year later. The former I met first at the time of the 1978 Thames visit, and the other became Chief Officer of the Waverley in 1979.

Several important and very progressive decisions were taken as we started this new era, the first being to provide a new boiler for the ship, the second to work towards obtaining another vessel for the company so that if an accident similar to 1977 were ever to occur again the company would not be left without income, and finally to attempt to provide facilities on board that maximised earning potential. A new catering officer had been engaged towards the middle of the 1978 season and some experiments were made in the dining saloon to maximise use of this large space, allowing it to be open at all times instead of just being open for meal sittings. Cafeteria-style catering was tried out, with considerable success, and so the decision was taken to refurbish the saloon with modern fixed seating and tables to accommodate this style of use for the 1979 season. The small cafeteria forward was not really earning much but the bar next door was more often than not packed out. The forward end of the ship was divided into two spaces as originally laid out, with a stairway coming down from the forward deck shelter above into a small foyer dividing the two spaces, with doors into each. Forward was a tearoom/cafeteria and the aft part was just a lounge, into which we had installed a bar in 1977. We also took note of the fact that passengers complained regularly about the ship having no space wherein people could sit in peace, undisturbed by through traffic. During January to March 1979, this was altered; the stairway was removed and two new stairways were installed, coming down to port and starboard direct from the deck above, with entrances just forward of the funnels leading down into a new large space. The partitions and doors around the bottom of the stairway had been taken away and the bar moved forward, creating what was later to be called the Jeanie Deans lounge, with the original name boards from the paddle box of that vessel installed above the bar. The new large space provided could be used by entertainers, and had a floor area for dancing when required. The conversion was generally well received.

A new service area complete with display cabinets and hot plates was installed at the after end of the dining saloon, with good access to the galley along with fixed seating and tables for the customers. The on-board team were extremely busy connecting up services for these new areas: electrical power, water and steam. A new entrance had been created at the rear of the forward shelter, instead of the original sliding doors to port and starboard, and this turned the space into a quiet seating area that became much sought-after in the years ahead, with the space being booked regularly for private parties. No dry-docking was required as this had been completed the previous November. Unfortunately, the directors were this year in complete unanimous favour of taking the ship south again, and so I had set a precedent the previous year, one that I was never going to get out of in the years ahead. It was a great worry to me that these long voyages in exposed waters would result in serious delays or damage to the ship. We ran trials during the first week of April and sailed on the Clyde on Saturday 7 April before setting off for the south at 5 a.m. on Sunday 8 April. It was a freezing cold spring in 1979 and the voyage to Southampton took until 11 p.m. on Good Friday, 13 April, to accomplish, with awful weather all the way. We eventually made it to Heysham for our first call for fuel and fresh water, then Fishguard for further supplies, from where we sailed on 11 April. Strong winds from easterly to south-easterly directions accompanied us, which is why the English and Welsh coasts were favoured all the way to Land's End. We reached St Ives Bay that evening, anchoring for the night, and we had a go at rounding Land's End the following morning but we had to turn back: the sea and swell conditions were just too great. It was, in fact, only one of two occasions during my twenty-three years in command that I saw the ship take a green sea over the bow. We also lost a paddle float while making the turn to return to St Ives. We now had to frantically try to get a small tanker of fuel to St Ives as we had insufficient fuel left to continue, and this had to be delivered at high water that afternoon, while our engine room team set about replacing the broken float. A small craft came out to take me ashore to examine the pier at St Ives at low water to ensure that we could get alongside to get the fuel on board, as there was only a two-hour window over high water to accomplish this. The mission went off as planned, without a hitch, and with quite unbelievable co-operation from Esso at Plymouth, who seemed to fully understand our predicament. They just pulled out all the stops to make a vehicle available and delivered the required fuel at the appointed time. Must have had an ex-seaman on duty as plant supervisor that day! With fuel on board and a new paddle float fitted, we set off at 5 a.m. the next morning and once through the long, heavy swell between Pendeen light and the Runnel Stone buoy, the ship made a rapid and uneventful passage to Southampton, following the liner *QE2* up Southampton water to arrive at 11 p.m. The ship missed a press conference arranged for that afternoon and a scheduled evening cruise that evening.

After that the ship traded reasonably successfully, but loadings were very poor in what was cold and miserable weather, with trade not really picking up until we reached the Thames in early May. The visit in 1979 was extended westwards from Weymouth to take in Torquay, Plymouth and the Lizard, with a final weekend on the Bristol Channel before returning to the Clyde. Notable events were taking the inside berth at Southend pier because the classic Belgian passenger ship *Reine Astrid* had arrived from Ostend and was alongside the outside berth, also swinging in Bridge Reach, Rochester, using the tidal eddies, no tug, no anchor. 20 May saw us at Plymouth and the Lizard before returning to the Solent for the Spring Bank Holiday weekend, 26–29 May. The *Waverley* arrived in the Bristol Channel for her first visit on the evening of 31 May; wow, what an occasion, what a welcome – sailings were packed for three days, with an incredible send off from Penarth at the end of it. We had been eight weeks away from home by the time we returned to the Clyde.

The Clyde service continued without incident or breakdown and the reopening of Helensburgh pier in July following dredging made a sizeable contribution to passenger loadings. Irvine was visited again, with no tug assistance this time, the ship swinging on her own anchor. The tug *Garnock* had been damaged by an explosion earlier that year while dumping expired and surplus explosives at the official dumping ground off Arran. The ship also made a visit to the Main Wharf at Ardyne, rather nostalgic for me, but the site was looking very inactive and forlorn compared to the hive of activity that it had been when I had been working there in *Sound of Islay* and *Sound of Sanda* 2–3 years previously. The 1979 season finished at the September weekend, as it had the year before. It was a year of fairly varied weather conditions, but we finished in a fairly healthy state, the financial result not as good as the previous year but acceptable. It was also the only season that I completed without a day off. Our efforts in the early part of the year had been justified, as we were at last seeing a decent return from the catering, which was to continue to improve as the years progressed, a great credit to our new catering officer and his hardy bunch of lads and lassies, who endured terrible living conditions to accomplish this outstanding result.

```
Tele. 213930                          41 Gigha Place
                                      Bourtreehill
                                      Irvine
                                      Ayrshire
                                      KA11 1DF
                                      22/9/79

       Dear Captain Neill,
                  As another season draws to
       a close may I take this opportunity to write
       to express my sincere personal thanks for
       all the enjoyable cruises I have had on board
       "Waverley" this summer - I especially enjoyed
       the cruise last Saturday to Ardyne and Loch
       Striven.
              It is my belief, and I am sure I speak
       for many thousands of others that the success
       of the "Waverley" is due for the most part
       to your own hard work since you became Master
       of the ship.
              As a small token of my thanks, I enclose
       an album of photographs which I would like
       you to have

                               Yours sincerely

                                 Harry Hay
```

An appreciative letter from Harry Hay, September 1979.

1980

The new decade dawned, and with 229,000 passengers carried in 1979 it was going to be a challenge indeed to keep the momentum up, and in fact it was going to be 1982 before these loadings were exceeded. The visit to the Bristol Channel was an enormous success and a ten-day visit was planned for 1980, encompassing two weekends and the intervening mid-week. Someone into statistics had calculated that it had been 4,297 days since a paddler had sailed in the channel until the *Waverley*'s first arrival! A cruise to off the Dunkirk beaches was planned to commemorate the fortieth anniversary of Operation Dynamo, with the first master of *Waverley* laying a wreath at the approximate position of the sinking of the previous *Waverley*. He was on board at the time and I remember him vividly describing how, being a non-swimmer, he held on to a piece of the bridge structure as the ship sunk beneath the waves, only to realise that he had to let go of the old girl as she made her way to the bottom, or otherwise drown! He had a lifejacket on so he soon popped up to the surface and was picked up by another ship. The ship was launched from Inglis at Pointhouse on 29 May 1899, the last Clyde steamer of the nineteenth century, and was sunk on Wednesday 29 May 1940, exactly forty-one years later. She had a full complement on board, resulting in heavy loss of life.

1980 proved to be the worst summer of weather in the whole of my period of command, with lots of wind and rain throughout the season. It nevertheless proved to be quite an incredible year all in all. A new manager was appointed on 22 March and he was to guide the shore administration of the company for the next eighteen years. He had been a former school chum of mine and we hadn't seen each other for over twenty years, so there was a bit of catching up to do. Another appointment was that of the purser from 1979, who had become the Southern Sales Manager from the previous November, but this appointment was much more short-lived. Waverley Excursions Ltd was born at the beginning of that season, to release the owners from the responsibility of the day-to-day running of the ship. Two of our visionary objectives were accomplished in that year too, the ordering of the new boiler and the purchase of a second ship for the company; it was just a quite incredible turn of events – we were certainly building the business alright, and at a pace way ahead of our own expectations. The ship came out in early April at Easter, sailed for a short period on the Clyde, visited Liverpool on the way south, sailing on a similar pattern of sailings to previous years then returning via the Bristol Channel for a ten-day stint there, returning to the Clyde by mid-June.

The winter refit had involved lifting the timber decking on the sponsons and replacing it with steel, a load of re-caulking work on the decks above the forward bar and the dining saloon; following the success of the traffic-free space in the forward shelter, the aft shelter received the same treatment. New doors were cut outside the purser's office to port and starboard and a cross alleyway created by the installation of new stylish timber partitions, complete with etched glass windows, to separate the shelter from the through traffic using the purser's office and heading down below to the main and lower decks. This again was a hugely popular improvement, creating another peaceful place to sit, apart from the never-ending problem of the leaky decks, which had been a feature of the ship since her construction in 1947. A new rudder stock was manufactured and installed in dry-dock, with the realignment of the whole of the rudder assembly taking place. The position of the bottom bearing housing had to be altered to allow for a twist in the ship's stern frame, a legacy from the 1970 grounding at Arrochar, when the rudder had been forced round to ninety degrees by the impact against the rocky shoreline. The result was very pleasing and transformed the way in which the ship steered and maintained her course, provided that conditions were calm and also that she didn't have a list, which was something that she hadn't done in all the years of our ownership. An additional benefit was a slight improvement in speed.

The Clyde sailings were now well established and the pattern continued with early season party bookings, schools and senior citizen cruises, and a few charters mixed in until the public sailings started for July and August, followed by the usual and familiar mixture of charters and unusual public sailings until the ship finished at the end of September. No sailings were missed despite some awful weather and some very bumpy days out of Ayr, with the ship running in an exemplary way throughout. It was as if the old boiler was saying, 'You're not really going to throw me out are you?' The catering produced a fabulous performance again, doubling the profit of 1979, which I am sure was due to the poor weather driving people under cover. Unfortunately, our catering officer was offered a more desirable position elsewhere and so left the ship at the end of the season. The boiler was definitely going and the final costings were arrived at by early June for its replacement. A Babcock Steambloc was chosen at a cost of £80,000, with the total cost for the entire installation, including two new diesel alternators and the associated switchboard, set at £176,000. A boiler appeal fund was launched and we were successful in obtaining a grant of £50,000 towards it from the Scottish Tourist Board. Confidence was such that the new boiler was ordered in early September, with the full installation projected to be completed by April 1981.

We had a lot on our plates, but the fire on the *Old Caledonia* that April had resulted in the ship being towed to a shipbreaking facility in Sittingbourne, Kent, and the company was persuaded to keep her in one piece until we were able to have a look. Two of the engineering team and one member of our winter construction team and I set off in my car to have an extensive look at the ship. We found the hull, machinery and boilers intact, as were the sponsons and paddle wheels, but virtually the whole ship would have had to be rebuilt from the main deck up, a task that we all thought to be beyond our limited resources at that time. In hindsight, I believe that had we known all that was to be accomplished by us during the rest of the decade we in fact could have restored the ship, but that is another story. The ship's engines were later removed and are still preserved down at the Hollycombe Collection at Liphook in Hampshire.

In the meantime, the MV *Shanklin* became available at Portsmouth and we found ourselves down there with our chairman to look at that ship. We were aghast – what a ship. Although the port engine was in bits, but repairable, the rest of the ship was in incredibly good condition, and you could have eaten your meals in some of the bilge spaces they were so clean and well maintained. The ship had been extensively refurbished and a new lounge had been created in 1978 at the after end of the promenade deck. It was an opportunity to purchase an economical motor ship with splendid accommodation to sail in support of *Waverley* and it was extremely unlikely that another vessel as suitable as *Shanklin* would become available again and certainly not one in such amazing condition. Despite all that we had to deal with, the purchase of this vessel had to be seriously considered. The Portsmouth trio, as they were affectionately known (*Southsea*, *Brading* and *Shanklin*), were all Denny-built ships of extremely high quality with a set of machinery that would have been the delight of many a deep sea chief engineer. They had huge passenger decks and loads of covered accommodation, akin to the Clyde's *Queen Mary II*, and were also magnificent sea ships, in other words really passenger friendly. We had to have her and I backed that up by putting my hand in my own pocket and one of the engineer officers did likewise, although the amounts that we could put in were insignificant in terms of the project as a whole. Thanks to our chairman, other directors and our friends in Harrison's, a new company was formed to own the ship and that company, later to be known as the Firth of Clyde Steam Packet Company Ltd, was entirely separately funded from *Waverley* as any spare *Waverley* money was allocated to the re-boilering project. The ship was purchased for £25,000 on 6 November 1980 and after underwater inspection at Husband's Shipyard, Southampton, she left the Solent for the Clyde on Thursday 13 November 1980. After a stormy passage north, the ship arrived at Helensburgh on the evening of Thursday 20 November, where some of her new owners came aboard to see her, and it was clear that they were astonished by her spacious and well-appointed accommodation and pleased with their purchase. The ship proceeded upriver the next morning and berthed at Stobcross Quay at 9.40 a.m., where there was a press conference with the ship receiving some good coverage by all involved. On that evening the PSPS branch meeting was cancelled and members were invited to make their way down to Stobcross Quay to have a look around the new ship.

1981

We now had our hands full to be ready for 1981 and something new and much more adventurous had to be planned to ensure that we had the money to see our aspirations fulfilled. I planned a trip that would circumnavigate Britain in 1981 and would embrace new markets in the Humber, the Tees, the Tyne and the Forth. Work continued on board in conjunction with the re-boilering project and more re-decking and caulking work was carried out in an effort to make the ship watertight at roof deck level. All the lifejackets had to be fitted with retro reflective tape and this massive task was undertaken by the PSPS volunteers. Twelve pieces of tape had to be glued to each lifejacket, over 1,300 of them in all, and it took a total of seven weeks, with the volunteers working every weekend to accomplish this quite enormous task: dedication, determination and enthusiasm of the highest order. The saving to the company was some £3,600 – it was an utterly fantastic contribution. Work commenced on the *Shanklin*, rebuilding the port main engine, and I was involved in all the necessary survey work, with two new landing platforms being created at bridge deck level for low water working in the Clyde area. New double tier navigation lights were a new regulatory requirement that year, at a cost of £1,000 per ship plus the cost of new switchboards. New radio equipment was also installed in the new vessel. The two engineers on *Shanklin* had both been in Campbell's ships but had to seek substantial advice from the ex-Sealink engineers in Portsmouth to accomplish their task.

Accomplish it they did and both ships were ready in April and commenced their sailing seasons, the *Shanklin* having been renamed *Prince Ivanhoe* in the meantime. Trials in the *Waverley* were very successful, with the ship lightened by some 10 tons by the replacement boiler, and I recall that when running speed trials the vibration was such that I went down to inform the chief engineer, to find the regulator full open and a Babcock engineer shouting from outside the boiler room door for him to open her up now! 'That's it', said the chief, 'and we can't go like this for much longer.' The boiler was still making steam with everything full open! There was therefore little doubt about the adequacy of the new unit in terms of providing steam. However, the noise from the diesel generators and the force draft fans of the boiler was excessive and very obtrusive in what had previously been a virtually silent ship on deck.

The spring trip by the *Waverley* was a huge success, with capacity loadings almost everywhere that she went once the April sailings were over, with the first capacity loading on Saturday 2 May, for a cruise which had started at Tower Pier and left Ramsgate for the French coast off Cap Gris Nez, where the new French catering officer gave a suitably accented description of some of the points of interest. The ship was overbooked on the Forth such was her popularity, with many ticket holders left behind on two of the sailings. It was quite a boost to morale after a very hard winter and the whole spring visit had carried an amazing 82,659 passengers. We had to remain in Scotland for a few extra days to effect some paddle wheel repairs once we reached the Clyde area, and we were also delayed by a few hours on the passage round when speed had to be reduced while rounding the north of Scotland due to dirt in the fuel filters. We had introduced a new regime on board with all the electronics involved in the new rotary cup burners which fired the boiler, in that any fault just resulted in the boiler shutting itself down automatically. The ship performed a couple of the sailings scheduled for the *Prince Ivanhoe*, while she in turn deputised for us in the Bristol Channel. The pattern had been south, then round to the east coast, returning via the north of Scotland with a call at Kyle for fuel, back to the Clyde for a few days in early June while paddle wheel repairs were carried out over the overnight periods, then to the Bristol Channel and back to the Clyde on 24 June – plenty of steaming! The *Prince Ivanhoe*, in the meantime, had made a few Clyde sailings before heading down to the Bristol Channel to introduce herself to the area, returning to the Clyde in late May to undertake her own Clyde sailings, only to be despatched south again within a few days to cover for *Waverley* while paddle repairs were effected. A full account of the short and sad life of this vessel is recorded in the next chapter – the whole thing was a total heartbreak. The Clyde season of *Waverley* was accomplished very successfully in poorish weather and the introduction of the Ayr, Troon and Ardrossan Sunday cruise to Loch Riddon proved very popular. The only change to the originally envisaged schedule was that *Waverley* remained on the Clyde during September to carry out the sailings originally intended for the *Prince Ivanhoe* instead of going to the south coast. Some good loadings were experienced in very pleasant weather before the season ended in the traditional way at the end of September. So the season that started with all the hallmarks of a new bright beginning for the company ended on a very sad note.

Just under 200,000 passengers were carried by the *Waverley* during the season.

1982

1982 was an utterly incredible year, with events that would have far-reaching consequences for the company. In 1979, during the ship's first visit to Avonmouth, I met Commander Tom Foden with his wife Daphne. He was a retired naval officer who had spent a large part of his time in Ghana and had been employed by Campbell's for the previous five years, organising school cruises, party bookings and charters in and around the Bristol area.

This appointment ceased when the *Prince Ivanhoe* was lost and arrangements were made to capitalise on his amazing knowledge and valuable contacts by inviting him to join the team as Bristol Channel agent for bookings of parties and charters on the English side of the channel from early 1982. This started a lifelong friendship between us which lasted until his passing in 2006, and together through the 1980s and 1990s we booked hundreds of thousands of pounds worth of charters and party bookings. He was responsible for the development of a very strong bond between all the port authorities on that side of the channel, from Sharpness to Clevedon. Together we encouraged and assisted wherever possible the reconstruction of Clevedon pier, which we both believed to be an essential ingredient in the provision of a reliable service with a good tidal window on that side of the channel, and it eventually reopened to passenger traffic in 1989. By the time that I made my first visit to his house at Clevedon in early 1982, Daphne had passed away, but one of my most vivid memories was that his cat Chan used to catch rabbits to supplement his diet and on rising from my bed on the first morning in his house, I was to find one of these deposited on the bedroom floor! Needless to say, I made sure that the door was tightly shut every night thereafter!

His persuasive tactics with charterers were amazing, often not at the rates laid down, but nevertheless always sufficient to cover operational costs and the clientele carried on these mostly charitable cruises spent huge amounts on the onboard services, with food, bar and shop sales well above the normal for each and every sailing. Much extra publicity for the ship was generated by these charitable does also. A letter from Stan Hammond of Bristol United Press demonstrated just how much these charters were appreciated and enjoyed. Tom was a very keen supporter of youth in general, but in particular the Sea Cadet Corps, and after much persuasion I eventually agreed to allow groups and occasionally individuals in the fourteen to sixteen age band on board for work experience training. It was very successful and resulted in us having a continuous supply of young, bright, enthusiastic, reliable and for the most part honest crew members each season, as many of them returned to work on board once they reached age sixteen. There were also sons and daughters of PSPS members, officers and crew members, directors and the chairman, including the son of a Board of Trade surveyor; all of them played their part in giving a high standard of customer service in all the departments that they worked in. My own son and elder daughter also joined the team in the second half of the 1980s, and most of them were to gain their first experience of paid employment on board the ship. It is true to say that without them the onboard services of the ship would not have kept running so smoothly throughout the decade and into the early 1990s, such was the family atmosphere on board in those days. What an enormous contribution their youthful energy and vitality brought and many of them made careers for themselves in both the Merchant and Royal Navies. I am aware of fourteen masters/pilots/harbourmasters out there who had their first experience of seagoing in the *Waverley* and there are a number of others who took up careers in coastal vessels and ferries after serving in the ship as mate. There is one maritime consultant, one maritime lawyer, several sub-mariners, several engineer artificers and three chief engineers as well, and those are only the ones that I know of. I am not aware of any of the girls that took part taking up sea careers but two who kept in touch are married with their own children and both viewed their time on the *Waverley* with very special memories.

In 1981, at the time of the commissioning of the *Prince Ivanhoe*, I had occasion to write a strongly worded letter to the Department of Trade about delays in the issue of documents and passenger certificates as she neared completion and this outspokenness was going to come back and bite me in the years that followed. I was only following and supporting similar action taken by the superintendents from Sealink and the Isle of Man Steam Packet Company who were facing similar difficulties in achieving completion of survey with their ships, but in their cases they had the power of big organisations behind them. I was summoned to the DOT offices a week or two later and given a dressing down over the tone of my letter. Regulations regarding the Safe Means of Access to Ships were due to become law in July that year and although I had studied them I just could not believe that the gangways in use for our type of operation, in use with an excellent safety record for over 100 years, would fall into the category described in the rules. However, I was later to find out how wrong that assumption was later in the season! Our gangways were manned at both ends during the short calls at piers and, apart from very low water in Glasgow, were always fairly level with a very short distance between ship and shore. However, in early July, when the new rules became law, I found myself in very hot water and had to quickly seek an exemption in order to allow the ship to continue trading until the end of the season. After that, the gangways were enclosed by nets and there had to be barriers extending 1 metre either side of each gangway at entry and exit. It was later agreed that these could be dispensed with, provided the gangways were manned at each end.

Two of my dogs featured on board during my time as master, the first being Grudie, who had a bit of a wanderlust and achieved considerable fame around the Clyde resorts for his exploits, having slipped ashore on one or two occasions when not noticed and as a result boarded the next ship to arrive at the pier! He was returned once with 'I've been on the *Glen Sannox*' stickers all over him, and then with an account for bed and breakfast attached to him having spent the night aboard the *Keppel*! Grudie passed on towards the end of that summer, aged twelve.

The winter refit in 1982 had been pretty extensive, with new plating in way of the forward windows and the removal of the wooden deck over the dining saloon, which was replaced with steel in order to finally make the saloon watertight. Extensive re-plating was also undertaken on the paddle drums under the landing platforms. At the end of it all, the Jeanie Deans lounge was completely refurbished with comfortable seating. Our second engineer had left us at the end of 1981 to return to Western Ferries and employment nearer home. His replacement was a familiar face from *Balmoral* and *Prince Ivanhoe* and also the chief officer from 1979 returned to take up a permanent appointment with us. A new suspended ceiling was installed in the dining saloon with modern recessed lighting, and much re-wiring was carried out in the toilets and alleyways, with new electric hand driers in the toilets also, taking advantage of the extra power supplied by the new diesel alternators. The souvenir shop was extended and doubled in size by the removal of a two-berth cabin located behind the original shop area. Most of this work was carried out in house. It looked as if we were going to lose the repair facility at Clyde Dock Engineering at Govan but eventually there was a reprieve and the ship entered dry-dock in early March. The job was completed on the 23rd, when the new five-year loadline certificate was issued, with the ship steaming to and from the dry-dock under her own power.

One of the features of the Babcock Steambloc boiler was a water tube transfer chamber at its back end which encouraged rapid circulation of the heated water. In a hurry, the boiler could raise a full head of steam from cold in under an hour, but we never, in fact, did it in less than four hours – what an improvement to the seventy-two hours required to do it with the original unit. In 1981 the fuel consumption averaged 700 litres an hour, compared with over 1,000 litres with the original unit, and the ship was about half a knot faster for the same settings. It wasn't to be without its problems, but in the aforementioned respects it was right up to expectations. The two sailings for Friday 27 August had to be cancelled when two of the water tubes in the transfer chamber failed, the fault being traced to blockage of the tubes by sediment, so some modifications would be required before the 1983 season. However, the noise problems experienced in 1981 had been greatly reduced and the ship could now make a thirty-six to forty hour passage without refuelling, an improvement of some ten hours. A sheet showing the comparison results from 1981–84 is attached to this section which shows really and truly how the business was being built. The ship entered service in early April and the pattern of sailings was beginning to develop that continues to this very day, except that the operation was more extensive back then. By way of a long weekend in the Western Isles, the ship proceeded round Britain, this time in a clockwise direction with no spring Solent or Thames sailings in 1982 to allow for an extended visit to the Bristol Channel and also to avoid the high cost of pilotage and port facilities at that time in these two areas. I had just successfully obtained my pilotage exemption certificates for the Bristol Channel at the start of that season, which reduced the cost a little when sailing in the area from then on. We also had to purchase one of the Lundy launches to land our passengers on the island and this craft became immensely useful, both in the Bristol Channel at Lundy and at Ayr for running ropes around when part of the Compass pier collapsed, rendering the bollards on the outer end unusable. The launch, named *Westward Ho*, was transported between the two areas on the deck of the ship.

The ship returned to the Clyde in early July until 29 August, then on to the Solent from 1–20 September, which included a special unscheduled sailing to watch HMS *Invincible* and HMS *Bristol*'s triumphant arrival back at Portsmouth from the Falklands War on Friday 17 September. The two lads pictured on the front cover of issue 90 (winter 1982) of *Paddle Wheels* with the ship approaching *Invincible* anchored at Spithead are two of the lads who started on the ship in their early to mid-teens and gave ten and fourteen years' service to the company respectively, a massive contribution. This was the year when the late summer/autumn visits to the Solent began, a trend that has continued right up to the present day. The ship returned to the Clyde on 22 September and closed down for the winter a week later after a very successful September weekend of sailings back on the

Clyde. At that stage we were expecting to flit back to Anderston Quay at the end of the year but the ship didn't in fact move until the following spring.

During the season news came that the MV *Leto*, ex-General Steam's MV *Queen of the Channel*, was on the market in Greece and keen to see us acquire a replacement for *Prince Ivanhoe*, I did a comparison costing projection between operating her and the *Southsea* or *Brading*, the two remaining Portsmouth ships. I considered that she would have been a fine vessel for Bristol Channel service, the same length as the Clyde turbine *Duchess of Hamilton*, slightly broader and with excellent sea going qualities. She was some 15 feet longer than the *Bristol Queen*, with a similar speed but much more manoeuvrable. However, she had been away from British registry for about fourteen years and without a visit to Greece to establish her condition, we had no idea whether or not returning her to the British flag would have been possible without substantial alteration and expense. The idea was not very well received by the other directors so as a result it was not pursued. I was a bit miffed at the time, as to have had a substantial seagoing ship in the fleet seemed to me very attractive, but I am sure that it was the right decision in the end. The one thing that you had to continually have was vision if the show was going to keep going, even if those visions could sometimes be a bit over-ambitious!

P.S. WAVERLEY - COMPARISON RESULTS

	1981	1982	1983	1984
PASSENGERS CARRIED	194,211	240,276	238,193	221,328
PASSENGER REVENUE	£406,310	£500,522	£546,656	£599,810
CATERING REVENUE	£113,000	£141,329	£168,739	£191,180
SHOP REVENUE	£ 45,000	£ 57,414	£ 63,664	£ 67,836

CLYDE SEASON

PASSENGER NUMBERS	1981	1982	1983	1984
JULY	40,947	59,652	52,989	58,015
AUGUST	51,257	45,719	53,170	51,258
	92,204	105,371	106,159	109,273

PASSENGER REVENUE	1981	1982	1983	1984
JULY	79,255	121,950	123,640	142,593
AUGUST	97,618	94,761	124,533	122,620
	£176,873	£216,711	£248,173	£265,213

AVERAGE DAILY REVENUE EX. EVENING CRUISES

	1981	1982	1983	1984
SUNDAY	£2512	£3001	£4460	£3904
MONDAY	£1881	£2480	£2425	£2441
TUESDAY	£3327	£5106	£5910	£6534
WEDNESDAY	£3957	£4428	£4965	£5170
THURSDAY	£2031	£3699	£4294	£4483
FRIDAY	£2629	£2958	£3288	£4159
SATURDAY	£3071	£4846	£5725	£6241

SEPTEMBER EX. FINAL WEEKEND

PASSENGER REVENUE	1981	1982	1983	1984
	£27,763	£76,547	£44,500	£108,512

The revenue sheet showing the comparisons for 1981, 1982, 1983 and 1984.

1982 also saw the end of Campbell's empire, which had slowly built up over the years following the deaths of its founders, Peter and Alex Campbell, to the extent that latterly there were nearly as many staff in the office to run one ship as there were on the ship itself. Peter and Alex started the business with the 1885 *Waverley* on the Bristol Channel in 1888, much as we had started with the *Waverley* in 1975, and built it up, hands on, through the years, with much of the management and administration coming from on board the ships themselves, all in days when communication was very much more complicated and difficult than it is today. Nevertheless, they became famed for the high standard of customer service that the company afforded and also the quality of the catering on board the ships. The *Balmoral* was sold to become a floating restaurant in Dundee and the *Devonia* went to Torbay for further service from that area to the Channel Islands. The last of the traditional Isle of Man ships, *Manxman*, also finished that year so we were fast becoming the only coastal cruising ship left. On the Clyde, the *Glen Sannox* had ceased her cruising role and the *Maid of the Loch* had also finished sailing on Loch Lomond; we were really the sole survivor. By November I was informed that there was going to be an official enquiry into the loss of the *Prince Ivanhoe* and that my accident of 1977 in the *Waverley* was going to be lumped in as well. My wife had informed me in a radio link call back in April, with the ship off Land's End at the time, that she was pregnant with our third child, and she was born on 2 December. It certainly had been a momentous and historic year in every possible way imaginable, both for the *Waverley* and for the family.

1983

1983 was to be another fabulous year for the ship but obviously started with me personally at a very low ebb due to the official enquiry that ensued and although I won my case I was determined to move on at the end of that season. Messages of kindness, support and encouragement poured in and when I read the article entitled 'A Family Matter' in Issue 92 of *Paddle Wheels* (summer 1983) my family and I were so moved that I put the matter behind me and carried on. All the ship's officers and permanent crew, present and past, also stood right behind me with some giving evidence in court; it was a really humbling experience.

Extensive further re-decking of the ship was carried out at Stobcross Quay, with the ship having the steel deck extended to midships on both sides to improve her watertight integrity at roof deck level. The area lifted on this occasion had the wooden deck relaid on top on completion of the steelwork. Babcock, in conjunction with the ship's engine room team, had carried out some modifications to the transfer chamber tubes in an effort to eradicate the problems experienced in 1982. The paddle wheels also received substantial attention, with many moving parts and bushes replaced. The first engineer had resigned at the end of 1982 and so his replacement was treated to a baptism of fire, which he accepted with marvellous enthusiasm. Improvements were also carried out to the lifesaving appliances, with two brand new fibreglass lifeboats replacing all three existing wooden boats, and one of the new boats had an engine. Having a motor lifeboat assisted us in obtaining an exemption from carrying three lifeboats as under the rules, ships of

Waverley's length had to carry three lifeboats. The exemption allowed us to replace the third lifeboat with additional inflatable liferafts, and the removal of the davits aft and all three wooden lifeboats, replaced by two lighter fibreglass ones, effected a net weight saving of almost 6 tons. The motor boat was very useful for crew training purposes and could also be used when required to land passengers on Lundy Island.

The ship was dry-docked from mid-March to 8 April and after a short berthing trial at her new berth at Lancefield Quay, the ship sailed to Ayr. The office had moved back to Lancefield Quay while the ship was in dry-dock and this was to be her new base until 1988.

From Ayr she sailed to Ilfracombe and operated the Lundy Field Society Charter on Saturday 16 April and the North Devon Hospitals Charter on Sunday 17 April from Bideford, both sailings carrying capacity loadings. It was then round to Plymouth for an evening charter cruise which attracted over 700 passengers, followed by a few days in Sussex based at Eastbourne, again attracting large loadings. A fortnight's visit to the Thames then followed, with people turning out in absolutely unbelievable numbers, with many days sold out and people being left behind on a number of occasions. The catering team was almost overwhelmed under the new catering officer, who had come to us from the *Kingswear Castle* restoration team – the support was totally uplifting for us all. Our first visits to Whitstable were undertaken that year. It was then to the East Coast, visiting the Tees, Tyne and Forth, returning to the Clyde via the north of Scotland.

No Easter sailings were given in 1983 because the ship was sailing on the Clyde to take part in the Pride of the Clyde celebrations being sponsored by Glasgow District Council over the Spring Bank Holiday weekend from 28 to 30 May and she continued to sail on the Clyde until 6 June, undertaking charters and public sailings. Then it was back down to the Bristol Channel for a three-week programme of very busy sailings, again in mostly good weather, with a number of packed evening charters tagged on to the public sailings. We returned to the Clyde in late June for the main season, with fantastic results obtained in home waters until 24 August, in mainly good summer weather. Off to the Solent to commence her season there on 27 August, we returned to the Clyde on 22 September. By 2 September, I needed a break; it had been an exhausting season, and I was able to hand over the ship to my chief officer, who was just completing his third season on board. He proved himself to be an excellent seaman and first class ship handler, now ready for command, and he finished the Solent season for me, in what was pretty indifferent weather. We would need to find another ship for him in order to keep him! I had some domestic problems to sort out, not the least of which was finding a larger property to accommodate my expanding family! I returned to the ship for her final week in service back on the Clyde, which encompassed a very successful September weekend of sailings and two charters. The ship laid up on 29 September and so ended another very successful season of sailings for *Waverley*.

Shortly after the end of the season, the chief engineer and I were invited down to the Medway to take the operationally restored *Kingswear Castle* out for her first sailings. We were honoured to accept and our *Waverley* catering officer for 1983 and 1984 was one of the project leaders. The ship ran a highly successful weekend of trials from 4 to 6 November to the satisfaction of all concerned, and in particular the insurance surveyor on board, who had to be sure that this anachronism could be safely operated! We had not been able to offer much support to the *Kingswear Castle* team except lots of encouragement and a little advice but I regarded it as an enormous privilege to be invited to take part in this momentous occasion, and so began the huge success story that *Kingswear Castle* has become.

1984

Our tenth year of operation began in April at Easter with sailings on the Clyde, which established the pattern of operation that continues to this day, with the exception of the time of the dry-docking. At that time dry-docking was nearly always in March, before the ship entered passenger service. Following the Easter sailings, a spring visit to the Western Isles was completed, then it was down to the Bristol Channel for a long spell from 16 May until 25 June, with a weekend in Plymouth (1–4 June), where she was to be available to *The Observer* for the start of the single-handed, transatlantic yacht race. Her first public cruise to the Lizard via Falmouth was offered and attracted a reasonable crowd, with about 500 on board for the cruise, 330 of those joining us at Falmouth. On 17 June the Church of St Helena on Lundy was packed to overflowing with *Waverley* passengers, the service being conducted by the ship's catering officer and the lessons being read by the relief mate (who had been the ship's mate back in 1976) and the chairman of the PSPS. There was only one cancellation and one altered sailing during the visit, both occasioned by weather conditions, and the ship undertook eight evening charters and two day charters during the visit. The ship returned to the Clyde on 26 June and the only sad note was that it was to be her last season using Millport Old Pier, the council refusing to fund the £90,000 worth of repairs required. However, a hard-won fight by a local pier action group would ensure that it was returned to use in 1992. The service continued until 21 August in a wonderful summer of weather, with people being left behind regularly, including two Tarbert Tuesdays when the ship left potential passengers behind at Tighnabruaich, the full Class IV complement of 1,016 having been reached, something previously unheard of. The seventh Solent season started on 25 August with a thirteen-day programme, the only incident being when a six-year-old girl wandered ashore at Ryde on the return call and the ship returned to Ryde to reunite her with her frantic parents. The ship then made a very fast passage back to Southampton in just under an hour, with the engine running at 47/48 RPM. Not a single sailing was altered or cancelled during the visit. The Thames programme that followed was a triumph, the highlight of which was meeting up with the *Kingswear Castle* on the Medway on 9 September. The small paddler had been running trips all season with the maximum permitted twelve on board, carrying a total of 350 for the season, and her popularity was such that the decision was taken to seek a full passenger certificate for 1985. One day was lost due to another water tube failure in the Steambloc, another baptism of fire for our new first engineer, who again handled it with great professionalism and skill. The repairs were carried out with the ship alongside at Chatham and Babcock's repair team provided superb and rapid service, a great tribute to them. They were of course involved with *Kingswear Castle* by this stage too. The chief engineer was off for a few days as he had become a married man the year before and just as I had done two years earlier, he had to get home for a break. The schedules were gruelling and the physical, mental and emotional strain experienced by the senior personnel was colossal, but in those days there was no fairy godmother waiting in the wings to help us: we had to earn every penny that we could. The *Waverley* had a very rough passage back to the Clyde but made it back for the traditional September weekend of sailings minus two paddle floats. She returned via the east coast because of the forecasted south-westerly gales and had a good passage, including a bunkering stop at Aberdeen, until Duncansby Head was reached, but the passage between there and Cape Wrath was very challenging with a huge swell running. This was to be her fourth and last, to date, circumnavigation of the British Isles, although on this occasion it was unscheduled. The ship was laid up on 25 September and had produced the best financial result ever, 221,238 passengers having been carried in the most lovely and happy season that I could remember in my time on board.

1985

At the beginning of 1985 the *Balmoral* became available in Dundee, where attempts to run her as a floating restaurant had failed. A new company was formed to own the ship and she was eventually purchased at the beginning of March and moved from her mud berth on the 7th after a colossal effort from *Waverley* personnel to achieve this. The full story of how this was achieved and set up is told in the next section. For 1985, it was time to look at some new ventures nearer home and it was decided to try the Isle of Man and the east coast of the Irish Republic between Dundalk and Rosslare, including a run out to the Tusker Rock. This might help to produce some money to help with the restoration of *Balmoral*. The ship would commission again at Easter weekend on the Clyde, with an extensive refit planned through the winter months. Interest in charters in the Bristol Channel was at an all-time high and some ingenious timetable planning was going to be required to fit them all in, a great problem to be dealing with. The surplus made in 1984 was all going to be used on further improvements to the ship and was to include the renewal and re-insulating of the boiler room casings, the provision of seating all the way round this area with seats that had been purchased from the Isle of Man Steam Packet's *King Orry*, and also the renewal of the paddle shaft pedestal bearings. Some re-plating was done in way of the windows in the Jeanie Deans lounge and the steering engine was given a complete overhaul.

 The ship went to dry-dock on Thursday 14 March and in dry-dock the wheelhouse and master's cabin were removed and replaced by a larger aluminium structure which would incorporate a chart room and radio room, a much-needed feature with the ship now making extensive sea-going voyages. New radio rules were on the cards, involving much more sophisticated equipment. The existing equipment at that time was located in the master's cabin – not really a suitable place for it when the ship was at sea in the days before mobile phones! The opportunity was taken to completely renew the radio equipment when the new wheelhouse was installed and as far as I know the *Waverley* was the first British ship to convert to GMDSS (Global Maritime Distress and Safety System), but if not, she was definitely the first coastal ship so to do. It wasn't until 1993 that she became a true GMDSS ship as many of the shore stations had to catch up before they themselves were fully operational in the new system. All was complete and the ship left the dry-dock on Good Friday, 5 April, for trials but was delayed until the Monday due to technical issues and some work still to complete on the new wheelhouse, this being the first time in our ownership that the ship wasn't ready to enter service on time. However, Clyde Dock Engineering put in a huge effort over what was a holiday weekend and the ship was ready for Easter Monday with a sailing from Glasgow to Brodick, with over 800 landed on the island for time ashore. The wheelhouse remained white until cladding was fitted the following month.

The ship left Glasgow on Thursday 11 April and proceeded to Stranraer for an evening cruise for West Sound Radio, which was supposed to be round Ailsa Craig but was confined to Loch Ryan due to the weather conditions. The next day the ship reached Garlieston after a rough passage round the Mull of Galloway and the weather continued to upset the programme for the whole weekend. Then followed another error of judgement on my part when, after much deliberation, I agreed to sail to Douglas in weather that at best was at the upper limit of what was allowed on our Class III passenger certificate, but being the first trip to the Isle of Man, with over 400 on board, many of them pre-booked and many of whom had also made long journeys to Garlieston to make the trip, I felt obliged to try and make the voyage for them. The voyage was accomplished but my lack of familiarity with how large the swell could build up on the east side of the island resulted in a very uncomfortable passage between Maughold Head and Onchan Head and despite leaving Garlieston on time at 8.00 a.m., the ship didn't arrive at Douglas until 1.30 p.m. The guidelines issued in those days for Class III voyages were sea conditions in which the sea state was such as to cause only moderate pitching or rolling. A well-known maritime historian and writer, Richard Danielson, was on Onchan Head taking photographs of the ship entering Douglas Bay which were quite spectacular but in my opinion did not show the ship to be pitching more than moderately when the angle of the deck was studied. I felt that the ship had handled the conditions really well and she had suffered no ill effects but with Garlieston tidal and the pier at Ramsay closed there was no option but to complete the voyage once the decision to sail had been made. The ship had to remain at Douglas thereafter for safety reasons to comply with the conditions of the passenger certificate as the forecast was dreadful for the next twenty-four hours, so the passengers had to be accommodated ashore for two nights and were not returned to Garlieston until 9.00 a.m. on the Monday morning. This was a quite amazing feat of organisation by some of the office staff who happened to be aboard at the time. It had been a very expensive mistake on my part, however, and resulted in my involvement in yet another enquiry into whether or not I had taken the ship to sea when the passenger certificate was invalid, i.e. it wasn't fine weather, a case which was eventually dismissed in court at Stranraer in October of the next year. There were a number of sailings in and around the island, including a voyage from Workington, between then, culminating with a cruise round the island via Calf Sound on 30 April, the only time that I know of when the ship was to make passage through the Sound, succeeding passenger certificates excluding it from the plying limits, something that I had difficulty in understanding as it was no more onerous than passage through the Kyles of Bute.

Between 20 and 28 April, the ship sailed in the Irish Republic between Dundalk and the Tusker Rock with a reasonable result in pretty indifferent weather. We returned to Campbeltown on 1 May and Ayr the next day, followed by the Western Isles and Clyde sailings until 22 May. The Western Isles included our first call at Crinan and the new wheelhouse had the new wooden cladding fitted at Glasgow over a period of five days when time permitted, to fit in with her sailings. The ship left the Clyde at 10.15 a.m. on 22 May for Barry and from then offered the Bristol Channel sailings that year, which again were hugely successful, with no less than twenty-one charters being carried out during the visit, which concluded at Mumbles on 26 June. Only two sailings were altered due to weather and no sailings were cancelled. The Clyde season started on 28 June with no Millport as the pier was closed because of its declining structural state and a new Sunday schedule was devised from Glasgow to Loch Goil, finishing at Ayr in the evening, one which I personally hated. The Clyde season was dogged with very poor weather following three very good summers and the results were disappointing. The ship left for the Solent on 29 August, starting her programme there on 31 August and operating until 13 September with no alterations or cancellations to sailings. One paddle float was damaged by floating debris on arrival at Southampton on 9 September, and on 6 September the steering gear and capstan from the PS *Ryde* were loaded on board. The capstan was used but the beautiful Hastie's steering engine was never installed, being scrapped a few years later. The Thames season ran from 14–23 September without incident and again was very well supported. The two paddlers rendezvoused twice, at Whitstable on 21 September and again up the Medway on 22 September, with both ships packed on both occasions and *Kingswear Castle* looking splendid, complete with her new passenger certificates issued at the beginning of that season. The *Waverley* left the Thames on 23 September and after a call at Plymouth for bunkers, the ship arrived back in Glasgow on the 25th. The usual September weekend of sailings went off with splendid results and special permission was granted for us to call at Millport, provided that the weather was good, to undertake the annual illuminations and this day proved absolutely incredible; we turned passengers away at Greenock, Helensburgh, Dunoon and Largs, an unbelievable estimated 600 being turned away at Largs, and over 1,000 were turned away in total. The ship landed 1,016, the full Class IV complement, at Millport. In all 205,282 passengers were carried, with the catering and souvenir shop revenue up on the previous year. The catering was in the hands of one of the young lads who had started in the work parties in 1975 and I am sure he felt a sense of pride at the results obtained.

1986

1986 saw us officially a two-ship company again as sufficient money had been raised, with promises of more to come, which gave us the confidence to proceed with a substantial refit of *Balmoral*, with the idea of giving the ship a further lifespan of between ten and fifteen years. The ship had lain idle since her delivery voyage from Dundee almost a year

1 *Waverley*'s twenty-fifth birthday! A PSPS commemorative plaque is being unveiled by Jean McGowan (then Miss Martin), watched by Terry Sylvester (with teddy bear), his daughter Sharon and John Whittle, managing director of Caledonian MacBrayne.

2 The experimental funnel colours with the yellow band tried briefly on *Waverley* in 1973, prior to the CalMac colours being applied.

3 The handover on 8 August 1974 at Gourock. From left: Douglas McGowan, John Whittle, Sir Patrick Thomas and Terry Sylvester, showing the famous pound note.

4 *Waverley* departing Gourock on a wet day in 1975, with *Queen Mary II* berthed at the pier.

5 Lynn McGowan, daughter of Douglas and Jean, on board *Waverley* in 1974.

6 Douglas McGowan with his two daughters, Lynn and Jan at Rothesay in the 1980s.

7 Terry Sylvester, Wilma Innes and Scottish Television personality Bill Tennant at the launch of the PSPS *Waverley* appeal (the first one) in February 1974, at the James Watt Dock in Greenock.

8 *Waverley* canting in the north basin at Ayr during her first berthing trials there, in June 1975. Ayr was a very different port in 1975, a working port full of activity.

9 The first publicity postcard produced by the famous marine artist John Nicholson in 1974. This was also used for many years as the heading for thousands of *Waverley* newspaper advertisements. John produced many paintings and drawings of *Waverley* and *Balmoral* for publicity and fund raising, completely free of any charge.

10 *Waverley* leaving Anderston Quay on the first sailing on 22 May 1975.

11 Leaving Ayr for the first time in 1975.

12 Following *Queen Mary II* homewards past Clydebank.

13 The captain's grandmother on her first visit to the bridge deck, 1978, looking out over the Firth of Clyde.

14 In Garvel dry-dock in the winter of 1975/6.

15 A well-filled *Waverley* heads into Rothesay in 1976.

16 At Liverpool with *Mona's Queen*, 1977.

17 'Where are they all going?' Passengers queuing for *Waverley* at Ayr, published in the *Ayrshire Post*, 27 August 1976.

18 The 1976 timetable for cruises from Glasgow. 1976 promoted the ship that YOU saved.

19 On a unique call at the car ferry berth at Cairnryan, 1977.

20 Rothesay Dock, 1977, on a special sailing for pupils from Clydebank High School.

21 *Waverley* at Dunoon Coal Pier at low tide after the Gantocks grounding, July 1977. Note the fire engine, ready to pump the steamer out in case of the pumps failing at

22 Being moved upriver from the James Watt Dock to Anderston Quay after temporary repairs, with a tug assisting the steering, 27 July 1977. The tug *Flying Demon* of the Clyde Shipping Co. is in attendance.

23 Outward bound past the Cloch lighthouse for her first visit to the south coast, 15 April 1978.

24 Departing Newhaven during her first visit there, April 1978.

25 *Queen of the South*, ex-*Jeanie Deans*, at Tower Pier, 1967.

26 *Waverley* outward bound from Tower Pier through an open Tower Bridge, 1 May 1978.

27 *Waverley* berthed at Irvine with the tug *Garnock* alongside, 22 August 1978.

28 Stormbound at St Ives on the passage south, 1979.

29 Passing through the tidal race off Portland Bill.

30 Backing out of Troon in a fresh north-westerly wind.

31 *Prince Ivanhoe* departing Ilfracombe on 29 July 1981, dressed overall for the Royal Wedding of Prince Charles and Lady Diana Spencer.

32 *Prince Ivanhoe* departs Swansea on 30 July 1981, a few days before she was lost.

33 Passing under the Forth Bridges, spring 1982.

34 Passing through the Thames Barrier. in 1984

35 At the quayside in Newcastle.

36 *Kingswear Castle* running trials, 6 November 1983.

37 At Aberdeen, 19 September 1984.

38 Passing Duncansby Head and the stormy waters of the Pentland Firth, 1984.

39 *Balmoral* being moved up the Clyde from the shipyard to the Waverley terminal after her refurbishment, November 1985.

40 *Waverley* in the Govan dry dock with the wheelhouse removed, 1985.

41 Crowds waiting to join the ship at Dundalk.

42 *Waverley* passes St Colman's Cathedral, Cobh.

43 *Waverley* moored outside *Balmoral* at Anderston Quay, February 1987.

44 *Southsea* off Rothesay during her spell on the Clyde, September 1987.

45 Three Ships Day at Lundy, 21 June 1988. From left, *Balmoral*, *Waverley* and *Oldenburg*.

46 Berthed at Tarbert (Harris) in 1989.

47 Heading off down the Orwell with a full load from Ipswich, 1989.

48 *Waverley* in the inner harbour at Yarmouth, Isle of Wight, with *Balmoral* at the pier on 4 September 1989, while *Balmoral* was on her fortieth birthday cruise.

Contributors to the WSN fleet

49 *Queen of Scots* and *Waverley* together at Anderston Quay, during the spell *Queen of Scots* was deputising for *Waverley* after the Gantocks grounding, between 21 and 23 July 1977.

50 *Queen of Scots* berthed alongside *Waverley* at Millport on the hand-back day, 31 August 1977.

51 *Shanklin* on the Husband's slipway at Marchwood, Southampton, November 1980.

52 *Shanklin* heading through the Kyles of Bute on her delivery voyage to the Clyde, 20 November 1980.

53 A view of the buffet on *Prince Ivanhoe*.

54 The after saloon on *Prince Ivanhoe*.

55 *Shanklin* and *Waverley* at Anderston Quay, November 1980.

56 *Prince Ivanhoe* at Ilfracombe.

57 *Galway Bay*, ex-*Calshot*.

58 *Balmoral* at Larne.

59 *Keppel* arriving at Kilcreggan in 1990, flying the Waverley Steam Navigation house flag. She was on charter due to the unavailability of Helensburgh in that season.

60 General Steam Navigation Co.'s *Queen of the Channel* disembarking passengers at Boulogne.

61 *Queen of the Channel* at Calais.

62 *Leto*, ex-*Queen of the Channel*, at Piraeus around 1980. She was sold to Greek owners in 1968 and renamed *Oia*. In 1974 she hit rocks off the island of Serifos and was declared a Constructive Total Loss. In 1976 she was sold, repaired and renamed *Leto*. She was sold for scrapping in 1983.

63 Berthed at Castlebay, Barra, in 1990.

64 *Waverley* berthed at Bournemouth Pier in September 1982.

65 Being tendered to by CalMac's Island-class ferry *Morvern* at Iona, May 1991.

66 Arriving at Portencross for a unique call at the pier there, Easter Sunday 1995.

67 *Waverley* berthed at Kingswear, showing the railway station, with trains at the platforms, and the steamer pier.

68 PS *Marion* (1897), near Mannum on the Murray River, Australia, 2001.

69 *Waverley* in her post-refit livery with *Oldenburg* at the pier, Lundy Island, and the cargo ship *Hoo Kestrel* anchored in the bay.

70 *Bowcliffe* outward bound in the Corran Narrows.

71 At Stranraer in 1975. This was *Waverley*'s first call there and her first ever sailing south of Ayr.

72 The new wheelhouse in spring 1985 before the application of the wood cladding.

73 *Waverley*'s funnel reflected in an instrument in a silver band on board, summer 1980.

74 *Waverley* berthed at Bournemouth Pier in September 1982.

75 *Waverley* post-rebuild off Penarth.

76 Heading into the sunset off Greenock.

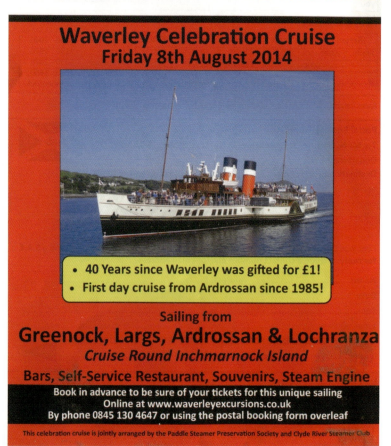

77 Flyer for the cruises celebrating the fortieth anniversary of the sale of *Waverley* for preservation, 8 August 2014.

earlier and more about the lead-up to this decision can be found in the next section. After a rebuild and trials on the Clyde, the ship arrived in Barry on 13 April to offload the company launch *Westward Ho* and then made her way to Bristol, where she arrived at 8.00 p.m. amid spontaneous applause from a crowd of over 200 people. Both her master and I had done a spell in a dredger during the winter months to familiarise ourselves with the River Avon prior to taking pilotage exemption certificates for the river, which we were both successful in obtaining.

The ship entered service on 13 April and apart from ten days in North Wales from 20 to 30 June, the ship continued sailing in the Bristol Channel until 8 September. A short visit to the south coast then followed between 10 and 24 September, with the ship returning to the Clyde on 26 September for a final weekend of sailings before laying up at Glasgow on 30 September. The ship made history when she sailed on the canal between Sharpness and Gloucester on 15 April, returning to Sharpness on the 19th. Financial results for her first season were disappointing and some let-downs regarding promised funding left us with a huge deficit, which was later cleared by one of the Waverley directors out of her own pocket.

The winter was hectic and because of the work on *Balmoral*, the *Waverley* took a bit of a back seat that winter, with only essential maintenance being carried out. She moved to dry-dock when *Balmoral* left on 27 March, and remained there until 23 April. The starboard spring beam was renewed and the capstan from PS *Ryde* was fitted, which proved itself to be a fantastic machine with a bigger drum and more power than the one originally fitted to the ship. The alternator engines were surveyed at a cost of some £2,000 and trials were booked for 28 April but one of them failed so the ship had to remain in Glasgow while the problem was investigated. No quick solution could be found so a portable generating set was placed on deck to avoid delaying the ship and this remained on board until Wednesday 7 May while parts were sought and the ship's main set repaired.

Successful trials were completed on 29 April and the ship set off for Campbeltown the next day to undertake the Ayr Show service on Thursday 1 May. Despite one of the best crowds ever for this cruise, it was not to be; poor weather meant that we headed to Brodick via Kilbrannan Sound, but a paddle float broke off Pirnmill and we had to terminate the cruise at Brodick while a replacement was fitted by the ship's engineering team. The weather continued to worsen and so coaches were arranged to take the passengers back to Campbeltown from Tarbert in the evening. I am afraid the whole day was a disaster so far as our customers were concerned, and as is often the case on the Clyde, the weather was fine by evening and so we also received much stick from the passengers over the coach return! We spent 2–6 May in the Western Isles and 8–15 May back on the Clyde before attempting our second visit to the Isle of Man, which was again dogged by bad weather, spending Saturday 17 May and most of Sunday 18 May stormbound at Peel due to gales. Only two out of the four sailings planned were carried out – again, a huge disappointment. An extended visit to the Irish Republic was then carried out between 23 May and 15 June and in addition to the ports visited the previous year, we added New Ross, Waterford, Youghal, Cobh, Cork and Kinsale. The visit was a huge success, with a crowd of some 2,000 trying to get aboard at Youghal for an afternoon cruise on Sunday 15 June!

The ship then made a fast passage to Swansea to begin her Bristol Channel programme, shortened due to the arrival of *Balmoral*, which had obviously diluted the market. However, record numbers of charters were carried out and during the first few days in the channel both ships were employed to cover them. There was a first at Lundy when their own ship, *Oldenburg*, *Balmoral* and *Waverley* all met up in the roads for the first time; it was indeed a great and historic occasion on Wednesday 18 June. Another interesting occasion was on Monday 30 June, when *Waverley*, *Balmoral* and *Westward Ho* were together in Swansea, the latter being loaded on to the *Waverley* for her return to the Clyde. The last channel sailing by *Waverley* was the day before and she had operated all sailings without alteration or incident.

The *Waverley* arrived at Ayr the next morning and after unloading *Westward Ho* proceeded immediately into her main Clyde timetable with the cruise from Ayr to Tarbert. The timetable was little changed from the previous year except for Thursdays, which now went to Tighnabruaich instead of the Dunoon and Holy Loch sailing of the previous year. All sailings were operated, with only minor alterations to a number, three as a result of poor weather, one by a condenser fault and another by a boiler fault which was once again blockage of two water tubes in the transfer chamber. An interesting charter to UIE took place on 9 August, when the ship berthed at one of the old John Brown's shipyard berths at Clydebank which had been especially altered to accommodate *Waverley* to embark guests for the 'Doon the Watter' trip to the container terminal and then onwards on a cruise to Loch Long. While at the container terminal the Royal Yacht *Britannia* passed with Her Majesty the Queen on board—the occasion being the naming of the rig *Mr Mac*.

The first engineer left the company in April after a row over something that had happened on the *Balmoral* and a new first engineer joined about a month later. The chief engineer left at the end of July and this was a terrible blow to me, and had the greatest personal effect on me of anything that had happened to date in the period of my command. We had become terrific friends and I had learned that I could trust his loyalty and support with my right hand if the need arose, which was a great comfort in the regulatory minefield that we faced in the operation of the ships day in and day out. He had had enough and I had to respect him for that, but it was a serious blow to my confidence and I really never was the same again. His engineering skill was enormous, his energy and drive unbreakable, and it was difficult for me to see how we were going to survive mechanically without him. In hindsight I should have left with him; he wanted me to, because in a sea career which spanned over fifty years until I retired in 2010 he was among only a handful of ship's officers that I had met who possessed such loyalty, tenacity and commitment to duty. He was absolutely open and would never go behind your back on any matter, was willing to admit his own faults and was quick to point out any of mine in a quiet, unassuming manner. I was bereft – I just didn't know what I was going to do without him. Perhaps he had already made the decision earlier in the year because this was the year that we started our first apprentice in the hope of building our own engineering team to run the ships in the future. Fortunately, my son had joined at the beginning of July and together with a couple of his friends helped give me a bit of a boost to bolster me on. What a dilemma, but we soldiered on and the new first engineer took over as chief.

The Clyde season ended on 26 August and we left for the South Coast that evening but it was discovered that the boiler had not been filled with water despite the presence of three engineer officers on board in readiness for the voyage south, so special arrangements had to be made to call at Fishguard for fresh water the next day. At 12.34 p.m. on the day after that (29 August), with the ship between the Runnel Stone buoy and the Lizard, there was a resounding and awful crash from the port paddle wheel and the ship stopped. A number of problems had occurred in 1986 which pointed to the lack of TLC that the ship had received the previous winter, due to the attention that we had had to lavish on *Balmoral*, and also to the loss of two of our experienced engine room team, and we were definitely paying for it now. In those days the ship was running really hard, as the mainstay of the business, and corners could not be cut in the standard of maintenance that she received. The damage was extensive and the swell conditions too great for the engineers to get into the wheels to cobble things together and get us to the nearest port. For the first time, I had to summon a tug to take us the 8 miles to Penzance Bay. The gods were with us; fortuitously, the tug *Proceed* was at anchor in Penzance Bay, awaiting another job, and her skipper agreed to come out and tow us in – what a miraculous piece of good fortune. He also agreed that he would not regard it as a salvage job and terms and conditions were agreed in my cabin on board without difficulty. Once we were safely anchored in Penzance Bay, the extent of the damage was assessed. It was most certainly an insurance job; one third of the outer rim of the wheel would have to be replaced along with two paddle floats. Penzance shipyard was informed by radio link, also the insurance surveyor, and both were on board before 5.00 p.m. What an amazing service – I was utterly gobsmacked. The repair berth could only be accessed at high water but it was a flat, sandy berth and the ship would be safe to dry out at low water. The tug could not access the berth as her draught was too great to get in even at high water, so the ship had to somehow get the half mile into the berth under her own power. High water was 11.00 p.m. and so, giving the new engineering team their due, they, together with all available hands, removed the damaged parts by whatever means that we had at our disposal, and the new chief skilfully welded in a temporary section of rim to link the broken parts together and all was ready by 10.00 p.m. What a superb effort, and the ship paddled into the berth under her own power, berthing at exactly high water. First thing the next morning Penzance shipyard were on board, and in two days they shaped and replaced the broken rim direct from the original drawings and replaced the two paddle floats; the ship was ready to start her south coast sailings on Tuesday 2 September from Bournemouth, having missed the first three days of the programme.

With poor results from the *Balmoral* and the loss of the first three days of the Solent programme, I decided that something special had to be planned to try and boost our revenue before the end of the season. Much against my better judgement, I decided to return to the Bristol Channel on the way north and include passages in the River Avon and a visit to Bristol city docks to wine and dine future charterers for 1987. Commander Foden and the chairman were absolutely delighted and publicity and plans for the visit, together with a schedule of sailings, were initiated. Meanwhile the Solent programme continued without incident, including a very successful charter for the Missions to Seamen, with no sailings being cancelled and only one modified due to weather, the programme being complete by

15 September. Sailings from Worthing and Eastbourne were given on 16 September and the Thames programme started the next day. This continued until 29 September without incident, except for a couple of days of late running, and the ship rendezvoused with *Kingswear Castle* on one occasion at Tower Pier and twice on the Medway.

Leaving the Thames on 29 September, she arrived at Penarth at 7.00 a.m. on Wednesday 1 October, proceeding to Cumberland Basin on the evening tide and then onwards to the Arnolfini berth at Narrow Quay in Bristol city docks. I was at a low ebb, exhausted and stressed with the strain of operating the ship in the River Avon and also knowing that I had an enquiry to face at Stranraer in the weeks ahead; however, the visit was a resounding success, with open days at Bristol on the Thursday and Friday during which ten charters were booked for the 1987 season and huge interest created in the ship, with the shop and catering doing a roaring trade, Commander Foden having arranged an occasional licence for the ship during the visit. Ex P. & A. Campbell master Captain George Gunn was on board for the first trip up the river and we became great friends thereafter. The ship offered cruises on the Friday night from Bristol to Avonmouth, a day cruise to Clovelly and round Lundy from Portishead and Penarth on the Saturday, and a cruise from Bristol to Ilfracombe via Portishead and Penarth with an evening cruise tagged on on the return journey, Penarth–Portishead–Bristol–Penarth–Barry, finishing there at 11.55 p.m. on the Sunday evening. The revenue for the three days was an all-time record, with the ship carrying capacity loads each day, and all the river trips were accomplished with considerable ease compared to what I had expected; however, I had opened a new door and River Avon trips were going to be the order of the day in the years ahead! The visit finished with a single trip, Barry–Mumbles–Milford Haven, with the ship returning to the Clyde carrying the UN peace flame and arriving back alongside *Balmoral* in Glasgow at

A letter from Jim Buchanan, chairman of the Firth of Clyde Steam Packet Ltd.

4.40 p.m. on 7 October. She was off service then until her final Clyde sailing on Saturday 18 October, with a charter to the BBC on the Sunday, and was laid up the following day, Monday 20 October. Passenger numbers were down on the previous year at 156,238, but revenue was up 10 per cent – not too bad a performance, all in all.

Just before we finished, I was contacted by the owners of the *Southsea* at Portsmouth, wondering if we would be interested in taking over that ship! More about this in the next chapter, but it began an interesting story and a long association with this vessel that had a very sad end.

1987

The fortieth anniversary season of 1987 had all the hallmarks of being the end of years of hard work building the business, devising the best timetables and patterns of sailings to optimise revenue, and generally setting the trend for the future. The ship had her first cellular phone installed and the use of computers was helping to improve many aspects of the shore administration, but alas a major fault with the Steambloc boiler was to put paid to our dreams for that year and delay matters for a couple more years. Big changes were taking place in the ship repair situation on the Clyde, with Clyde Dock Engineering struggling to survive at Govan dry-docks and much happening on the lower Clyde at this time also. It was a very sad state of affairs but it was decided to take the ship elsewhere for dry-docking this year to establish a presence for the future, just in case the worst came to the worst. The *Balmoral* went to Clyde Dock and they were paid all debts outstanding to them from the previous year by one of the directors, as mentioned earlier, and as it happened the yard did close down later that year. This was a great sadness to us all as they had been very involved in the purchase and rebuild of *Balmoral* and had provided free berthing and watch-keeping services for the ship during the summer of 1985 while we were all sailing the *Waverley*. The *Waverley* moved from Anderston Quay to Windmillcroft Quay (the site of Euroyachts at the time) to load on board the serviced inflatable liferafts and the *Westward Ho* and thereafter returned to Anderston Quay. This was the first time that she had moved under the Kingston Bridge.

The next day she left the Clyde for Cardiff and was in dry-dock there from 2 to 14 April while a complete overhaul and re-bushing of the paddle wheel feathering gear and eccentrics was carried out. The Perkins (P6) engine in the *Westward Ho* was also overhauled on the dockside. Changes to the water treatment in the boiler were also instigated by the new chief engineer in an effort to eradicate the blockages that had been experienced from time to time in the transfer chamber tubes. Undocking took place on Tuesday 14 April and after successful trials we moved to Portishead dock for a couple of days to store up before making her first sailing from Bristol on Saturday 18 April. The rest of Easter weekend was spent in the channel and the ship returned to the Clyde on 23 April, operating a number of sailings there until commencement of the Western Isles sailings on 1 May. The Campbeltown to Ayr Show sailing went well on this occasion and an afternoon cruise round Ailsa Craig was given out of Ayr while the Campbeltown folk were ashore.

On completion in the Western Isles, we went direct to the Bristol Channel landing a crew member at Douglas on the way. Fourteen charters were operated in the Bristol Channel during her visit between 9 May and 14 June; the other runs of significance were a centenary cruise to commemorate P. & A. Campbell's *Waverley* on 25 May and the first visit to Tenby on 31 May. One sailing had to be altered and one cancelled because of weather during the visit.

The ship was back in Scotland in time for her fortieth anniversary cruise on 16 June. The Clyde season continued successfully with the same schedule as previous years, except that the Sunday was changed to a cruise around Bute from Glasgow, until on Sunday 26 July a serious bulge and rupture was found in one of the boiler furnaces. The ship was off for repairs until 9 August and the fault was traced to oil contamination of the boiler water. She continued until 23 August, when further bulges were found in both furnaces, resulting in the ship being laid up and her passenger certificates being withdrawn. It was clear that the whole matter was going to have to be thoroughly investigated before a suitable plan for the future of the Steambloc boiler could be implemented. The ship would not sail again in 1987. The alternatives were looked at and it was decided that *Balmoral* would take over the *Waverley*'s schedule from early September and that we would charter Sealink's *Southsea* to run a service on the Clyde until the September holiday weekend. I have to take full responsibility for the decision regarding *Southsea*; it was a case of my heart ruling my head because on paper the proposed operation looked very marginal in terms of projected costs against revenue, and that was assuming reasonable weather, when in reality the weather was lousy and the whole exercise ended up losing money. More about the ship in service in the next section.

After dry-docking at Govan during the first half of May, the *Balmoral* had a greater variety of cruises in 1987, starting on the Clyde for a week in late May. In addition to her early season Bristol Channel cruises, during which she took part in the Three Ships Festival at Lundy along with *Oldenburg* and *Waverley* on Wednesday 3 June, she made a visit to North Wales from 5 to 10 June. She also visited the Solent area in early August, where she performed the Missions to Seamen charter from Littlehampton and had a capacity crowd for the Cowes fireworks night. There were also good loadings for three cruises from Weymouth to view the tall ships, together with an evening charter as well. She covered for the failed *Waverley* on the Solent and Thames from early September until 4 October, did a sales visit to Bristol for two days on the way north, and arrived in Glasgow for lay up on 13 October. The results for the ship were much improved on 1986, but regrettably the company was plunged into another financial crisis as a result of the problems with the boiler in the *Waverley*.

1988

Our accountant had done a magnificent job again while the marine staff were on holiday and had once again saved the day by obtaining a moratorium from all of the major unpaid creditors, including the Inland Revenue, and we were as a result able to continue trading but with extra-careful monitoring of expenditure. The technical side was working hand in hand with Babcock Power and the decision was taken to fit two new furnace sections to the boiler and because of the nature of the failure this work would be the subject of an insurance claim. The new system of chemical cleaning introduced in 1987 was considered for the most part to be responsible for the failure, together with some over-firing caused by misalignment of the flame from the rotary cup burners. New methods of operation for the boiler were to be introduced, together with a mandatory overhaul of the burners by the manufacturers at the beginning of each season. The old system of water treatment was to be brought back into use and thermocouple sensors were to be fitted to each furnace in the water space to monitor the temperatures at various positions considered to be vulnerable. Filters were also to be fitted to the feed water system to ensure that any oil carry over from the reciprocating machinery was trapped before it reached the boiler. It was a very thorough process and although it had taken almost four months to complete, it proved itself to be a very worthwhile exercise as the boiler performed very satisfactorily for the next ten years with only minor faults to deal with in all of that time. The contract for repair was put out to tender and was eventually won by NEI Cochrane International Combustion of Annan, who proposed the prefabrication of two new furnace sections, to be installed by cutting a hole in the deck between the funnels and lowering them into position by portable crane from the quayside. The contract was for a fixed price and would be carried out to a predetermined time scale. An appeal was launched to assist with the cash flow as marine insurance claims at that time took notoriously long periods of time to settle.

The first job for the marine staff that year was to move MV *Caledonia* from Greenock to Dundee for her new owner, Mr J. Docherty of Broughty Ferry. An attempt to extricate the vessel from alongside MV *Columba* in James Watt Dock had been made at the very end of 1987, with the vessel in collision with the *Columba* and the harbour wall in the process. The move was then abandoned! Almost as soon as we opened in the New Year of 1988, a ship broker friend of mine arrived in the office and asked if we would do the job. Terms were agreed and six of us went down to the ship, signed on and had a good passage round in less than two days. The new owner was on board and the engine room was in the capable hands of two Cal/Mac engineers, all contributing to making the whole job a most enjoyable and pleasurable experience. Our efforts seemed much appreciated, which made it a most pleasant start to the New Year.

Now that we knew *Waverley* was going to be operational again we had to turn to timetabling and crewing matters for the new season. By the end of February, NEI Cochrane were ready to commence work and on the last day of that month the tugs *Point Spencer* and *Bantry Bay* arrived at Anderston Quay to tow the *Waverley* to Yorkhill Quay, where the work was to be carried out as the heavy plant required for the work would have easier access to the ship in this location. The tugs were too big for the *Waverley* and the whole move provided a series of calamities as a result. The forward tug took the weight up on the towing line with such force that the bitts on the *Waverley* were torn from the deck and the fairlead damaged. The resultant sudden movement and turbulence caused sucked the *Balmoral* off the quay, as she was tied up inside *Waverley* at the time, and her gangway was displaced as a result and fell between the ship and the quayside. The *Waverley* was off down the river in the hands of one tug while the crew frantically tried to make fast another rope to the forward tug but this proved impossible and the ship struck one of the navigation columns on the approach to Bells Bridge, and then the starboard bridge wing, which was completely shattered by the impact against the bridge itself. On she trundled and I couldn't remember ever feeling so helpless standing on the bridge – it just all happened around me without having any control whatsoever over the situation. At one stage, the mast stays caught the edge of the bridge momentarily as well, and I thought the mast was going to come down a second time, as it had done back in 1971, but the telegraph cables, which also went down below at this point, mercifully escaped without damage. What a debacle – yet another insurance claim on our hands. The tug skipper did a great job and managed to work us alongside Yorkhill by very skilful use of the tug, which was so powerful that even with her engine at dead slow ahead she was towing the *Waverley* at almost four knots. Repairs proceeded thereafter to the boiler furnaces, the damage done on the mooring deck forward and the smashed bridge wing and were not completed until 22 April. During all of this we also had to accomplish a move of our offices to portakabins during the second half of March as the building that we were in had been sold to Wimpey for a housing development. A berth for the company's ships was going to be provided a little further upstream, with new access gates to the quayside provided, and the new arrangement proved to be excellent and lasted until 2005. Office accommodation and workshop facilities were incorporated into the new development, which continues to be the headquarters of the company to this day.

Meanwhile, the *Balmoral* was pressed into service towards the end of March and left Glasgow for a weekend of sailings at Easter between 1 and 3 April before heading for dry-dock at Milford Haven on Wednesday 5 April, where she remained until the end of the month. A new mate was interviewed and subsequently engaged while we were at Milford Haven and he was to be with the company for a number of years. A new purser also came into the company and he was to serve for the next twenty-three seasons and became a hugely important part of the *Waverley* story in his own right, both ashore and afloat, quickly grasping the complex nature of passenger and crew management, especially when things didn't go according to plan. For me, it was a great pleasure to sail and work with him over the last nine years of my command of the ship. His first season was a particular baptism of fire as we were let down by a new catering officer, who decided not to take the position at the last minute. There was no time to interview and make another appointment and so I was faced with taking responsibility for the catering myself that season, becoming very heavily involved in the day-to-day running of the food side of it. The purser was an incredible support and help with this, and my son and one of his friends were in their third seasons on board, with one running the forward bar and the other the after one. Without all of their help and unstinting loyalty I would have been totally unable to carry the workload that this enormous challenge presented.

Waverley ran satisfactory trials on the Clyde on 23 April and proceeded direct to Milford Haven for a short dry-docking between 26 and 29 April before returning direct from there to Oban to pick up the Western Isles schedule the next day. During the visit between 30 April and 6 May she made her first visits to Portree, Armadale and Raasay. She sailed on the Clyde for a week then, and on 9 May she took part in an episode of STV's *Take the High Road*. She managed two successful sailings from the Isle of Man on 15 and

16 May and reached the Bristol Channel to start her programme there on Wednesday 18 May. The visit started with her first call at Briton Ferry for an evening charter and during the visit she was also to visit Padstow, the first call there by a paddle steamer since the *Bristol Queen* in August 1967. She also made another visit to Tenby on 19 June, with the final sailing in the area given on 21 June before returning to the Clyde.

The Clyde season ran from 24 June to 30 August and this was the year of the Garden Festival, with a new swing bridge for foot passengers constructed to link the north and south banks of the river now in full operation. During the season a number of sailings by both ships had to be diverted to Yorkhill Basin because the bridge could not operate in winds greater than force five. Glasgow trade on *Waverley* benefited from the Garden Festival by the very fact that she was seen passing up and down. 1988 was a very windy season and a number of sailings were disrupted down Firth. There were also a number of technical issues, mainly associated with the ship's circulating pump, and it was decided to order a new electric pump from Weir's of Cathcart and also give the steam one a thorough overhaul in the winter ahead. The ship had always had a habit of losing the vacuum when the engine was put ahead with sternway on, which was caused by the paddles interrupting the sea suction for the circulating pump, causing it to draw air, which in turn immediately caused the condenser to overheat due to lack of cooling water to condense the steam. Very complicated, but the provision of an electric pump controlled by a switch on the manoeuvring platform was to go a long way towards preventing this from happening.

The Clyde season finished on 30 August and we proceeded south on 3 September. Swanage Pier was reopened, with the first visit by a paddler since September 1966. The Solent programme went really well, with no alteration or cancellations to sailings, and on the last day, 18 September, so many passengers were left behind at Worthing that we worked an extra evening cruise back to Southsea Clarence Pier, with coach return to accommodate those who were disappointed. The Thames season was also very successful and the ship took part in the filming of *Great Expectations* on 26 September. Only one sailing was altered during the visit as a result of weather conditions and once again we rendezvoused with *Kingswear Castle*, with both ships again packed to capacity. On 1 October, after a short oral examination by one of the senior pilots on board the ship, I was granted a Pilotage Exemption certificate for the Thames. I was spared the written examination due to changes in the pilotage rules, and also in recognition of the fact that I had sailed for eleven consecutive seasons with qualified pilots on board. We left the Thames on 10 October and were back at Bristol Narrow Quay at 10.35 a.m. on 13 October, where she was open ship until the evening of the 14th. Once again, both ships had run a record number of charters in the channel and more were booked for 1989 while the *Waverley* was berthed in Bristol. She sailed publicly the next two days, de-stored at Barry on 17 October then proceeded to Milford Haven to complete dry-docking work and repairs deferred from the spring due to the delay in completion of the boiler modifications. She was in dry-dock from 20 October until 20 November while substantial work was carried out. The boat deck companionway was relocated to make space for new toilets which included facilities for the disabled at the after end of the after shelter, and two of the former toilets at the after end of the main deck were converted to provide improved washing facilities for the crew on one side and a TV room on the other with mess room facilities also. New rudder pintles were fitted and some minor plating work carried out. After undocking, the ship remained in Milford Haven until the end of the year.

The *Balmoral* had an interesting season of sailings also, which in addition to her Bristol Channel base saw her cruising on the Clyde, Tay, and Moray Firth, and off Northern Ireland, Liverpool and North Wales, and the south coast. Between the two ships, over 249,000 passengers were carried during the season and the company had cleared half of the debts amassed as a result of the previous year's boiler failure. The *Balmoral* finished on 29 September and laid up in her new home at Bristol for the winter.

A very sad note during the season was the passing of the *Waverley*'s first master, who had died aged eighty-one. He was a wonderful man and had always been a huge support to me, particularly at times of crisis, when his huge wealth of maritime experience kicked into play with advice and words of support and encouragement.

1989

1989 started with us all settled into our new purpose-built premises at Lancefield Quay, with the workshop facility set up and ready for action. The new berth was also ready, with brand new railings and gates, landscaped gardens, a small car park for office staff and a large access area for fuel wagons and other heavy vehicles delivering stores to the ships. It was a revelation and demonstrated the esteem in which the company was now held in the local area. The developers, Wimpey, chartered the ship for an evening cruise to celebrate the opening of the new development in April. It was time to fetch *Waverley* from Milford Haven and introduce her to her new home, leaving on 17 January and arriving alongside the new berth the next day. Shortly after this, a letter arrived at my home in Troon from the procurator fiscal's office in Edinburgh, stating that I was to face criminal charges for my part in failing to produce the annual return and accounts for 1987 on behalf of the company. I was dumbstruck as, although a director, I did not consider the production of accounts to be within my area of direct responsibility; this was the last straw. I immediately set about obtaining new employment and was successful in obtaining a position as master of the new *Hebridean Princess*, ex-*Columba*, which ship I had sailed in during my years with MacBraynes. I considered it a great honour, accepted, and tendered my resignation. To cut a long story short, for some reason I was persuaded to stay on, and I had to withdraw my acceptance to Hebridean Island Cruises, a decision that I have regretted ever since as a couple of directors and the company solicitor considered that it would be a great opportunity for me. Whether or not I would have risen to the position will never be known, but the clientele sailing in *Hebridean Princess* were certainly very different from those in *Waverley*, being resident on board, and the master was expected to play a much greater part in the entertainment of the passengers. The atmosphere would certainly have been much more relaxed.

The season commenced on 25 April and what a season it was to turn out to be. There was glorious weather in July and a number of historic events, probably the most significant of which was the reopening of Clevedon Pier on 27 May. It was also *Balmoral*'s fortieth anniversary; she had been launched on 27 June 1949 from Thorneycroft's Woolston, Southampton yard by Mrs C. D. Pinnock, wife of the Chairman of Red Funnel. The *Waverley* was in the Western Isles from 28 April until 8 May, adding Lochmaddy, Tarbert (Harris) and Stornoway to her schedule. Sailing on the Clyde between 11 and 14 May, she carried out the centenary cruise for the Caledonian Steam Packet Company on 13 May, and in association with this a new video production by Video Productions of Gourock entitled *Sail of the Century* was launched. This was quite magnificent, with aerial shots of outstanding quality showing the ship all over the Clyde and Western Isles.

The ship was in the Bristol Channel from 19 May to 17 June and enjoyed a very successful month, particularly after the reopening of Clevedon Pier. Many charter sailings were worked, as in previous years. The weather was good and all sailings were operated as scheduled, including another visit to Tenby, finishing with a bird watchers' cruise out of Milford Haven on Sunday 18 June. Back on the Clyde from 20 June, she had a marvellous season, with glorious weather through July providing excellent loadings coupled with an unusually high number of charters. August proved to be less productive, with many days of high winds and rain, and for the first time in my period of command all Ayr calls were lost during one week of sailings. We made it to Troon on one of the days but were unable to continue and this was the only day completely cancelled. I did have the great pleasure of entertaining my mentor on board during one of the Campbeltown sailings during that month – a unique and great occasion and one of the few times that I was to be seen in the ship's bar during the whole of my twenty-three years in command!

The South Coast programme from 31 August until 20 September started with a charter from Torquay, followed by a charter to Swanage Steam Railway the next day from Swanage. Another charter was worked from Southampton the following day to view participants in the Round the World Yacht Race, following the yachts as far as the Needles then wishing them well for their voyaging before returning to Southampton. The *Balmoral* was also down south for this event and both ships berthed at Yarmouth, *Balmoral* on the face of the pier and *Waverley* in the inner harbour. The public timetable continued, with charters worked from Southampton on both Friday evenings, 8 and 15 September. A charter to the Missions to Seamen was worked from Worthing on 11 September and the ship made her first call at West Cowes pontoon to land the passengers for time ashore. There were no calls at Sandown during the visit as the pier had been fire damaged and calls were made at Ryde instead. The only casualty for the whole visit was a sailing from Worthing on Tuesday 19 September when, after trying for forty minutes, I couldn't get the ship safely alongside the pier due to swell conditions.

We continued on to Ramsgate to start the Thames programme. I had been able to study quite a bit in the 1988/89 winter and now had pilotage exemption certificates for Southampton, Portsmouth, the Medway, the Orwell and the Stour. Cruises from Ramsgate were given on 20 September in conjunction with paddle steamer week, followed by a charter to the BBC to film scenes in the series *Portrait of a Marriage*, during which the mate and I, together with some other members of the ship's company, were kitted out in period costume. This was centred around Folkestone and was great fun for all, some of the directors and cast having a marvellous time with some of the ship's crew. The public programme commenced on Saturday 23 September and was the same success as in previous years, with trips up the Orwell to Ipswich, meetings with the *Kingswear Castle* and the celebration of the centenary of the construction and opening of the present pier at Southend all taking place. The ship left the Thames on 9 October and arrived in Clevedon on Wednesday 11th, when she proceeded to Bristol, where she spent the next five days centred around Bristol, offering two single-journey evening cruises from the port with two day cruises at the weekend. Support was huge once again but such frequent and regular passages up and down the Avon, most of them in the dark, were really telling on me! *Waverley* arrived back in Glasgow on Wednesday 18 October to lay up; 192,332 passengers had been carried in the season and the company was now in the black again following the 1987 boiler failure.

The *Balmoral* had an amazing season too, with her birthday cruise a sell-out, new trips up the River Wye to Chepstow, and the reopening of Clevedon Pier providing record numbers from the upper channel. Such was the success of Clevedon that pre-booked passengers had to be turned away a number of times because the ship was full. In all, nine channel sailings were fully booked, with only two sailings cancelled because of weather. She gave an extensive pattern of sailings in Scottish waters off the east coast, including visits to Invergordon, Wick, Inverness and St Andrews, and her Clyde sailings included her first calls at Renfrew. The south coast was visited on two occasions and following a visit to the Clyde for the autumn holiday weekend, she finished the season with a charter to the RNLI from Portaferry in Northern Ireland. Bristol was reached on 28 September for lay-up, so the season, which started on a worrying note with misalignment of the main engines caused by bottom repairs, turned out to be a record for the ship so far. She had carried 109,504 passengers for the season, a company total of 301,836 altogether for both ships.

Our ten years of building the business were over. The *Waverley* was re-boilered and running reliably, the second ship was bought and established twice (the first one being lost), and there was money in the bank at the end of it, all achieved with pretty minimal external financial support. The PSPS had worked tirelessly throughout the decade to achieve charitable status for itself, the *Kingswear Castle* and the *Waverley*, a quite incredible accomplishment. Waverley Excursions had been born to look after the day-to-day running of the ships and in 1989 the *Waverley* had been the winner of the water section of the Scania Transport Trust Awards Scheme. A cheque for £250 had been presented to Waverley Steam Navigation Company Ltd for 'outstanding endeavour in preserving our National Transport Heritage', with a handsome brass plaque to go along with it. Not bad for a bunch of amateurs who had through the years fought themselves towards at least a modicum of credibility and without doubt an outstanding accolade to all those involved. The company would enter the new decade a stronger force, with two ships in good condition, both with no encumbrances (mortgages or the like), and a credit balance in the bank.

A Captain's Memories: Part 4
Other Ships and Projects

Queen of Scots

The loss of the *Waverley* to Clyde service at the height of the season due to the Gantocks grounding required some innovative thinking, and in an effort not to be defeated the Waverley Steam Navigation (WSN) board actively sought a vessel to charter in order to cover as much of the service as possible. The *Arran* was available, the pioneer Clyde car ferry from 1954, but she would come fully crewed and as a result was a very expensive ship to charter and really not that suitable a craft for passenger cruising. Sealink were approached at Portsmouth because it seemed that the Ryde passenger service was by then reduced to a two ship service, with the third ship available at times of peak demand. However, this was not a goer, the third ship being employed on cruising duties during the day except on Saturdays. We were left with the much smaller *Queen of Scots*, which had just finished service as a ferry running from Rothesay to Ardyne with workers engaged at the McAlpine concrete production platform construction yard there. The ship had just been laid up, as the yard had run out of work, and as a result the ship had become surplus to requirements. She was in certificate (Class IV and V) and was available immediately. Her previous Class III certificate for 452 passengers, which she had on the south coast, had not been renewed by her new owners when she came to Scotland. No sailings from Ayr or Brodick would therefore be possible and in any event the ship's speed would not have enabled her to cover the distance in a day that could be achieved by *Waverley*. However, with some adjustments to the timetable, we all believed that she could make a contribution in the *Waverley*'s absence. A bareboat charter was agreed with her owner, Sir Robert McAlpine, and the ship was delivered to Anderston Quay by *Waverley* personnel on Thursday 21 July, where she was immediately painted in WSN livery. She entered service on Saturday 23 July, covering as much of the paddler's schedule as she could, and ran impeccably until 31 August, carrying over 14,000 passengers during the period. The ship had quite an interesting history, being built at New Holland in 1935 as *Coronia*, and sailed out of Scarborough for various owners until 1968, enjoying quite distinguished war service based in the Portsmouth and Isle of Wight area, with unconfirmed reports that she ventured as far as the Mediterranean! She moved to the south coast in 1968 and was renamed *Bournemouth Queen*; she sailed between Poole, Swanage, Bournemouth and the Isle of Wight, also using Totland Bay pier at times. She was purchased by McAlpines and brought to the Clyde in 1974 and following the 1977 charter the WSN looked after the vessel at Glasgow until she was sold on for further use in 1978.

Shanklin/Prince Ivanhoe

The *Shanklin/Prince Ivanhoe* was really my baby. I could never be accused of having a real love for motor ships, but at pre-sea training school at East Cowes on the Isle of Wight I had grown very fond of the Portsmouth trio of *Southsea*, *Brading* and *Shanklin*, the latter becoming my favourite. Denny built the first two in 1948, followed by the *Shanklin* in 1951. They were ships of outstanding quality and comfort, with smooth-running engines and loads of open deck space, which was steadily improved throughout their working lives. They all had a small cargo hold forward for the carriage of baggage, newspapers and fresh consumable produce to the Isle of Wight.

The *Shanklin* was particularly smooth running and on passage on board she felt like the Clyde turbine steamers. I was later to learn that this was because she had direct acting Sultzer engines, built under licence by her builders, whereas the other two had been fitted with engines direct from the manufacturers in Switzerland. These Swiss engines were controlled through gearboxes, which created more noise. The *Shanklin*'s engine room was fully insulated whereas the *Southsea* and *Brading* were not, and all three were converted to bridge control quite early in their lives, which obviated the need to have an engineer at the controls in the engine room. This was not successful in the *Shanklin*, which caused her to have a number of accidents at piers, caused by the failure of the engines to respond quickly enough to commands from the bridge. Much of the blame for this was put down to the officers handling the ship from the bridge, who were said to have failed to recognise the need for a short delay between ahead and astern to allow for the engines to stop and be restarted in the opposite direction.

Shanklin therefore returned to being manually controlled from the engine room, with an engineer responding to telegraph orders from the bridge – the same system as that employed on *Waverley* and *Balmoral* today. The manoeuvring console in the engine room was cleverly designed so that one man could easily manoeuvre both engines on his own and interestingly enough, a very similar console was built into the MacBrayne ferries *Clansman*, *Columba* and *Hebrides* when they were introduced in 1964, some thirteen years later. I became well-known on *Shanklin* as a schoolboy from 1957 to 1959 and got to know many of her officers at the time, both on deck and in the engine room.

One of those officers, who had become a senior master and subsequently assistant marine superintendent down at Portsmouth in the interim, came up to Newhaven to accompany me in the *Waverley* on our first voyage into Clarence Pier, Southsea, in 1978, which he had used regularly while master of PS *Ryde* and also while cruising in the *Shanklin* later. On the voyage we enjoyed many reminiscences, going back many years, and he was able to reveal that he didn't think that it would be long before one of the trio became surplus to requirements. I was therefore able at that time to ask him to let us know as soon as any decision in that direction was taken. That was done in early October 1980, after the ship had lain idle at the odds and evens moorings in Portsmouth Harbour since the previous March. My visits to the bridge and engine room of the *Shanklin* had become something of a distant memory until November 1980, when the ship became the property of a new company, Gorto Ltd, later renamed Firth of Clyde Steam Packet Co. Ltd (FOC).

I remembered the engineers back in the 1950s remarking on the quality of the machinery and the level of equipment in the engine room, likening it to a much larger ship. The ship was quite new then and obviously very impressive to those that worked on board. However, once our engineers had seen over the ship, I remember one of them remarking that the kit out of the engine room would have been the envy of many a deep-sea chief engineer! The day that we took over the ship, I stayed on board at Portsmouth because I had so much administrative work to complete before moving the ship to Southampton the next day and the generator was left running for me when the others left at about 5.00 p.m. that day. Later I went down to shut it down before going to bed about 11.30 p.m., looking around the machinery space myself, remembering the engineers' words and thinking yes, my goodness, this does feel like a big ship. We had to operate the ship on one engine as the other was stripped down for repair and required some work to be carried out by Metalock before reassembly could take place and this would not be done until early the next year at Glasgow.

The ship was steamed to Southampton, where an underwater survey was undertaken and preparations made for the voyage to the Clyde. We left Southampton on 13 November and reached the Clyde a week later, having amply demonstrated the seagoing qualities of the vessel on the way with a two-day stop at Torbay for shelter, during which we put into Brixham for stores and some extra fuel. The approach to the Clyde was made via the Kilbrannan Sound and the Kyles of Bute in an effort to keep her arrival a secret from the media, with the vessel arriving at Helensburgh in the evening for an overnight stay. Many of those that had provided financial assistance towards the purchase of the ship came aboard to see her and were astonished at her condition and spaciousness. She did look magnificent as the lads had worked really hard to ensure that she looked her best. A reception for the ship was arranged in Glasgow for the media and for all those interested in seeing her, hosted by our chairman, and what a day it was – one of the councillors on board wondered if she could be pressed into service on the Arran run immediately! The ship was just an instant hit with everyone that saw her and later sailed in her. Various uses for the vessel were discussed during the following month until it became apparent that there was going to be no service on the Bristol Channel in 1981.

P. & A. Campbell had ceased trading at the end of the 1979 season and a new company had been formed, primarily to maintain the service to Lundy Island, called White Funnel Steamers Ltd. The directors of the new company were Mr S. C. Smith-Cox, P. & A. Campbell Ltd, and Mr John Smith of the Landmark Trust, owners of Lundy Island. This new company chartered the *Balmoral* from P. & A. Campbell Ltd to operate the Bristol Channel services for the 1980 season. The ship was to be managed by P. & A. Campbell Ltd, a company within the European Ferries Group, but the arrangement wasn't a success. It was a summer of awful weather and the *Balmoral* seemed to spend most of her time down at Swansea that year, with the result that the Landmark Trust withdrew support in December and White Funnel Steamers Ltd closed down.

The decision was taken that *Shanklin/Prince Ivanhoe* would become the Bristol Channel ship for 1981, and that rightly or wrongly, P. & A. Campbell would be retained as the managers in that area, something the writer had very serious reservations about. Back in Glasgow, we set about getting the ship ready for service, with engineer officers engaged later in January to rebuild the port main engine. Meanwhile, the *Waverley* engine room team supervised the repair of the cracks to the entablature of the port main engine and were also able to arrange that any further work on the machinery could be deferred until the next winter due to the extensive and detailed records which came with the ship, showing the utterly amazing quality maintenance regime that had existed with her previous owners at Portsmouth right up to March 1980, when the cracks in the port main engine were discovered.

All went according to plan and the ship was dry-docked and ready to run trials at the end of April. Around £60,000 was spent on the refitting of the ship with, in addition to the work in the engine room, a complete upgrade of her safety equipment to enable her to operate on Class III service. The ship had only been used on Class IV and V service by her previous owners, although she had been built as a Class III ship, and so this was a massive job involving a complete revamp of all the life saving appliances to incorporate the inclusion of inflatable liferafts, in addition to what existed on board, new fire fighting equipment, a brand new CO_2 room, breathing apparatus, new compasses and navigational equipment. To facilitate operation in places with a bigger tidal range than the Solent, new upper deck landing platforms had to be created, and also accommodation for the crew including mess room facilities, as the ship's company had not been required to live on board in Solent service. A new galley had also to be constructed and for all of this detailed drawings had to be submitted to the Department of Trade for approval before it could be carried out. This was a very lengthy and frustrating process but it was accomplished and I was lucky enough to be able to retain some of the drawings submitted at that time – very nostalgic. There were some absolutely brilliant young surveyors involved at the time.

In addition to this, the *Waverley* was being re-boilered during the same period and so we were all stretched to the limit to cope with it all. After a couple of runs on the Clyde, where one or two teething problems were ironed out, the ship left for the Bristol Channel, where she arrived on the evening of 30 April. It had all been an incredible achievement and surely deserved success, but it was not to be; on the way up the Avon, the bad luck that seemed to embrace the *Prince Ivanhoe* from then on commenced and she grounded between Miles Dock Upper light and Leigh Woods Lower light, damaging the starboard bilge amidships in way of the engine room double bottom tank. The ship was taking water into the tank and inspection on the Grid Iron outside Bristol Cumberland Basin locks on the morning of 2 May confirmed our worst fears that she would require to be dry-docked again. She successfully completed her static visit to Bristol and was in dry-dock at Barry by 10.15 p.m. on Tuesday 5 May, which lasted a week at a cost of over £20,000.

Following successful visits to Watchet and Minehead on 16 May, she returned to the Clyde to cover her own sailings scheduled up there, but was recalled to the channel again at the end of the month to cover for *Waverley*, as she had sustained paddle damage on the way round the north of Scotland which required the facilities at home base to put right. On this visit she covered a number of charters for the paddler, including the one for North Devon hospitals out of Bideford, which, it was reported, was accomplished in weather that might well have been too much for *Waverley*. The charterers were absolutely delighted with the ship and sang her praises for years afterwards.

On the return passage to the Clyde, around 10 June, the ship only got as far as Tenby when she was recalled to Avonmouth to carry out a fully booked schools cruise as the *Waverley* couldn't get down in time because of the weather, which was particularly stormy for that time of year. Finally, on the return journey to the Clyde she sustained heavy weather damage as a result of the huge swells created by the continuous blustery weather and this resulted in a further repair bill for £7,500, both this and the incident in the Avon being covered by insurance. Included in this sum was damage caused to five beam knees when the ship collided with the wall on arrival at Glasgow on 15 June. Recovery was still going on almost a year later – such is the pace in the world of marine insurance!

She returned to Bristol Channel for the season on 21 June to begin her scheduled sailings in accordance with the advertised timetable, which didn't appear until early July – the first fortnight of sailings, I believe, were covered by advertising provided by P. & A. Campbell Ltd. When the *Waverley* returned to the Clyde towards the end of the month, I was approached by a couple of the directors of FOC, who believed that we were going to have to give up on the operation of *Prince Ivanhoe* because of the critical state of the cash flow. I pointed out that there was about £25,000 of insurance recovery to come back and that as I had an investment in the ship I would like the opportunity of having a go at it myself.

Arrangements were made for me to join the ship on 6 July to do just that, and I travelled down overnight to join her at Penarth, complete with my wife and family. Thank goodness they were there because I felt like an alien in our own ship, surrounded by Campbell's officers and paraphernalia. It was clear that I wasn't welcome on board. The engine room was being run like a deep sea ship with 'Stand by' having to be given before manoeuvring could commence, something that I had never experienced in coastal ships in fifteen years of handling coastal vessels, except when the vessels were on a long passage.

The timetable header for 1981, showing the two ships.

All the catering staff that the FOC company had supplied had been driven off and the chief steward, another Campbell's man, was openly helping himself to drink from the bar. I had a letter from his predecessor explaining his reasons for leaving, which I still have in my possession today.

We set off with 200 odd passengers on board for Minehead, I was tired and fed up and made an utter mess of taking the ship into Minehead harbour. Forgetting that I was not still in the *Waverley*, I entered too fast and the ship over-ran about 50 feet, causing the port propeller to foul small boat moorings in the harbour and doing minor damage to a couple of the moored boats as well, another £2,000. What next?! I returned to my cabin totally demoralised, wondering if the ship would ever settle down. I then made the huge mistake of being persuaded to take the ship onward to Ilfracombe on one engine, incurring another £1,200 worth of expense in coaching the people home because once at Ilfracombe the propeller could not be cleared without having the ship dried out at low water. She could have done this at Minehead while the passengers had a day ashore and we could have returned to Penarth in the evening at the scheduled time if only we had stayed put – what a shambles my first day on board had been. However, great things were to follow; the ship did settle down and apart from one day altered and one missed call at Minehead, the ship ran perfectly until Monday 3 August and revenue receipts steadily increased in fairly average weather. During her last week in service, 27 July to 2 August, the ticket revenue was £26,290 and the catering revenue £4,647, and this from a single outlet. The month of August produced good weather that year and so with the schools on holiday there was no reason to believe that she would not have continued to earn at that level for the rest of the month and there were several evening charters booked for August also.

Ticket revenue of £100,000–120,000, with catering revenue at around £20,000, would certainly have made a huge difference to the position of the company by early September in those days. The ship could carry 896 passengers on the Class III and over 1,300 on the IV and believe me you could lose 1,000 on board that ship, she was so incredibly spacious. We left Penarth that morning and voyaged via Minehead, where a facing fender was burst berthing on this occasion – what a pain the place was with that particular ship. I had devised a method of berthing her for future occasions by screwing her round the corner instead of the straight run in generally used, which I believed would have worked effectively but I was never going to get the opportunity of trying it with that vessel. I was able to try it later with *Balmoral* and it worked a treat.

We continued on to Mumbles, where I handed the ship over to the chief officer, who had been master of the *Balmoral* the previous season. I was asked in a letter from the owners to act in my position as director and company representative during the course of a Department of Transport survey to allow continuation of her loadline certificate and the issue of a special extension to her Class III passenger certificate to allow for two evening cruises to take place later that month from Swansea. The surveyor joined at Mumbles pier and the ship left at 2.15 p.m. for the afternoon cruise. After we had completed a thorough inspection of the ship, the surveyor, the chief engineer and I were in my cabin, inspecting ship's certificates and documents, when at 3.30 p.m. there were several sharp bumps and a screech indicating that the ship had made contact with something under the water. The ship didn't stop and so I have always assumed that it was some unknown and uncharted underwater obstruction off Port Eynon on the Gower Coast and not the ground.

I had been unfortunate enough to be involved with two groundings during my time as second and chief officer in MacBraynes, and of course the famous Gantocks grounding while master of the *Waverley* in 1977, and believe me there is no doubt when a small ship runs aground. If it's rocks, there is an awful rumbling noise with huge loss of speed, the ship more often coming to rest completely. The ship was catastrophically damaged. The engines were stopped within a few minutes due to lack of lubricating oil pressure and by the time that she came to rest she was almost a mile off shore. My report of the incident and last log entry are copied, with apologies for the condition of the copies. On this occasion the damage had breached the engine room double bottom tank by way of the port main engine lubricating oil tank, which was situated within the double bottom, and so on this occasion the engine room started flooding rapidly as opposed to the accident in the River Avon back in May, when the tank top held. From the time of contact until the ship was beached about a mile away was twenty minutes, during which I had declared a full emergency on board, ordered the ship to be sounded, ordered a Mayday call, ordered the lifesaving appliances to be made ready for use, started the passengers donning their lifejackets and despite a number of interruptions had managed to plot a safe course to the beach and safely navigated her there without hitting anything on the way in. There is little point in making for a beach if you are going to run over some obstruction on the way!

I recall the chief engineer visiting the bridge on three occasions, once to say the ship was finished and that we should go in there, pointing to the beach. Having asked whether or not we could run the engines, he went below again and returned to say that he thought that we could, but for a very limited period. Once I had rung for astern on the engines, he reappeared on the bridge again to ask why we were going astern, which in hindsight was unnecessary on my part, but my thinking at the time was to keep the ship in the shallowest possible water in case the engines didn't run long enough to get us to the beach. I remember finding this odd as I felt that the chief engineer's place was in the engine room, doing all that he could to reduce the ingress of water to the machinery space, without which the ship truly was finished. This had been the case in the previous incidents that I had been involved in, where the engine room teams were hard at work in their respective machinery spaces, dealing with the emergency. Perhaps this assessment was unfair because he was a very young man, in his first job as chief engineer, having not sailed in a rank above fourth engineer previously, and in that rank only in a large seagoing ship where incidents involving bumps, scrapes and contact with the bottom are rare compared with the likelihood of such events in coastal vessels. However, running the engines with the valves set as they were was just exacerbating the inflow of water into the space, so that by the time that we reached the beach she most certainly was finished and all I could do was make sure that everyone was evacuated as quickly and safely as was possible and watch the ship slowly sink from under me.

Once the ship had sunk, there wasn't enough insurance value to repair her so there was nothing for it but to declare her a CTL (Constructive Total Loss). It was a sad end for me to a project that had been years in the making, was one so close to my heart and one which had such huge potential for the future. Life would never be quite the same again for

The log book entry for the evacuation of *Prince Ivanhoe* after her grounding, 3 August 1981.

3rd August, 1981.

Extract from Official Log Book of "Prince Ivanhoe"

This is to certify that, at 15.30 hours this afternoon, the vessel struck an underwater obstruction off Port Eynon Point, South Wales, when on an afternoon cruise from Mumbles to the Gower Coast. Mr. T. Goldie, First Officer and number 46 on Ships Crew Agreement, was on watch at the time. I was in my cabin with Mr. T. McMillan, Chief Engineer, and number 9 on the Ships Crew Agreement, and Mr. C. Darlow, a Department of Trade Surveyor working on ships business. I proceeded immediately to the bridge and ascertained the position of the ship, also giving instructions for soundings to be taken of all compartments. The engines were stopped within five minutes, due to lack of lubricating oil pressure. Reports came back to me that the ship was making water rapidly in three of her six watertight compartments. The Chief Engineer informed me immediately that we could perhaps have the engines for up to a maximum of twenty minutes, although he pointed out that this action would almost certainly finish the engines. We discussed briefly what we considered to be the only option open to us in order to safeguard the lives on board, due to the total immersal of the vessel in an estimated thirty minutes; and this was to beach the ship in the best possible area of the sandy beach at Port Eynon. At 15.37 hours, a call for immediate assistance was sent out and by 15.40 hours the engines were started, full astern at first for a distance of about one and a half cables, to reduce the ingress of water, as the ship struck going ahead, and also to check that the steering gear was still functioning and, above all, to ensure that at all times she was kept as near the shore as possible. The approximate heading of the vessel at the time was 80°(C), 170°(T) and she went astern about 3 0°(T) about one and a half cables from a point 110° (T), two cables from the East Helwick Buoy in a charted depth of about ten metres. The engines were then put to full ahead and the rudder hard aport, until the vessel was heading for the sandy section in the middle of Port Eynon Bay. By this time, approximately 15.45 hours, the ship was just inside the five cable ring, using the one and a half mile range on the radar, from the beach and had already settled bodily, by visual inspection, about 1ft. 6ins. in the water and was beginning to develop a slight list to port. The vessel beached at 15.50 hours just below low water mark and immediately steps were taken to evacuate passengers, using all available small craft and the ships own lifeboats and inflatable liferafts. During the period 15.47 until 15.50, all passengers were issued with life jackets and the crew were engaged in making sure that they were correctly donned. The tide was rising and the water level in the ship was soon at tide level, except for the forward end which remained afloat until 19.25 hours. All passengers were safely landed by 18.00 hours and all crew transferred to the Mumbles lifeboat at 18.40 hours. I remained with the ship until she finally settled on the bottom at 19.25 hours and left on the Horton Inshore lifeboat at 19.27 hours.

A typed extract from the log book of *Prince Ivanhoe* for 3 August 1981.

me, and for the company it was going to be years before it would recover enough to have another go. The opportunity to the company of ever owning such a magnificent ship again was over for good. A few days after the incident, I recall discussing with senior members of the ship's company and representatives from the managers, P. & A. Campbell Ltd, the possibility of quickly recommissioning *Balmoral* in an effort to salvage what remained of the season and being absolutely staggered at how little grasp the people present had of the gravity of what had just happened.

Without the enormous skill of the FOC company directors, particularly one of them, in dealing with the aftermath of it all, with massive help also from the ship's chief engineer and a bit from myself, we were able to keep ourselves out of the bankruptcy courts and also keep the *Waverley* sailing. We really were seriously underfunded and had not been ready to undertake all that went on that year. Re-boilering the *Waverley* and commissioning another vessel in the same winter was an incredible achievement but a huge financial risk and one that required a big bowlful of luck to achieve success, luck

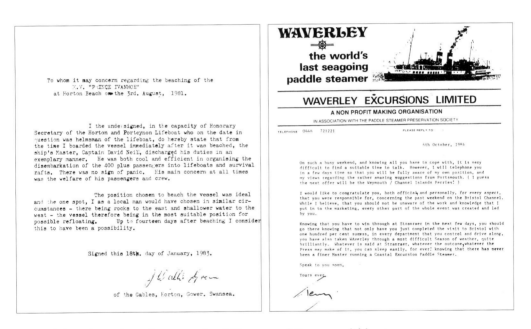

Above left: A letter from the coxswain of Horton and Porteynon lifeboat.

Above right: Letter of encouragement from Terry Sylvester to the captain dated 6 October 1986, following the offer of the *Southsea* and prior to the enquiry at Stranraer.

that did not prevail. I conclude this sad episode with a reprint of my last entry in the ship's log book, on 5 August 1981 at Swansea: 'This is to certify that the vessel *Prince Ivanhoe* has this day been abandoned to the underwriters by the owners the Firth of Clyde Steam Packet Co. Ltd, as a constructive total loss. With sadness the log book is closed and the ship becomes a wreck.'

Galway Bay

After a good season in 1984, we were all beginning to recover from the loss of the *Prince Ivanhoe* and thoughts turned to looking at other craft again. *Southsea* and *Brading* were still the mainstay of the Portsmouth–Ryde service and so they were not available. In November that year I was in the Irish Republic, planning the first visit of *Waverley* to that area for 1985, when I received a telephone message from the chairman asking me to have a look at the *Galway Bay*, which had come up for sale. The ship was laid up in Galway harbour at the time as she was every winter and had previously been the Red Funnel tender tug *Calshot*, built in 1930. Since being renamed, she had been employed running out of Galway on passenger services to the Aran Islands since 1964, and also acted as tender to any large passenger liners visiting the area, especially those of the Holland America Line, which made regular calls at Galway on transatlantic services in her early years there.

Although she had previously been steam propelled, the steam engines had been removed and the ship had been completely re-engined with diesel machinery prior to taking up this service. The hull was very strong and the price tag of £50,000 was not unreasonable as she was in certificate and ready to go with Class IIA, III and IV passenger certificates with numbers ranging from 420 to 600 passengers. This was, however, under the Irish flag and had we wanted to return her to British registry we could have encountered some difficulties. The ship had a very interesting history, having taken part in the Dunkirk evacuation, and was also tender to most of the famous transatlantic liners during her career at Southampton. Much as I liked the ship, I had to reject her, as with a draft of 12 feet and a service speed of 11 knots she would not have been a suitable running mate for *Waverley*. She is now preserved statically at Southampton, restored to her Red Funnel appearance with a tall steamer-type funnel.

Balmoral

In December 1984 news came to us that the owners of the *Balmoral*, Craig Inns Ltd, had ceased trading and as a result that ship was available. We all knew that the ship was in a dreadful state and would require massive reconstruction work and alteration before she would be any use to us in service. The passenger accommodation was going to have to be completely refurbished, with the bridge and some of the other superstructure only fit for scrap. There was also substantial hull damage, propeller damage and most of the ship's belting (rubbing band) was smashed to bits. An anchor was also missing and the two main engines had been a source of considerable trouble in her last season, with the holding down bolts for the entablatures regularly fracturing. There were no lifesaving appliances at all except the wooden lifeboats, both of which were condemned. What a nightmare! However, she was about the last suitable ship for the job left.

She had a very good operational track record but had failed to make any money for any of her owners through the years. Not much of a resumé, but nevertheless we all went to Dundee in February and were faced with virtually digging the ship out of the mud. The main engine lubricating oil tanks had been turned into effluent tanks and the ship was land-locked, except at the biggest of spring tides. We went ahead with the purchase and the ship became ours in late February for the princely sum of £20,000. It was decided that if we could get her to Glasgow, the decision regarding her future could be decided over a year, during which time we would investigate what funding support might be obtainable and if none was forthcoming she could be sold for scrap.

No tug would come into Craig harbour, where she was berthed, because of the level of siltation and so we had to find a way of getting the ship to the harbour entrance. The engine room team reckoned that it might be possible to get the windlass at the bow running using power from the emergency generator, which would allow us to warp the ship across the dock. Long ropes had to be rigged to achieve this, which meant that some of the lads had to wade through the mud at low water and haul the ropes across to the other side of the harbour. It was a dirty and horrible task and very hard work, with no power other than their own arms and legs to assist them. We even tried pulling a flat dinghy across the mud but it kept getting stuck and in the end proved more trouble than it was worth. One of the highest tides of the year was on 7 March and we calculated that we might have a maximum of a two-hour window over high water to complete the task of moving the ship across the dock to the waiting tug, which had been duly ordered to attend that day.

The generator ran, the windlass ran and the ship left Craig harbour under tow for dry-dock as planned; it seemed as if the *Balmoral* herself wanted to be saved! A ten-day period in dry-dock revealed no serious defects in the hull and the *Waverley*'s engine room team had been hard at it, changing the ship from static use to an operating unit again. The day after we left dry-dock the main generators and switchboard were back in operation and eventually the main engines, too, were coaxed back into life, with a smoke screen that seemed to envelope the whole of dockside Dundee. I spent two gruelling days with one of the lads, finding the cables for the engine room telegraphs, identifying them, and then reconnecting them so that we could once again communicate engine movements from the bridge. Fortunately, they were all still there and had just been cut and dropped down into the ceiling panels below. On Friday 22 March 1985, we became a company with two operational ships again when *Balmoral* went out on successful trials under her own power, with the old Sirron engines pounding away once more. Compass adjustment followed two days later and the ship left that night for Glasgow, where we arrived at 10.30 p.m. on 26 March. The ship had completed the passage in about fifty hours at an average speed of just over eleven knots and total fuel consumed for the voyage including trials was just 8 tons. The only hiccup was a blocked air vent in one of the fuel tanks, which caused a short stop while it was traced and rectified. The next day she moved to Clyde Dock Engineering at Govan for inspection and remained there until 10 April, returning to Anderston Quay to transfer some fuel to *Waverley* that day.

She returned to Govan for lay-up for the rest of the summer as all the company's seagoing staff were then busy operating *Waverley*. Estimates were prepared and the Balmoral Restoration Fund was set up to raise the required estimated £300,000 to return her to full operational service. She was returned to Anderston Quay on 19 September as Clyde Dock needed the space and she remained there until the end of the year. Work continued throughout the year in an effort to raise the required funding and at a meeting in early January 1986 the owners decided that sufficient funds were available and promised to allow us to proceed with restoration of the ship.

She moved under her own power to Govan dry-dock on Tuesday 21 January 1986 to begin a major rebuild which was designed to extend the ship's life by ten to fifteen years. The hull was shot blasted and primed from bow to stern, the lower belting was removed completely and the remainder of the belting was renewed in virtually its entirety. The heavy shell damage aft was completely cropped away and new steel was inserted. Bottom repairs were carried out in way of the engine room and much of the steelwork at the forward end of the aft deckhouse, where a new purser's office and cabin was created, had to be renewed. The service area at the purser's office was designed more like a reception desk rather than the old railway ticket windows found in the *Waverley*. A new aluminium wheelhouse and chartroom was built and installed using the same drawings as those used for *Waverley* the previous year. The entire bridge deck was re-decked, while below the former upper deck bar was converted into an observation lounge and souvenir shop. A new dining saloon and galley were built over the former car deck space and the large lower bar beneath this area was refurbished. The galley ranges were gas-fired, as in *Waverley*, but the hot counters had to be electrically powered as there was no steam on board and this required the fitting of a new AC electrical supply. Gravel ballast, about 4 tons' worth, was removed from the bar bilge by the ship's master and I personally! This was no longer required as the weight of the new superstructure, dining saloon and galley above was more than ample compensation for it.

In the engine room new fitted holding down bolts for the engine entablatures were installed and the engines were opened up as required for survey, with very heartening results. No need for major replacement was found and the engines were considered fit for many more years of reliable service, which indeed proved to be the case as the years progressed. The generator engines, on the other hand, were found to be close to the end of their working lives and many new parts had to be sourced and fitted in the hope of getting a few more years out of them. Already they were operating at their maximum loading, due to the ever-increasing demands for electricity required in a modern age, and at times both generators had to be in operation to meet the demand for electricity on board, especially at night. This was a worry but eventually new generator engines from the same manufacturer were found around 1990 and somehow the engineering teams on board were able to keep the old ones running until then. I am afraid that I do not have a record of the exact circumstances under which we came upon these replacement engines but they had been in some establishment ashore and had done very little running, resulting in them serving the ship right up to the time of her lay-up in 2012.

Forward, a new lounge bar was created and named the Britannia Lounge, with furnishings and carpets to a high standard and a small dance floor included in the centre of the space. A completely new kit-out of all fire fighting appliances had to be carried out, and on deck the original lifeboat davits were overhauled and two brand-new lifeboats fitted, one of which was a motorboat. New buoyant apparatus was purchased and most of it was arranged as seats on the new upper deck, above the new dining saloon and galley. On the bridge, new navigating and radio equipment had to be purchased and installed, also a new engine room telegraph transmitter as one of the originals had disappeared while the ship was in Dundee. Just as we were nearing the end of it all, the foremast broke in a storm and a new one had to be sourced (in the form of a telegraph pole), shaped, painted and quickly installed.

The livery chosen for the ship was that of the General Steam Navigation Company ships, a white hull with green lining, green boot topping and a buff funnel, which was chosen for the ease and cost-effectiveness of maintenance. Fancy colour schemes are very labour intensive and as a result costly to maintain. The new look and very smart *Balmoral* arrived at Anderston Quay at 6.00 p.m. on Friday 28 March 1986. She ran trials on 31 March and returned to Govan for further finishing work until 4 April. Further trials were carried out on 7 April and she left Glasgow on Thursday 10 April to start her new life as Britain's most far-travelled excursion vessel, a life that was to last much longer than the ten to fifteen years originally envisaged at the start of her rebuild.

The whole exercise had cost well in excess of £360,000, well above budget, but the ship did give many years of reliable service. We owed a huge debt of gratitude to the many companies, professionals and individuals who all helped to make this dream become a reality. Unfortunately, at the beginning of 1987 there was a shortfall of around £136,000, caused by the failure of some of the promised funding to materialise (£50,000–£55,000) and a trading deficit following her first season in operation. It looked bleak but one of the company directors cleared this debt out of her own pocket, which allowed the ship to continue to trade. The rest of the *Balmoral* story is well recorded in a number of magnificently produced publications.

Southsea

During the period from 1974 to 1986, considerable rapport had developed between the management of Sealink British Ferries at Portsmouth and I, with a number of officers and crew of the ships becoming good friends. I had been responsible for picking up the *Lymington* for her new owners, Western Ferries, in 1974, been advised by one of their senior masters on the occasion of the first visit to the Solent by *Waverley* in 1978, not to mention all the negotiations that had gone into the use of their facilities at Clarence Pier, Southsea and Ryde for *Waverley*'s Solent visits. Again, I was involved in taking over the *Shanklin* in 1980 for our ownership, and in early 1986 was on board the *Freshwater* collecting some equipment no longer required by her new owners, Western Ferries, but needed for our *Balmoral*. I was asked a couple of times if I was getting a job down there! The events of early October 1986 were to eclipse all that went on before when we were invited to the manager's office at Portsmouth Harbour station and asked literally if we wanted the *Southsea*. A huge, detailed document was prepared, giving all the various

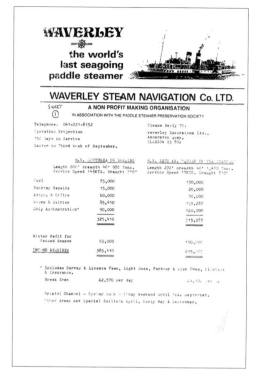
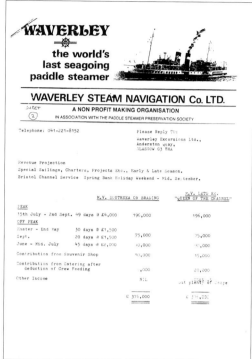

Above left: Cost comparisons for *Southsea/Brading* and *Leto*.

Above right: Revenue comparisons for *Southsea/Brading* and *Leto*.

options, but the bottom line was that the ship had to be available on eight Saturdays in July and August between 10.00 a.m. and 8 p.m. to supplement the Portsmouth–Ryde service. Recognising our position at the time, having just commissioned *Balmoral*, WSN would have the choice of a low price purchase or bareboat charter (with purchase options built in), the price to represent and discount the Saturday ferry sailings for Sealink. In other words, Sealink would not pay for the Saturday sailings for a period of three years, i.e. twenty-four Saturdays, but in return the ship would be released to us for £10,000. In addition, Sealink would restrict any sale of *Southsea*'s sister ship *Brading* to static use only.

WSN could have free use of Clarence pier, Ryde and Yarmouth, with a free lay-over berth at Portsmouth harbour, either on the odds and evens hulk or on the south end of the Railway jetty. The sale would include £100,000 worth of machinery spares and should we need anything else, there was agreement to pick *Brading* for spares within reasonable limits before that ship was released for sale. All navigational equipment would come with the ship, together with all the Department of Trade reports on the vessel including one for reduced manning. The survey reports showed the hull and machinery to be in excellent condition, with no major work required, and all the asbestos insulation had been removed from the ship only the previous year. Substantial electrical work, together with substantial rewiring, had also been carried out at the same time. Additionally, the project came with 100 per cent blessing of all the councils on the Isle of Wight.

What an incredible offer – if only it had come a year earlier, we would have been in a position to take full advantage of it. Negotiations continued and as time progressed it seemed that we were becoming the meat in the sandwich between in-fighting taking place at Sealink headquarters in London and the local management in Portsmouth. At WSN, we agreed to give the deal a try with the ship operating a service on Class IV, V and VI certificates in an area bounded by Poole and Bournemouth in the west and Sandown and St Catherine's Point in the east, trips round the island not being possible on a Class IV certificate.

The ship was prepared for the voyage to the Clyde, where we were going to overhaul her in-house at Anderston Quay. The passenger accommodation was adequate but nowhere near the standard on the *Shanklin*, as the *Southsea* had endured a further gruelling seven years on the ferry service, so some minor refurbishment and improvements to the catering were planned. The ship was ready by early January and the voyage was planned to commence on the 14th when suddenly, without prior warning, we were summoned to Sealink headquarters in London on 13 January to be told that the deal was off and that they had decided to operate the ship to their own account in 1987. In some respects I think that we were all relieved because the whole thing was once again a huge financial gamble at a time when we were far from awash with funds. The local manager at Portsmouth resigned a few weeks later and a number of top level and quite heated meetings took place between the local Isle of Wight councils and Sealink management in London over the future of the *Southsea* in respect of the Portsmouth to Ryde service. With the events that occurred in 1987 with regard to the *Waverley*'s boiler, it was a blessing in disguise.

We were already well aware of the fact that the running of a ship continuously all season in the Solent was bound to dilute the market in that area for *Waverley* and *Balmoral*, valuable revenue that would have been hard to replace elsewhere. When the boiler failed in the *Waverley* on 23 August 1987, I contacted my friends at Sealink regarding *Southsea* again, regarding availability of the ship for charter. At that time the ship was operating a limited range of short cruises on the Solent and down as far as Sandown, with additional sailings to and from Ryde at peak periods. The reaction to my telephone call amazed me as I was told that the ship would be taken off her cruising service immediately after the August Bank Holiday weekend if we wanted to charter her.

After a good deal of discussion it was decided that although it looked very marginal, a Clyde operation in September, we would take the ship on for a month. The timetable embracing the Friday, Saturday and Sunday services operated by *Waverley* would be supplemented by two new services added for Tuesdays and Wednesdays. It was therefore Glasgow–Rothesay on Fridays and Glasgow–Tighnabruaich on Saturdays, both including all intermediate calls, with the Glasgow Round Bute via Dunoon, Largs and Rothesay on Sundays. Tuesday's schedule was rearranged to start at Helensburgh at 10.30 a.m. and pick up the normal schedule to Tarbert and cruise on Loch Fyne from Largs at 12.00 p.m. via Rothesay and Tighnabruaich, returning to Helensburgh at 8.15 p.m. A new schedule was devised for Wednesdays, leaving Helensburgh at 8.30 a.m. and sailing via Dunoon, Rothesay, Largs and Brodick, thence via Kyles of Bute to Rothesay, with time ashore before returning via Garroch Head and the same calling points, arriving back at Helensburgh at 8.20 p.m. There were no sailings on Mondays or Thursdays except the

September weekend, Monday 28 September. The September weekend sailings between Friday 25 September and Monday 28 September planned for *Balmoral* were carried out by *Southsea* as the *Balmoral* was down south, deputising for the broken-down *Waverley*.

I travelled to Portsmouth with a couple of the lads on 1 September and started making preparations for the Loadline Exemption certificate required for the voyage to Glasgow while the ship was still on the run in the Solent on Wednesday 2 and Thursday 3 September, with the rest of the *Waverley* crew arriving in the evening of the 3rd, together with all the safety gear transferred from *Waverley* which was required for the loadline passage, including the navigational charts. It was all stowed appropriately and the ship was satisfactorily closed down for the voyage to Glasgow in the presence of the Department of Trade surveyors that evening and the loadline certificate was issued. Ship's articles were opened and all crew members signed on, including two representatives from Sealink, an engineer and a master. The Bareboat charter was signed and I took command of the ship at 10.00 p.m. that evening. The representatives from Sealink took no part in the operation of the ship other than as technical representatives of the owners. I did avail myself of the pilotage qualifications of the Sealink master on the outward and inward legs of the Solent pilotage area, as at that time I did not have pilotage exemption certificates for the district.

The exact reason for these lads being there was not fully revealed. Perhaps the owners were afraid that we would sink that ship, as we had done the *Shanklin*, but I rather feel that they were on a fact-finding mission into the world of day excursion cruising as the manager arrived on board half way through the charter, asking very pertinent questions and taking a great interest in what was going on. The day that he was on board was blowing a full gale and he did remark that he thought the ship to be in good hands. The complement was gratefully received and I felt to an extent vindicated! The loss of the *Shanklin/Prince Ivanhoe* was a terrible thorn in my flesh. Our second engineer, who was also second in the *Prince Ivanhoe*, did notice considerable differences in the way that the engine room was run under Sealink, who of course had run the ships summer and winter for nigh on forty years. I prepared the passage plan for the voyage to Glasgow and we sailed from Portsmouth just before midnight on Thursday 3 September and had a pretty unpleasant passage up. I recall particularly, on the way round Land's End, in weather which neither the *Waverley* nor the *Balmoral* would have looked at, a couple of the deck crew coming to the wheel house and saying, 'Wow what a seaboat she is,' and a reply coming from the *Waverley*'s famous bosun, who was on the wheel at the time, 'Aye you could cross the Western ocean in this one.' He had been in the *Shanklin* on her delivery voyage back in 1980. It was a joy for me to be back on one of the trio again and we arrived in Glasgow at 3.45 a.m. on the Sunday morning after an almost fifty-two-hour passage.

The Glasgow Department of Trade surveyors arrived on board at 8.00 a.m. and after various drills and tests the passenger certificates for Clyde service were issued and the ship left on her first sailing at 11.00 a.m. on Sunday 5 September with ninety-nine passengers onboard. The ship made every scheduled sailing, seventeen in all, plus one charter, kept perfect time on the schedules detailed above and was a joy to handle. The weather was awful, the resorts seemed empty, and few people seemed interested in a sail on this wonderful cosy and dry ship. Dry at deckhead level, not in so far as the bar was concerned! The main difference compared with the *Prince Ivanhoe* in so far as I was concerned was the amazing astern power that the ship had – it was a revelation. This may not have been due to lack of power in the engines in the *Prince Ivanhoe*, as the engines were the same power, but rather down to what power the engine room team were prepared to give you. In the *Southsea* the ship's engines were directly controlled from the bridge! It was a wonderful experience for all of us on board from the *Waverley*. I was astonished that none of the lads gave up as all those who couldn't go home at night in Glasgow had to rough it on board, as the ship had no crew accommodation at all apart from four small officers' day cabins. For the company it was a total commercial failure and in the whole of the operation she grossed only £35,580 and lost between £8,000 and £10,000. During one overnight stay in Helensburgh, the small makeshift souvenir shop set up on board was broken into and all the cigarettes and some of the souvenirs were stolen. Her fuel economy was pretty amazing, however, and for the whole charter, from leaving Portsmouth to returning there on 1 October, the ship used only 60 tons of diesel at a cost of just over £8,000 and almost 20 tons of that was consumed on the delivery voyages to and from Portsmouth.

The return voyage to Portsmouth was completed in just under forty-six hours in glorious weather, the best weather of the whole charter. The ship was used once or twice that month on the Portsmouth–Ryde crossing and then laid up until the 1988 season, when she resumed her duties again for one last season. A little mileage was gained from the fact that she was forty years old in 1988, and a slightly more adventurous cruising programme was offered in addition to her ferry duties.

At the end of that season the ship left under her own power for lay up on the River Fal, and indeed was very carefully and commendably mothballed. Sometime later, I believe around 1990, she was towed to Newhaven, where she was similarly laid up and carefully looked after. What the intentions of her owners were I don't know, but they can take full credit for the fact that she was completely undamaged and still kept in remarkable order throughout the remainder of their ownership. I know that in the late 1980s they believed that she would fetch in the region of £100,000 on the open market, for either future service or static use, and that they considered the *Brading* to be valued at some £50,000 for static use. However, these sums were never attained and the *Brading* ended up being broken up at Pound's shipbreaking facility at the top end of Portsmouth in 1994.

At the end of the 1996 season, once again the *Southsea* became available for sale, and on this occasion the WSN board were completely uninterested in having anything to do with the ship, and so together with a number of friends and interested PSPS members, more than £70,000 was raised, including a sizeable sum from my own family, to purchase the ship and have her on stand-by for future operational use. The ship was purchased in February 1997 for £25,000 and arrangements were made to have her towed to Southampton, which was successfully carried out the following month. I had developed a friendship with Husband's shipyard in Southampton, who agreed to look after her for the summer at a very nominal charge while I operated *Waverley*. My hope and vision at that time was that WSN would recognise the value of this unique ship and that she could be utilised at the time of the *Waverley* rebuild, which was due to be announced a few months later. The *Balmoral* was coming to the end of her ten to fifteen year new life that we had envisaged when she was rebuilt in 1986 and was going to require major expenditure and rebuilding herself in the years that were to follow, a judgement that very much proved to be the case.

In the *Southsea* we had a motorship in perfect condition, fit for at least another ten years' service without major expenditure apart from a bit of refurbishment, and with space on board that would provide huge earning opportunities for the future. She could first be available to run with the *Balmoral* while *Waverley* was rebuilt and then become the motorship of the future for the company. It was all a dream and although I was able to work on board the ship in July and August that year when, together with a couple of lads and volunteers, we did substantial work in preparation of the vessel for re-entry into service, the whole idea was doomed to failure, and we all lost our money. By early September most of the lifesaving appliances had been overhauled and made ready for use and with help from Sealink engineers and former engineers from the *Waverley*, the ship was passed ready to go, subject to successful underwater survey. It was a shame, a wasted effort – she wasn't wanted and was towed up to Bristol, played about with up there for a number of months then resold and towed back south again. A sad story, a dreadful waste of money and the end of a fine ship, being scrapped, I believe, around 2001.

CalMac Ships

In 1990 the structural condition of Greenock Custom House Quay and fire damage at Helensburgh precluded their use and the *Keppel* was chartered to feed in passengers from both Gourock and Helensburgh, flying the WSN house flag for all the main season calls that year and occasionally coming alongside the *Waverley* at Kilcreggan pier. On one occasion, both the *Kenilworth* and the *Keppel* were alongside.

On 28 September 1991 the *Jupiter* was chartered to operate the Rothesay rebels' cruise from Gourock and Dunoon as *Balmoral* was deputising for *Waverley* on the south coast. She also flew the WSN houseflag that day.

In the 1993 Clyde season, Brodick pier was being reconstructed to accommodate the new *Caledonian Isles* and was out of action for the whole of July, so the *Rhum* was provided by our friends at CalMac to ferry *Waverley*'s passengers in and out from the link span. With the help and co-operation of CalMac's Marine Superintendent, a former colleague of the writer, two new piles were incorporated into the new works to allow *Waverley* to keep using the pier.

For many years, when the *Waverley* and the *Balmoral* visited Iona, the *Kilbrannan*, *Coll* or *Morvern* were chartered to ferry passengers to and from the island.

Projects

The main projects that we were forced into to ensure our continued operation were those involved in the repair and maintenance of piers and other shore installations that the vessels used. Consultancy work, guidance, assistance and just pure encouragement were offered at Clevedon, Penarth, Minehead, Ilfracombe, Mumbles and Newport with varying degrees of success. Complete success was achieved at Clevedon and Penarth, and berthing retained at all the others except Mumbles.

On the south coast we advised regarding berthing bollards at Worthing, supplied greenheart piles for installation at Eastbourne and offered advice and assistance on the reopening of Swanage Pier in 1988. We helped to keep the berths at Sandown open with advice and assistance where we could in the installation of new piling. Information was provided at Yarmouth (IOW) and at Totland Bay in an endeavour to keep them open. Unfortunately Totland Bay was not a viable proposition, but Yarmouth has been retained. We managed to get Walton Pier reopened for a few seasons and encouraged Clacton to retain their berthing facility, and at one time towards the end of my time with *Waverley* we discussed the installation of new corner piles, with us supplying the timber as we had done at Eastbourne. Unfortunately, this came to nothing during my time with the company.

We also were instrumental in reopening Britannia Pier, Great Yarmouth, for calls for a number of seasons, which provided very lucrative business on single trips to London. I was also at Deal Pier in the early 1980s, when storm damage destroyed the fendering, but we were unable to persuade the council to reinstate it for a few calls each year.

Back in home waters, we campaigned hard when it seemed as if Tighnabruaich Pier would be closed to traffic and we also pushed hard for the reopening of Millport in the late 1980s and early 1990s. We were also instrumental in reopening Helensburgh Pier to traffic, successfully encouraging the council to dredge it on our behalf.

In our workshops in Glasgow, some small engineering projects were undertaken for other people, together with a huge amount of in-house repairs to our own ships, with parts for the paddle wheels being made in our own shed up until 1986. Radius rods, stays, bushes, paddle arms and small parts for the auxiliary machinery were all made, together with new second-hand steam engines being suitably altered and then fitted to the circulating pump and a new AC generator in the ship. The lathe was never idle!

One of the last major jobs that I had responsibility for arranging was the complete overhaul of the *Sir Walter Scott*'s main engine. This was removed from the ship at Loch Katrine and was transported to Anderston Quay, where our new chief engineer and his team completely dismantled it and meticulously reassembled it, returning it to the vessel in pristine order in time for the 1998 season. We had certainly come a long way from the band of amateurs that we were said to be back in 1975.

A Captain's Memories: Part 5
The Slow Decline 1990–98

The title of this chapter might seem rather negative but huge changes were coming about which were to change the original concept of the company forever, although much was achieved in the 1990s nevertheless. The small business nature of the operation was going to progressively disappear as the company became more corporate and the autonomy given to me back in 1976 would vanish as more and more people came into the operation, and on to the board of directors, who wanted to show how it all should be done, in their view. The *Balmoral* was allowed to be moved to Bristol at the end of 1988 and although she developed her own band of faithful followers and volunteers, the tight cost controls applied to expenditure on the ships in the 1980s vanished as we had created two separate organisations. The whole shipping industry had changed out of all proportion since we had started in 1974, with technology progressing at an alarming rate. In 1974 there were still loads of ships with a standard ship's wheel for steering and telegraphs giving orders to the engine room, where engineers operated the control levers to supply the movements requested. By 1990 there were only a handful of ships left using this age-old system. In nearly all ships, particularly coastal ships and ferries, the machinery was directly controlled from the bridge and powerful lateral thrust units had replaced bow rudders almost entirely. Electronic aids to navigation and communication systems were appearing and being improved at an incredible pace.

New regulations were being formulated on escape routes, seating, damage stability and survivability, life saving appliances (LSA) and fire protection, all in the wake of the capsize of the *Herald of Free Enterprise* off Zeebrugge, the loss of the *Marchioness* on the Thames after collision with the cargo ship *Bowbelle*, and the loss of the ferry *Estonia* in the Baltic, with a combined total loss of life involving over 1,000 people. All this required submission for approval of new muster stations for passengers with an updated muster list for crew, which in turn led to new manning approvals for the ships being necessary as well.

In addition, new effluent disposal regulations were being introduced whereby raw sewage could no longer be disposed of directly into the sea untreated, but compliance with this was deferred until the first stage of the millennium rebuild in 2000. The phase in date for the ships was 1995 and an appeal was launched to provide funds to enable the ships to comply in time, with the aim of raising £350,000. This was hugely successful and achieved the magnificent sum of £360,734 by the spring of 1995. The results of the new works were going to improve the ships enormously in terms of safety, especially in respect of the LSA, which had changed little since new regulations were introduced following the loss of the *Titanic* back in 1912. New, stronger window frames with thicker safety glass were to be fitted in the sides of both ships to improve the watertight integrity at main deck level. In the *Waverley* the spray-tight doors that were fitted at the forward and after end of the sponsons at main deck height in 1978 needed to be altered by cutting each in half so that the lower halves remained closed at all times, with the option of having the upper halves open in good weather. However, there was a downside to all of this; passenger numbers had to be reduced to: Class III, 740; Class IV, 860; and Class V, 925; but with these new numbers, each passenger would have a seat. Nearly all the joinery and glazing work involved in manufacturing these new windows, together with refurbishing or renewals on board both ships, was entrusted to the hands of a well known PSPS member from Sussex who provided work that was quite magnificent in every respect. Much of this remains in place to this day, a testament to its outstanding quality. A new bar was constructed for the Jeanie Deans lounge in the *Waverley* in 1994, and new bridge wings in 1996.

1990 was to be my last season in full charge of *Waverley*, except for 1996, until I finished with the ship in 1997. It was the last season also of the chief engineer, who had taken over in 1986, and also of my son, both of whom had given five years service to the company, my son finishing up as catering officer in the *Balmoral* in 1990. Finding crews that would accept the primitive living conditions available on the ships was becoming increasingly difficult. The two engineer apprentices taken on in the mid-1980s had both moved on, one only after a few months' service, the other completing his apprenticeship but moving on immediately thereafter. Long periods away from home in cramped and poor conditions were becoming increasingly unattractive to the people that we so desperately needed to keep the ships running. A new engineer apprentice was started and he was to excel in all respects, gaining his higher national diploma in engineering, and was selected as prize winner for general excellence. The famous shipyard personality Jimmy Reid presented him with the Salveson Cup at the Glasgow College of Nautical Studies' annual awards ceremony, held at Glasgow City Chambers on Thursday 17 November 1994. He became chief engineer of the *Waverley* in 1997, but he too was going to eventually succumb to the massive physical, mental and emotional pressures that were so much a part of keeping the ship running.

1990 was a season with a few special ingredients added to what was now becoming a regular pattern of sailings each year. Spring was in Scotland, where the piers at Castlebay (Isle of Barra), Lochboisdale (South Uist), and Lochmaddy (North Uist) were added to the 1990 Western Isles programme. Early summer was in the Bristol Channel, main season on the Clyde, late summer and early autumn on the south coast and the Thames, and an October long weekend in the Bristol Channel, finishing with a couple of sailings on the Clyde in mid- to late October completed the *Waverley*'s programme throughout most of the 1990s, with occasional deviations for special events.

A spring visit to Bournemouth was made in conjunction with the Forties Festival in 1990, followed by a visit to Brighton marina to take part in the Brighton Festival. Handling the ship in the confines of Brighton marina was a challenge to my ship handling skills, involving the careful co-ordination of two small craft to accomplish the necessary manoeuvres into the berth. One of them was the ex-Newhaven pilot boat and the other a workboat belonging to a contractor working in the marina. The crews of each were a joy to work with. We then proceeded to Dover to take part in the Golden Jubilee sailings commemorating Operation Dynamo (the evacuation of the Dunkirk beaches in 1940, where the previous *Waverley* was lost on 29 May) and the ship sailed all the way to Dunkirk on this occasion with a reduced passenger certificate. The main event was organised by Holts Battlefield Tours and later the ship was chartered by the Royal British Legion on a voyage from Ramsgate to welcome home all the Dunkirk Little Ships that had taken part. A very positive and encouraging article appeared in the *Evening Echo* during the Thames October visit that year, showing the ship approaching Southend pier in winds gusting Force 8 yet with still a sizeable queue awaiting her on the pier. The Brits can be a hardy race, and I think this was the time that I berthed on the inside of the pier!

Earlier in the season, on the Clyde, the ship had commemorated the diamond jubilee of the turbine steamer *Duchess of Montrose* by sailing all the way from Gourock to Inverarary and from Gourock round Ailsa Craig. The *Montrose* was the writer's favourite turbine steamer, launched by Denny's of Dumbarton in 1930, and with the *King George V*, launched four years earlier, she would revolutionise Clyde passenger steamer design. Returning from Campbeltown during one of the regular Ayr sailings, the No. 1 or King rod in the port paddle wheel fractured off Holy Isle and the engineers managed to cobble it together with two chain blocks and we staggered into Brodick pier at dead slow speed. By the time a replacement was fitted at Brodick Pier we had run out of daylight to return the passengers to Ayr, which resulted in many of them roughing it ashore for the night. Surprisingly, there were few complaints and we returned them all early the following morning after a hearty breakfast! After this event a bridging piece was made out of a piece of stout angle iron and on both future occasions that the No. 1 rod broke, this was fitted over the fracture and it took us safely back to the next port. I am pleased to say that we never had to employ the services of a tug to tow us home on any passenger sailing during my twenty-three seasons in command.

At the end of the season, the ship finished up in Avonmouth, where the start of a major programme of improvements that would take place throughout the decade was begun by the fitting of a new set of paddle wheels. In my early days back in the 1970s, the *Waverley* was often described by her previous owners and masters as a ship with a Rolls-Royce engine in a Ford Ten body! We had steadily been trying to improve that Ford Ten body through the years but the 1990s and into the millennium were to see huge improvements to the ship's structure using modern materials and repair techniques. Many new ideas were introduced on the commercial side of the business in the 1990s, with live commentaries being given from the bridge in each area of operation, covering all points of interest, and with the commentators being on the bridge they were able to pass on details of passing ships and navigational information as it became available on the ship's radio. I wasn't to appreciate what a distraction all this was until many years later, when I was sailing a cargo ship up the Thames in almost total peace and tranquillity! However, all the commentators were highly professional local people and provided a much appreciated service to the passengers, and in many cases much improvement to my own knowledge of the areas that we were visiting, this generally tending to be restricted to what was required to safely conduct the navigational and operational requirements of the ship.

Many new means of increasing earnings were developed also, with huge research going on in the winter months preceding each season to establish what maritime events that the ships could be linked into and quite innovative scheduling was then devised to have the ships present at as many of them as possible: festivals of the sea, Tall Ships events, barge races, parades of steam, yacht races, fireworks displays, meeting famous liners and warships, D-Day events and many others. The development of single trips to London from towns, resorts and even cities within a day's sailing distance from the capital city were offered from places as far away as Eastbourne and Great Yarmouth, with return by coach, and proved very popular and successful. Eastbourne Pier was reopened in 1991 after a gap of four years and I remember a sailing from there about 1995 or 1996 grossing nearly £30,000 for the day! Just before the end of my time in the ship, I was involved in trying to link in with rail returns from London as a number of our customers had commented that they would like to have spent some time in the city before returning home rather than being piled into a coach immediately after the ship arrived. Another development proving very popular was where our trips included a trip on one of the preserved steam railways in a number of locations. I had been responsible for hiring an eight-coach train to run from Littlehampton to Portsmouth on the occasion of the Missions to Seamen charter due to a poor weather forecast and this met with such customer approval that the charterer made a substantial contribution to the extra cost involved. Unique, one-off sailings were operated to commemorate the diamond jubilees of all the famous Clyde steamers built in the 1930s, often taking the ship to unusual destinations. Sailings were made with great success to ports, piers and harbours seldom visited, and as a result very useful publicity was generated for the ship.

The visit by *Waverley* to Yarmouth (IOW) inner harbour attracted great attention and *Balmoral* joined her there, berthing at the head of the pier. Unique visits were made to Salcombe, Kingswear, Mevagissey, St Mawes, Padstow, Sharpness (Old Dock), Portencross and Otter Ferry, and that was by no means all. Trips in the River Avon by *Waverley* increased every year, until in 1997 the ship made no less than twenty river trips between 2 May and 7 June, operating eight passenger carrying sailings and one charter, with a gross revenue of over £155,000 being attained. New berths were introduced at Knightstone Wall, Weston, and at Barry inner harbour, while on the Thames Estuary we started calling at the outer wall of the Old Harbour at Margate.

All these extra services were provided in an effort to earn more and more revenue yet, in 1994, with a total turnover for the whole company of almost £2.5 million, there was no profit at all. We were earning well but costs were running out of control. No greater testament to this was when the *Balmoral* was painted in umpteen different liveries between 1992 and 1996, with all the cost of materials and labour involved in that, with not a word of censure or disapproval uttered from the board of directors other than from the souvenir shop director, who had to throw away sizeable sums worth of souvenir stock because they were all inaccurate in detail and therefore unsellable. Eventually, the directors insisted that the ship adopted the livery of P. & A. Campbell, which she has had since 1996, and in the opinion of the writer she looks her finest in this condition. One of the original founder directors was brought back in 1995, in an effort to sort things out, but I think even he found it hard to make the necessary changes to cost control that were required.

The *Balmoral* had an enormously successful 1991 season, with her doing the Brighton Festival that year followed by a very lucrative week on charter to the Isles of Scilly Steamship Company to deputise for *Scillonian III* on the ferry service due to a lengthy engine repair being required in that vessel. She had a very good visit to the Tall Ships event at Milford Haven and a great August in the Bristol Channel due to glorious weather. A problem with *Waverley* at the end of the Solent sailings meant that she deputised for the paddler on the Thames at the end of the 1991 season also. In 1992 a special sailing to Campbeltown was operated by *Waverley* to commemorate the diamond jubilee of the formation of the Clyde River Steamer Club and the former flagship of the Caledonian Steam Packet Company, turbine steamer *Duchess of Hamilton*.

The *Waverley* backed up to off Glasgow Bridge Wharf in early 1993 to celebrate the diamond jubilee of the Glasgow boat TS *Queen Mary II* before sailing off to the Kyles of Bute, and in 1994 both ships took part in the D-Day commemorative celebrations at Spithead. *Waverley* followed the fleet as it sailed to well south of the Isle of Wight and on the return met the last unaltered Liberty Ship, SS *Jeremiah O'Brien*, heading out across the Channel. We turned round and steamed with her for a few miles to cheers of vocal and visual compliments from her crew of veterans, a unique and emotional meeting at sea of two steamships powered with the same machinery. In fact, a few days earlier our chief engineer had been in touch with the engineering team on the *Jeremiah O'Brien* to see if they had any United States gland packing that would fit *Waverley*'s main engine high pressure cylinder, which had developed a noisy steam leak. Unfortunately there was nothing to be had the correct size. The *Jeremiah O'Brien* went on to Chatham, where she met *Kingswear Castle* at Bullnose Point. The *Balmoral* was present at the Tower Bridge Centenary celebrations, with the Royal Yacht *Britannia* and *Kingswear Castle* also taking part. Our faithful bosun retired at the end of the 1994 season, together with a long serving able seaman who was always employed at the aft mooring position, and both would be sadly missed. In 1995 the Isle of Skye ports of Broadford, Uig and Dunvegan were added to the Western Isles schedule.

In all this time I slowly disappeared into the background and just drove and attempted to staff the ships in the summer and looked after the refit work on the *Waverley* in winter. To make cost effective use of the pilotage certificates that I held for the Solent, Southampton and Portsmouth, the Medway, and the Thames, also Harwich, Mistley and Ipswich, I was found to be in whatever ship was operating in those areas while the Clyde and Bristol Channel sailings were shared between the two permanent masters between 1992 and 1995.

In 1991 I spent most of the season in *Balmoral* for personal reasons and it was tinged with sadness when my mother passed away very suddenly and unexpectedly on 2 October. She loved the ships and was frequently on board, being instrumental in booking parties, school children and general public for Sussex sailings, all from her home in Eastbourne without charge, in the late 1970s and, unknown to me, also bought tickets for her sailings on board in support of the cause. She also made a sizeable commitment to the *Southsea* project proposed for 1986. It was fitting that I left *Balmoral* at Eastbourne Pier to attend her funeral – a place where I would miss her presence dearly, as she waited to join our ships there every time we called, and back in the 1950s she had introduced me to trips from the pier on P. & A. Campbell's PS

Glen Gower to France and MV *Crested Eagle* on a couple of coastal trips in 1957. A special sailing was operated by *Balmoral* from Eastbourne to Boulogne in 1996 to commemorate the cessation of these sailings by *Glen Gower* at the end of the 1956 season.

In 1993 my border collie Tip was to join me on board the ship and she became a great companion and well known to all the regular passengers. She was with me on board until I finished sailing in the ships in 1997 and was unbelievably intelligent, learning how to blow the ship's whistle and answer the office telephone! No security system was required on the ship's bridge while Tip was there, a growl or snarl being sufficient to deter any unwanted guests. Tip had pups in August 2000 and I kept one of them, Tippex, who survived until 20 February 2014. Tip died on 27 April 2004 and I had the joy of over twenty-one years of unconditional love between both of them.

By the early 1990s the *Balmoral* was steaming round Britain and operated the spring Western Isles programme in 1994, while in 1995 she tendered the liner *Queen Elizabeth 2* during the Tall Ships' visit to the Forth. Each winter, refit work progressed towards the phase in dates for the ships and up in Glasgow, from the 1991/92 winter and each winter thereafter until the beginning of 1997, the seagoing crew in *Waverley* were replaced by a squad of either four or six skilled ex-shipyard personnel, who were employed directly onto the company payroll to undertake major structural and engineering works. In 1991/92 it was mainly engineering work, with some work in and around the paddle boxes. A new low pressure cylinder main bearing was installed, with the paddle shafts being realigned and the port support bearing renewed, while the main engine valve gear was also overhauled. One of the landing platforms was removed to facilitate this work and holes were cut in the decks to allow heavy pieces of equipment and machinery to be lowered into the engine room direct from the quayside. A new end cover for the condenser had to be specially fabricated and fitted that year, and it is doubtful that this could have been got on board in any other way due to its sheer size and weight.

In October of 1991 a very critical letter was received from the chairman of the PSPS regarding the condition and operation of the ships, which was very demoralizing for us all because we were in fact giving it our very best with the personnel available to us. The *Waverley* had never been so hard run in her life as she was in the 1990s. From 1947 until 1977, her annual running hours were between 700 and 1,000, as they are today. In the 1990s they topped 2,000 hours every season. We took the criticism very much to heart and tried to address most of the issues raised during the 1991/92 winter after the ship returned to the Clyde from Southampton in November 1991. The following winter the phase in work started in earnest and replacement of the shipside windows commenced, with the first four windows each side of the Jeanie Deans lounge, together with necessary work to the surrounding steelwork, and the new style windows described earlier were installed. They looked quite magnificent and met the approval of the Department of Trade surveyors, with whom we had some quite lengthy and detailed meetings to discuss the work, both at their headquarters in London and also at local level.

In 1993 they too were undergoing change, with a move taking place to new premises in Glasgow and a change of name to MSA (Marine Safety Agency) taking place. This was eventually changed again to the MCA (Marine Coastguard Agency) five or six years later and that name has stood the test of time right up to this very day.

In the winter of 1993/94 we undertook the remainder of the work in the Jeanie Deans lounge bar area, removing the stairways that entered the bar at the after end, linking it to the deck above, and turning them round so that they came down from the promenade deck into the cross alleyway behind the bar. This meant that those not wishing to use the bar/lounge facility could proceed on down the engine room alleyway. New enclosed entrances were created to the stairways on the port and starboard sides of the forward shelter, with sliding doors to give access to the deck, and beautiful wooden screens with etched glass windows were made to separate the forward shelter from the stairways. The bar in the lounge was replaced with a beautiful horseshoe shaped wooden bar, especially designed to fit into the space between the stairways at the after end of the new room, and a new emergency escape was provided at the forward end of the space, where an area for entertainers and a small dance floor was also created. The heating system was improved and the entire area was refurbished, with new deck head panels and lighting being installed. I was really pleased with the end result and it received many favourable comments from our customers, who found that in daytime it provided a relaxing, peaceful place away from through traffic. Above, the ship was completely re-decked, with an extension of the steel deck from midships to the bow, and unlike the after end over the dining saloon, sufficient funds were available to buy new timber and relay the wooden deck on top thanks to the PSPS fund raising campaign.

In 1994 the ship was slipped in Southampton and started on the south coast that year and it was a real rush to have her ready due to additional hull plating work that was required, but thanks to an incredible effort from contractors, ship's staff and many volunteers, including the PSPS chairman, she entered service on time.

The final winter of the phase-in work took place in 1994/95 and involved a colossal amount of work and many meetings with the MSA to seek agreement and approval of the suggestions submitted, and in particular one for the dining saloon, in which I particularly wanted to avoid the installation of an escape stairway in the middle of the space with the consequential loss of part of the best open deck space in the ship at the after end. This approval arrived in February and it was all systems go to implement the required work in that space, which involved a complete rearrangement of the seating, with lifejacket stowage underneath. New, fully upholstered bench seating ran the full length of both sides of the saloon under the superb new windows, which in turn provided a stepping stone out of the escape windows into new open reversible liferafts (ORLs), inflated and afloat outside. We were able to demonstrate that the height of the ORLs when inflated were within an inch or so of the bottom lip of the window, allowing people to escape into the survival craft in the unlikely event of the exits at the fore end of the space being unusable, and sufficient lifejackets were stowed under the seats to accommodate everyone within the area as well. There was, in addition, a vertical ladder at the after end of the galley which would provide an extra escape for the more agile. The lower bar was re-decked and both that space and the forward shelter were reupholstered.

Less visible to passengers was another element of the new regulations – the provision of a more modern emergency bilge pumping system. The new electrically driven pump had to be installed by regulation outside the machinery space and so was located in the lower bar. The pump was capable of pumping all bilge spaces and meant that the old Downton brass hand pump could be removed from its position outside the shop and dispensed

Above left: The open reversible liferafts inflated, ready for use.

Right: A letter from the MSA, approving the escape arrangements from the dining room.

with. The companionway from the promenade deck outside the purser's office down to the main deck below was also renewed, another piece of outstanding joinery work from our friend down in Sussex. The engine room alleyways received a new colour scheme and a new 'period' lighting system was installed.

A new after mast was fashioned out of a magnificent Douglas fir log at Noble's boatyard, Girvan, and was made to the quality of the other new timber work in the ship, with new hounds bands and halyard sheaves to suit any combination of flags required to be flown. A stout block was made with a gantline to allow a man to be hauled up to replace bulbs in the navigation lights, which were mounted on stainless steel tables. The mast was the exact height of the one originally fitted to the ship, which was about two feet shorter than what was specified in the original builders' drawings. It was an outstanding job, costing nearly £10,000, and would have lasted the ship another forty years or so, yet in the second phase of the rebuild, for some reason, it was removed and destroyed. The new lifesaving appliances were fitted and the new life boats that were fitted to *Balmoral* in 1986 were removed and replaced with rigid rescue boats fitted with outboard motors. The motor boat from *Balmoral* was transferred to *Waverley* and the two rowing boats became surplus to requirements and were put up for sale. The *Waverley*'s was sold for £500 but the *Balmoral*'s was stolen from the Quayside in Bristol. The revamped dining saloon, which incorporated a private alcove for the ship's officers on the port side forward, also received much favourable comment from our customers and also, for its ease of operation, from the catering crew. It also provided seats for 118 people, an increase from the 100 that were available previously. The phase in work was completed and approved and the ship entered service at Easter with four well supported sailings and went on to have another successful season.

At the end of 1995 plans were being developed to apply for Lottery funding, which proved to be successful, and were announced on her golden jubilee sailing on 16 June 1997. This money was required to provide much needed attention to the sponsons and midship section of the ship, and new boilers. Installation of a bow rudder or bow thrust was also supposed to be included in the work, to improve the handling characteristics of the ship, but this work was never done. During the winter of 1995/96 we were at last able to improve the accommodation for catering staff, and the alterations provided four two-berth and one single-berth cabin in the former eight and four-berth space on the lower deck just forward of the boiler room and meant that we could provide reasonable live-aboard accommodation for stewardesses, who for the most part had lived ashore previously. Improvements to the toilets for both crew and passengers were also made at this time. The cantilever beams under the sponsons were replaced by a new and cleverly designed new structure inside the sponsons behind the toilets and this alteration improved the performance of the ship both when she had a list and in rough weather. The only disadvantage was that anything large in the water could travel into the paddle wheels when previously it would be hit by the cantilever beam and deflected outboard before reaching the wheel.

The trading loss in the accounts for *Balmoral* in 1995 was £103,169, and for 1996 £64,896 – a worry, but once the *Waverley*'s trading was added in, the figures were sufficient to gain the company approval for Lottery funding, which would take her into the new millennium. In 1995 two important members of the marine staff left the operation and the other captain, Robin Barr, died in December, so in 1996 I was back on my own again, as I had been away back in 1975; it was time for me to move on as well and I sought and found a successor, who joined in early 1997. It was all over for me in so far as the operational side went and I left the ship in the middle of June 1997, when she returned to the Clyde and just before her golden jubilee cruise. There was money in the bank, the Lottery funding was in the bag and the ship was in spanking form; my job was done, and in any case I could not have carried on for much longer – the stresses and strains of the job were becoming difficult to cope with as I grew older. Big changes were on the way; the accountant had moved on and the manager resigned in 1998, so it was over to the new team to show us all the way forward.

I was asked at the tail end of 1995 if I would like to be guest of honour at the centenary sailings of paddle steamer *Marion* on the Murray River in South Australia, an invitation that I was delighted to accept. I was therefore off to the Antipodes in October 1997, and with my hosts based at Mannum, who were the owners of the *Marion*, following the centenary celebrations I was taken to various locations along the banks of the Murray River, sailing in at least ten different paddle steamers. I gave five lectures and slide shows about the *Waverley* to amazingly interested and appreciative audiences and I am sure that many Aussies have travelled on the ship as a result. I was able to take in the cities of Adelaide, Melbourne and Sydney, where I hadn't been since the mid-1960s. It was a quite amazing end to my time with *Waverley* and I gained a huge number of new friends, and didn't return to the UK until December! The whole story is quite another tale but perhaps some of the accompanying illustrations will give a little flavour to one of the most momentous occasions of my life, a fitting end to twenty-three years of hard graft.

A Captain's Memories: Part 6
A New Beginning 1999 Onwards

The writer and former captain had nothing whatever to do with the ship from the spring of 1998 on and has stayed right out of the affairs of *Waverley* ever since, except for the fact that as a shareholder he continues to get the annual accounts. The following comments are only casual observations put together from sightings of the ship at sea in the Thames, Bristol Channel, the Clyde and Western Isles from other ships, and also include comments from friends who have either worked on the ship or sailed in her as passengers. I leave the blanks to be filled in by Iain Quinn, who has been outstandingly helpful in the editing and proof reading of my story. The ship proceeded to Great Yarmouth at the end of 1999, where the first part of the millennium rebuild took place. She emerged a new and much-changed craft with a new livery, and as a result a completely new appearance. At sea in the distance, she just looked like a blob with two red funnels as opposed to the crisp appearance of pre-rebuild days.

I was invited on board when the coaster, *Hoo Kestrel*, that I was in command of was anchored in Lundy Roads, awaiting the tide to go into Briton Ferry to load for the Continent, and the *Waverley* came into the pier at Lundy. I refused on this occasion but took up the offer of a visit later, when the ship was in Great Yarmouth for the second phase of the rebuild and I happened to be in the area at the time and as a result able to go on board. Some of the work carried out was very interesting, especially the new sponsons and the layout of the boiler room. The dining saloon looked as if it would be a nightmare to work in but the fittings were in keeping with the original design, except of course for the stairway in the middle of the space.

Obviously the company was continuing to become more and more corporate and the management, crewing and operation of the ship had completely changed. It was also obvious that money was no object in the management of this new and transformed organisation. The regime for officers and crew seemed to be much easier, with more regular time off and easier schedules combined with a much shorter season. In so far as the writer and former captain himself was concerned, he had moved on to pastures new in cargo vessels of the 2–3,000 ton range, running feeder cargoes from the Continent in and out of east coast ports, with more occasional runs to the west coast, Northern Ireland and the Irish Republic. During this trade, there were invariably visits by port officials, surveyors, pilots, colleagues and other visitors on board who were aware of my involvement with the *Waverley* and wanted to talk about her. It was truly astonishing how well the ship was known, far and wide.

In late 2003 I returned to where my coasting career had started back in 1966, in the Clyde and Western Isles, in a ship called *Bowcliffe* but now carrying logs, fertilizer, aggregates and later, in another ship, food for the many salmon farms dotted around the lochs of the Highlands and Western Isles. I visited an incredible variety of ports: Sandbank, Portavadie, Ardrishaig, Troon, Ayr, Lamlash, Brodick, Campbeltown, Gigha, Crinan, Corpach, Craignure, Lochaline, Mallaig, Kyle, Kishorn, Gairloch, Ullapool, Uig, Lochboisdale, Lochmaddy, Scalpay, Stornoway and a host of small islands and inlets in between as well. On one occasion while the *Bowcliffe* was berthed in Avonmouth, three friends from my *Waverley* Bristol Channel days visited and we had a great get together and trip down memory lane.

It was a marvellous climax to a career at sea lasting over fifty years, thirty-five of it as a master. My employers latterly were friendly and outstandingly appreciative, which made the last decade of my working life a total pleasure, with several of them asking me to stay on when I retired at the end of March 2010, but at almost sixty-six I had really had enough and was finding it difficult to keep up with the rapidly changing technology.

Acknowledgements

The text has come from my own archives, log books, diaries, magazines and other articles of the time, and also from my own memories and records. Photographs are from my own personal collection except where marked and if I have used any inappropriately then I apologise unreservedly for that. My thanks go in particular to Iain Quinn for all his support and encouragement, also for his proof reading and editing of the text where necessary.

Forty Years of Waverley Steam Navigation Company
A Purser's Eye View of the Early Years

Despite all that has been written and published, it seems ever more challenging forty years later to recall, recapture and recreate the emotional charge of those far-away days. As we mark the fortieth anniversaries of the gift of *Waverley* to the PSPS, the setting up of the original operating company, and *Waverley*'s first sailings under that new flag, it's worth reflecting for a moment just how distant these days really are. The mid-1970s are as far from today as the mid-1930s were from the years of which I write. And I can assure you how far away the 1930s seemed to us in the era of long hair, flared trousers and skinny ribbed pullovers. 1974 was the year when the unknown group Abba won the Eurovision song contest, when a pint of beer cost 17p, when inflation was running at almost 20 per cent, and petrol hit a new high of 67p per gallon. There were two general elections, a three-day week, and frequent power cuts. The first McDonalds opened in London, Monty Python's final series was shown, and Robbie Williams was born. And if some of these mean nothing to you, that's my point exactly. The world that existed at the time of the 1934 launch of *Caledonia* from Denny of Dumbarton seemed to lie in the unbridgeably distant past to us in the 1970s. During one of the many conversations of steamer reminiscences which filled the pauses in the routine inside the ticket office, I recall the sage and supportive relief purser, Fraser MacHaffie, recounting an old *Caledonia* story and asking the assistant purser, Derek Peters, if he remembered the event. 'No,' came the answer. 'I was only two at the time.' So if I labour the passage of time, it is in the spirit of acknowledging that many *Waverley* supporters and steamer enthusiasts are from younger generations, and for her to sail into the future, more such supporters must be recruited and encouraged. I want to do my part to ensure that some of the colour, some of the astonishing electric feeling of the remarkable beginnings of WSN, gets remembered and passed on. Passion has become an overused and devalued term, but it's exactly what we had then, what we have now, and it's what we need for the future.

Writing 'Waverley Steam Navigation Company' brings back to me the frisson that once accompanied these words. As names and institutions, both the Caledonian Steam Packet Company and David MacBrayne seemed as old as the hills, as solid as Scots granite. Although Caledonian MacBrayne was still a fairly new term, it seemed to carry with it much of the gravitas and professional history of both traditions. It's hard to imagine today how astonishingly upstart Waverley Steam Navigation Company sounded to many ears, almost grandiose in its pretence. I'm sure that was never the intent, but from the beginning it seemed like a name whose reputation we had to create and live up to. A constant theme of the early years of WSN was the almost superhuman efforts of those involved to create both the reality and the perception of high professionalism, often in the face of real adversity and at times unkind criticism. I remember arriving back at Ayr harbour after an evening cruise, a charter by the Scottish National Party, in late May 1975, when for the first time Purser Harold Jordan allowed me to broadcast an end of day farewell on the ship's tannoy system.

> On behalf of the Waverley Steam Navigation Company, the captain, officers and crew of *Waverley*, I would like to thank you for sailing with us this evening. We hope you have enjoyed your cruise, and that you will come again this summer, and encourage your friends to come and sail with us too. *Waverley* is the last seagoing paddle steamer in the world, and can only continue to sail if she is supported by people like you. Thank you, and please have a safe journey home.

Such an announcement was considered rather an odd thing to do back in 1975. Nice enough, but distinctly odd. Especially on a Clyde steamer. It was a bit 'American' perhaps? Laying it on a bit too thickly for Scottish tastes, a bit too explicit in its closeness and in its advertising. Surely safe, efficient and timely arrival at the destination was what was required, and once achieved, quite enough? For a ferry, maybe. But *Waverley* had not carried a car for a long time, and the last sheep were 180 in number on a ferry run from Rothesay to Keppel in March 1972. The inimitable Terry Sylvester insisted, from that day to this, that *Waverley* must always focus on the idea of pleasure cruises, for her success and for her survival. Terry periodically sent evocative typed or hand-scrawled memos to the purser's office, with infinite variation around this core theme. The first of them was received with drily frosty humour by Harold. The memo was ceremoniously set alight in the ticket office, and the singed remains added to the already bulging bulldog clip full of operational memos hanging on the inner bulkhead, unseen to passengers at the ticket window. But the point was well made, oft repeated, and is still as valid as ever. The welcome on board and final arrival announcements, in a more humanly touching style than was prevalent on the old railway boats or Cal Mac, quickly became part of the normal ticket office routine. Looking back, I recall how we pronounced Waverley Steam Navigation Company clearly and in full, and I daresay with a measure of pride. I for one am proud to count myself as a small actor in the cast of these early years. But that is in retrospect. At the time, we were driven by pure energy, living and working in the moment, and determined beyond words that these days would not be just a final flash at the end of the history of paddle steamers on the Clyde, but would be the beginning of something enduring.

The award of a £30,000 grant from the newly formed Strathclyde Regional Council was made in early March 1975, and thus one of the final parts of a complex jigsaw fell into place. *Waverley* had been very well covered in the media in recent months, and now a short paragraph appeared in the *Glasgow Herald* to the effect that she would sail again in 1975. I read the statement of fact with astonishment. Living in rural Ayrshire, finishing my school days and preparing to go to university, I had not been closely connected to the unfolding story. Perhaps, like many Clyde steamer enthusiasts young and old, I had seen the departure of *Talisman*, *Caledonia*, and *Duchess of Hamilton* with end-of-era sadness, and assumed that while *Waverley* might be preserved, she would only ever paddle again in our triggered memories. Was it really about to happen? Might we hear again a hypnotic paddle rhythm of over 300 beats per minute, smell again the whiff of hot oil and steam from the high pressure cylinder, stand again at the forward rail as she lines up to pass through the Narrows? If so, I wanted to be part of it. A terse teenage diary entry for Monday 10 March 1975 reads: 'Chemistry exam hard. Didn't get finished. Posted letter to Douglas McGowan.' The latter turned out to be the more important by far, and two weeks later I stood on the threshold of Douglas's Mount Florida flat as we took each other in with astonishment. Being interviewed for an assistant purser job seemed a serious matter, and I was dressed to impress with shiny boots, my best suit and a CRSC tie. Douglas, on the other hand, sported a very open neck shirt, the most relaxed of well-lived-in cardigans imaginable, and the sort of slippers more fitted to a Sherlock Holmes novel than to the south side of Glasgow. Douglas was charming and jocular, and I was treated to a whirlwind update on all things *Waverley*. Only later did I learn that he was holding down a full-time job in parallel to his burgeoning WSN commitments. We reminisced about steamers and routes, and as I began to relax, like all good interviewers he lobbed the key question: 'So why do you want to work on the *Waverley*?' 'Because I'm daft about steamers, I love everything about it, and want to spend as many hours on the ship as I can', was what I was thinking. Of course, something more measured was said, which nevertheless communicated the generally unspoken emotional and aesthetic passion of the steamer enthusiast. Douglas gave me optimistic signals, and I drove my old Beetle back down the Fenwick Road with a happy heart. A few weeks later came a written offer of a place as assistant purser for the first half of the 1975 season, at the princely wage of £5 per week.

Some days persist in the memory forever without fading. One such was the inaugural sailing of Thursday 22 May 1975. Anderston Quay at 9 a.m. was a scene of gentle frenzy. The cobbled quayside had not been used routinely for many years, and there was much last minute beautification to be done before invited guests began to arrive. Deliveries for the dining saloon, for the bar, for the tearoom, for the shop, for no precisely known destination began to arrive with speed and volume, and a deluge of enquiries of every description landed at the door of the ticket office, conveniently located at the foot of the starboard landing platform, and facing the quayside. A heady mixture of stress and anticipation filled the air. Derek Peters had joined the ship a few days earlier and filled me in on some of our shared duties. For today at least, it was mostly manning the gangways and acting as runners, message carriers from one part of the ship to another. We joked then, and by no means for the last time, that the role of the pursers was to keep chaos at bay! The guests started to arrive after midday, and we checked the invitations and adjusted the gangway ropes as the tide fell. Over 300 guests had been invited, but a significant crowd of onlookers, well-wishers and quite a few potential passengers had gathered on Anderston Quay. This was our first experience of turning away potential passengers who did not have tickets. Counting the passengers on and off, entering the numbers in a traffic book and thereby ensuring that the number on board is known at all times was one of the purser's responsibilities. The ebb and flow of the crowd made this almost impossible that day, but 336 passengers were recorded disembarking at Dunoon a few hours later. Speeches were made from the landing platform, and there was much to be said: words of thanks, sentiments of optimism. Terry Sylvester was on ebullient form, and Glasgow Lord Provost Sir William Gray ran him a close second. It felt like a wedding, a prize-giving, and a garden party all rolled into one. The exceptional factor being that the venue was about to sail away in just a few minutes.

The sun seemed to strengthen as the formalities ended, and the Strathclyde Police pipe band struck up and began to march on the quayside. That first passenger-carrying WSN departure seemed to happen in slow motion. A first single bell on the ship's telegraph, and we started ahead at little more than walking pace, the disturbance of the water by the paddles raising a faint but evocative scent of Clyde river ooze. The ship's steam whistle was already into overtime as she gave a final long blast of farewell and picked up to a faster but still gentle pace. Perhaps many on board were indeed carried away on a wave of nostalgia, but this moment alone was a concrete achievement beyond many expectations. The mid-1970s were not the easiest or happiest days for Britain or for Glasgow, and all could be excused for bathing deeply in warm sentiment on that sunny afternoon. Video cameras were the preserve of professional television crews, and convenient personal video recording was still part of *Tomorrow's World* in 1975. Traditional movie cameras tended to be the privilege of a few aficionados, and required a degree of affluence beyond the means of most folk. So it seems likely that the great, long, warmly echoing cheers raised by workers at Upper Clyde Shipbuilders in Govan as *Waverley* passed are lost to posterity. I remember with pure pleasure the paddle beat gradually quickening as we sailed out along the Long Dyke and towards the Firth. I recall we came alongside Dunoon pier exquisitely gently, and with absolutely no fuss whatever. It was my first experience of the exceptional mastery of handling the *Waverley* that Captain Neill was already demonstrating. Without it being spelled out, I had gathered that assistant pursers were responsible to the chief purser for their whereabouts while on duty. 'Disappearing off' was viewed very dimly. So having counted the crowd off at Dunoon, with Harold's permission Derek and I duly disappeared to the long viewing gallery atop Dunoon pier, to watch *Waverley* set off on a short cruise down the Cowal coast to allow the press to get more shots of her. Condor pipe tobacco smoke on the gentle breeze transported me back to a summer holiday with my grandparents in Dunoon early in the 1960s. I was interested then only in taking a self-drive motor boat around the Gantocks, climbing to the vantage point behind Highland Mary, and above all being on that same viewing gallery to see the tableaux of Maids, ABCs, Duchesses, *Jeanie Deans*, *Caledonia*, *Waverley* and others which daily processed right and left along that perfect Victorianesque viewpoint. When *Queen Mary II* came alongside Dunoon at the same time as *Waverley* on that day in 1975, it seemed as if the hands of time itself were twitching a little. *Queen Mary*'s deep red CalMac funnel still gave an impression of novelty, and the white bands on *Waverley*'s gleaming tricolour stacks seemed to reflect all the way home to Craigendoran. If parallel universes do exist, then it felt on that day as if we had jumped the points from one possible version of the future to another. The last two Clyde steamers, briefly sitting together at Dunoon late on that May 1975 afternoon, certainly looked and felt like a poetic time warp. Derek and I reflected as we returned to the reality of counting passengers that 'it feels like it hasn't happened yet'. Whatever it was we meant, looking back from now to then, it turned out to be the auspicious start to a long and continuing story.

So the summer of '75 unfolded. Like childhood holidays, even in Scotland, there is a tendency to remember only the sunny days. There were plenty of ups and downs, well recorded elsewhere, but left to myself I remember only the good bits. Harold Jordan and Fraser MacHaffie taught us first the essentials of the purser's office, then gradually the trial balance, banking and wages. We were eager and pretty fast to learn, and in our assumed self-confidence soon thought we know pretty much how it all worked. We felt remarkably well treated as young adults, and indulged in our youthful energy by the officers and the crew, and the directors of WSN. I look back with unqualified fondness to that summer on *Waverley*. I think we were very aware that the eyes of the Clyde were upon *Waverley*, and everything that she did, and so we felt a self-imposed pressure to do everything right, to the best of our ability, and to do our part to ensure professionalism, courtesy and competence was projected from the ticket office, in our responsibilities and in our interactions with the passengers we needed for survival. This could be something as apparently trivial, but in our view iconic, as always having the right destination boards showing on the correct side of the ship at every single call. It was small, but deeply emblematic, and a source of internal ragging if we ever slipped up on our own standards. We were sure that all the old hands on the Clyde piers noticed such things, and we were not wrong. First calls at Millport and Ayr were special highlights for me.

I had spent almost every summer so far in Millport. Closing my eyes when on Cumbrae, I see *Talisman* gliding into the long side berth at the Old Pier; the plumes of sand rising through the clear shallow water as her bow makes contact with terra firma at low tide; her slow canting around the huge rope fender which hung permanently from the corner of the pier, the paddles gently turning astern for what seemed like an age to a speed hungry youngster; her big cruiser stern gradually shrinking from view as she pulled away to port around the rocky islets in the west bay. The last time I had seen *Waverley* at Millport was an evening Showboat cruise in 1973, and it was simply a wonder to see her there again. If there was a commonality to these first visits, it was the regularity with which Captain Neill was turning the extraordinary into the routine, in the best way possible. This was certainly the case at Ayr. There had been much scepticism about the suitability, practicality and overall wisdom of *Waverley* sailing from Ayr, but Captain Neill had all the images of *Caledonia* operating from Ayr in his professional memory, and knew precisely how he intended to manoeuvre *Waverley* there. My recollection of our very first call at Ayr is that we entered the harbour at a brisk pace, which was maintained longer than anyone had imagined, and that we turned to port with a good way still on, almost heading *Waverley*'s bows towards the centre of the entrance to the northern wet dock. The powerful braking effect of the astern movement, and the resulting sideways movement, seemed to have *Waverley* at part of the way to the correct angle for backing across the River Ayr even before we touched the north corner. It's hard to imagine today how vibrant and busy Ayr harbour was then. *Waverley*'s ensign staff was only a few metres ahead of the end of a raft of fishing boats on many an occasion. Time after time, as the summer went on, *Waverley* arrived at Ayr without a fuss. I had the chance to be on the bridge wing during her first visit to Troon, as we swept around the awkward harbour corner, and with a definitive astern movement came to rest alongside, perhaps 15 or 20 metres or so short of the unyielding harbour south wall, and so elegantly close that heaving lines were scarcely needed. *Waverley*'s forays into the lower Firth seemed to have catalysed the retelling of a tome of half-forgotten steamer lore, including an incident where *Caledonia* had not stopped soon enough when performing the same entry to Troon, crumpling her bow and lifting the planking of her foredeck, like so many matchsticks, it was said. But for *Waverley* that day, to the casual eye, the berthing seemed no more remarkable than parking a mini car. During that summer, Captain Neill continued to show how *Waverley* could and should be handled. The intervening years, perhaps unsurprisingly, have shown that others too have the necessary ship-handling skills. But Captain Neill deserves exceptional credit for extending the range of the normal and the possible at that time, and for keeping skills alive that were almost lost, so that others could learn and follow.

I ended my full time duty as June came to a close, and Mark Beveridge joined to become the third assistant purser. But such is the lure of the paddler that every waking moment not otherwise gainfully engaged was spent in voluntary duties in the ticket office. Sunday 10 August was a magnificent charter by the BBC Scotland social club, from Glasgow to Tighnabruaich in glorious sun and warmth. Monday 11th dawned with thick clouds of sea fog hanging over the Firth. We sailed light from Glasgow to Dunoon, picking up only twenty-nine passengers there, but a more respectable 179 came aboard at Largs despite the unusual looking weather. As we headed south down the Largs Channel the fog thickened, and the mate, John McCallum, sounded her whistle at regular intervals. During the approach to Millport, visibility dropped further as the outer Eilean came abreast. The light post on the Eilean was visible, but Millport Pier was not. The ship came to dead slow, stopped, then retreated astern into better visibility again. Arriving later at Brodick, instead of sailing directly for fog-bound Ayr as per the sailing instructions, we waited at Arran in the hope the fog might lift. The sun indeed broke through, and 240 passengers joined at Ayr for a cruise only slightly delayed. Every loading was important, every little helped. Looking back at my instructions for the end of the summer, Tuesday 26 to Thursday 28 August are described as 'normal sailings'. With the vision of hindsight, it seems remarkable things were being described as 'normal' only three months after her return to service, and given all the events not recounted here. But there was a very real sense in which normality was the goal. Not a shoestring operation, but a well-managed, attractive and reliable pleasure steamer, which was also the world's last sea-going paddler. The summer of 1975 was remarkable in that, by the close, it seemed reasonable to expect that given a long-needed full renovation of the boiler, and a base of financial support similar to that in 1975, *Waverley* would be back carrying passengers on the Clyde again in 1976. That was our hope and belief as we applied the rubber stamp 'Waverley Steam Navigation Co. Ltd, 8th September 1975' below the final entry in the traffic book.

It's rare enough to see a purser on the engine control platform more than fleetingly, but to find three assistant pursers in the boiler room itself is even more unusual. But such was the case on a couple of Saturday afternoons late in 1975, when the preparations began for the long-overdue re-tubing of *Waverley*'s then double ended, fire tube Scotch boiler. Under supervision, a group of us set about pulling out the long twirly rods one by one from each of the flame tubes and slowly laying them in piles on the bilge plates to the sides of the boiler. It was filthy and dusty work, the soot and ash remnants penetrating our weekend clothes and coating our faces and hair. Even cold and unlit, the boiler room was a strangely claustrophobic space, and in coming summers under pressure in the ticket office, I remembered to count myself lucky and remember those down below. Whether a few such afternoons made much difference can be debated, but it was in the spirit of these days, and was just one example of the activities that continued to give a sense of solidarity to those determined to see a 1976 season come to fruition. January and February are generally the greyest, most damp and dismal months of the west of Scotland winter, and early 1976 was no exception. January saw the maiden passenger-carrying flights of Concorde. February heard foot stomping in appreciation when slides of *Waverley* were shown at the CRSC 'Highlights of 1975' monthly meeting.

But in closed circles, word was spreading that the regional council might not award *Waverley* any of the grant money essential to support the boiler repairs and the coming season. Time heals, but the decision of Strathclyde to give the full cruising grant to CalMac left *Waverley* supporters with a scar of frustration and anger. In the event, the funds were raised by a public appeal led by the *Sunday Mail*. Perhaps this was a blessing in disguise, for the media noise led to a public awareness and recognition of *Waverley* which by the summer of 1976 was very high indeed. The *Sunday Mail* of 7 March ran a double centrefold with the banner headline '10 Days To Save The Waverley', and the rest, as they say, is history. *Waverley* was towed to Stephens of Linthouse (Govan) at the end of March, firstly to dry-dock, then spent the remainder of April in Stephens' basin, where the boiler re-tubing was done. The summer of 1976 was looking both certain and optimistic again. But still in tight financial straits, WSN understandably could not afford CalMac assistant purser rates, let alone stretch to a junior purser, and I needed to earn more than an inflation-adjusted fiver a week during my first student summer vacation. I called Douglas from a payphone in the Wolfson student halls at Garscube, and we agreed I would do as many voluntary days as I could manage. Lunch with Harold and Fraser a few days later seemed to confirm that all was falling into place. Interviews for the deck crew and catering staff were scheduled for the first Monday and Tuesday of May. It was all a bit tight, but tight was the norm. Spring was in the air, and the atmosphere was electric again. I was buoyed up about *Waverley*, but very down about my own need to find another summer job.

On the Wednesday evening, the thump of 'Phone!' came at my room in halls. Mobiles were still twenty years away, and incoming calls to a distant payphone were answered only if some kind person had time to take a message or fetch you. It was Douglas and he came straight to the point: how would I like to be purser on *Waverley* for the summer? Harold had decided to leave for the attractive and rather more predictable position of purser on *Queen Mary II*. Once again, I felt that strange and wonderful feeling of the instant jump to an alternative future. My surreal week was capped off by the surreal vision of *Glen Sannox* at Ayr, arriving late Friday evening and leaving early next morning for a CRSC charter cruise to Campbeltown and round Arran.

Waverley was back in steam again on Monday 10 May, and it was a joy to be on board for the short trip from Linthouse back to Anderston Quay that Friday. The sense of anticipation grew as seating and stores were loaded back on board from the Anderston Quay warehouse over the weekend, and the ship was looking and feeling smart as she headed off down-river for sea trials on the morning of the 17th. Sailing across Cardwell Bay and viewing the recently renamed *Queen Mary* at Gourock, perhaps a few of us thought of how close *Waverley* had come to financial failure, and of the machinations of the local government of the day. But we were all focused on making the season a success, and relations between *Waverley* and *Queen Mary* were always cordial and professional in my recollection. Perhaps there was the mutual respect needed between two characters who both knew they were living on borrowed time. Certainly, it seemed sad that a note of competition for survival had been created between the two, for few doubted that the grand old turbine also merited operational preservation in her own right. Seeing the two ships together fairly frequently was one of the pleasures of these early WSN years. We turned off the Cloch, and headed back up-river.

The rhythm of life in the ticket office differed between the early season days of mostly charters, and the full season of individual fare-paying passengers. Ostensibly the work load was lighter on the charters, with no need to sell individual travel tickets. The pursers were nevertheless very keen to ensure not only that charters went smoothly in every way possible, but that the charterers somehow became fully infected with the enthusiasm for the ship that we felt. It was never discussed as such, nor an explicit strategy – we simply didn't think in these terms. We just knew word of mouth and repeat business were very important, and being open, engaged and helpful was a good starting point when the inevitable 'events' happened. Whenever wind, weather and work activities permitted, we kept the ticket office door open as much as possible: a symbolic open door which possibly predated the management fashion, and certainly gave the best office door views that most of us ever had.

An evening cruise on Friday 21 May was the first sailing, a standard and oft-repeated four hours down to Tail of the Bank and back. *Queen Mary* had made her first ever departure from Anderston Quay at 11 that morning, and we had enjoyed both the spectacle and just a little schadenfreude at the paucity of passengers. Mostly we stuck to our own business, which had plenty of challenges in store. That much became clear just a few days later when on charter to Radio Clyde. Details of our delay due to a problem with the port wheel were broadcast on live radio to Glasgow and the West of Scotland.

It was just a foretaste of the challenge of literally keeping *Waverley*'s wheels turning in 1976. If 1975 had been the season of boiler problems, 1976 was the year of the wheels. The pursers thought of themselves as a pretty stress-resistant bunch, but any unusual grind of a bush, clank of a connecting arm or rattle of a board or float was noticed immediately, and put our anticipatory anxiety up a notch or two. On the occasional days in 1976 when we sailed with a few boards or, rarely, a full float missing, the deviation from the perfect eight-beat rhythm seemed to create a slightly less relaxed atmosphere in the ticket office.

A lovely *Waverley* myth was born on Sunday 30 May. Passing through the Narrows of the Kyles of Bute had seemed to me the most magical, beautiful and exciting part of any Clyde cruise ever since a steamer trip to visit distant relatives in Kames at an impressionable age. I had noticed in 1975 that the transit that meant so much to me passed unremarked to many passengers unfamiliar with the Clyde, and I resolved to change this. I had read somewhere of evening cruises to the Kyles in the late 1800s with silver bands playing Strauss waltzes and other romantic fare. Music aboard Clyde steamers has always been a matter of personal taste and sometimes debate. Too much piped music is certainly unpleasant and perhaps in poor taste, but I had in mind the idea of a piece of music which would fit the sense of anticipation and excitement on approaching the Burnt Islands and Narrows. The 'Arrival of the Queen of Sheba' from Handel's oratorio *Solomon* seemed to fit the bill perfectly. It was played a few times in the 1975 season, but not regularly. The drama works better heading west past Colintraive, where the visual narrowing of the channel is most striking.

On the day in question, we were busy in the office on the outward trip, and I prepared to play the track heading back from Tighnabruaich towards the East Kyle. As we approached the Narrows, we could see the palatial turbine in the middle distance, heading towards us on her regular Sunday roster from Glasgow to Loch Riddon. To the background strains of Handel, *Queen Mary* turned to port and passed westward through the dog-leg channel as *Waverley* passed east through the Narrows.

It was a beautiful, symmetric moment, a gift to those who had ingested the word pictures in MacQueen and in Alan Paterson's *Golden Years*, and never thought to get a glimpse of such scenes. In fact, the music had not been chosen with *Queen Mary* in mind, and although we met her periodically in the Kyles, I believe our meeting at the Narrows that day was unique. Trial and error showed that the best place to start the tape, given normal ship speed, was just after Colintraive church, so that the music ended just after passing through. We elaborated an announcement relating the beam of *Waverley* between her sponsons to the width of the channel gap, just to enhance the interest. Not just a lump in the throat, but a clear image of that day came to mind on hearing the piece played on *Waverley* in that same place half a lifetime later.

June continued with a full timetable of schools and pensioner charters and cruises. A trip downriver to Dunoon and back which had seemed magical in 1975 began to feel banal and we looked forward to the Millport and Tighnabruaich days, and to the start of the scheduled full season from Ayr. Most importantly, *Waverley* was carrying good passenger loads, and covering her operating costs.

The light trip down to Ayr on Friday 25 June was made under brilliant blue skies, and *Waverley* steamed along at a good clip, almost 15 knots on the Skelmorlie Mile, reaching Ayr from Glasgow in just over four and a half hours. The weather was a taste of the glorious days to come in 1976, and the cruise around Holy Isle that evening gave a first taste of just how busy the ticket office would be on Ayr sailings that summer. Although advance bookings could be made via the *Waverley* office, and at Scottish Express travel agents in Newmarket Street, Ayr, and a few other outlets, the vast majority of passengers chose to turn up and pay on board. That evening, we took a good loading of just under 500, selling tickets as rapidly as possible after leaving Ayr.

The thin, yellow bus-type tickets and the Almex ticket machine were difficult, but necessity was the mother of invention. The cost and complexity of Edmondson-style stiff card railway tickets were unthinkable and unfeasible. An insert type Almex ticket of the type introduced later and still in use today was discussed, but did not materialise. In fact, a major disadvantage of the insert-type ticket is the slower speed of ticketing, which was potentially a real issue when there was still only one ticket window and relatively few shore bookings. The Almex machine (for initially there was only one!) needed handling with respect. The lever needed to be pushed forward with a strong but steady movement, and jamming seemed to happen at the tensest moments. Letter codes were varied according to the destination, allowing in principle a cross-audit to be performed between tickets sold and collected, and passenger numbers entered in the traffic log book. Collecting and checking the thin yellow paper tickets varied between frustrating and comical, especially on wet and windy days, but attempts at fare dodging were taken seriously. An evening cruise brought the simplicity of a single destination and no need to vary the destination letter slider on the machine.

As in railway days of yore, assistant pursers collected the tickets and bagged them up, but cancelling such flimsy tickets to prevent the fraud of resale was unnecessary and unfeasible. Instead, used tickets and the audit roll from the Almex machine were sent up to the office and never seen again. That evening was a perfect return to Ayr, crossing back to Culzean and sailing up the Carrick coast, a rare event in the early days.

The summer timetable began on the following Monday, and the ship began to settle into an intense kind of routine. She was looking and feeling smart, and the passenger numbers were rising steadily as that exceptional summer warmed up. The bicentennial cruise on 4 July was an early highlight, a crowd of 750 or so sailing from Anderston Quay at 9.30 a.m. The noises of revelry on *Waverley*'s departure possibly disturbed the early morning calm aboard the palatial turbine, which enjoyed a more leisurely 11 a.m. departure from Anderston on Sundays. A special American Thanksgiving-style roast turkey menu was offered in the dining saloon, and rapidly sold out. *Waverley* routinely operated a traditional dining saloon, with waitress service of a simple three-course lunch menu served at the long, communal, white cloth covered tables. Three and often four sittings of lunch were offered, and the same number of high tea sittings later in the day. Traditionally lunch and high tea sittings had been spaced at forty-minute intervals, with brisk serving and clearing, and a clientele who knew pretty well how the system worked. The sittings were announced by the loud ringing of a handbell at the entrance to the dining saloon, and those who had booked a place were rather expected to be ready, if not already in a queue on the lower deck at the appointed times. Thus the ticket office sold meal tickets for specific times, as well as travel tickets, and ensuring that the meal timings and destinations chosen did not clash often prolonged the interaction with each passenger at the ticket window. Eight coloured rolls of tickets, corresponding to each of the four sittings of luncheon and high tea, were spooled on a piece of dowelling, sitting in a wooden box to the left of the window. A long day cruise could see over half the passengers enjoying meals, and a full sitting could be as many as 100 diners and occasionally a few more.

Among the possessions I have carried from country to country over the last forty years is a framed artist's print of *Waverley*, on the back of which is written: 'Summer 1976 – two to Brodick, please!' I had almost forgotten why it was so inscribed. We sailed with our full certificated passenger complement of 571 from Ayr to Brodick and Campbeltown on Saturday 26 June, and the regular Tuesday 10 a.m. sailings to Brodick and Round Bute had a full load of 571 on both 6 and 13 July, with well over a hundred disappointed and none too pleased passengers turned away and left behind on Ayr harbour on both occasions. The ticket office was working flat out on these days to try to clear the queues during the ninety or so minute crossing to Brodick. Steamer tickets, lunch tickets, high tea tickets, Round Arran and Brodick Castle coach tickets, and explaining the relative merits of Brodick, Arran or a cruise Round Bute to the uninitiated was demanding but fun. We took spells on the ticket window, since more than about thirty minutes non-stop tended to introduce a note of irritation to our tone – which we did not want! The replacement of *Waverley*'s number four lifeboat with liferafts sufficient for a larger number of passengers allowed the increased number of 819 to be carried from Ayr and elsewhere on the Class III certificate. She immediately carried her full complement of 819 from Ayr on 20 July, still leaving a few score behind. I vividly remember negotiating with first officer Murray Paterson and deck hands to let the passengers on board fifteen or twenty minutes earlier than usual to have some chance of clearing the ticket queue before Brodick. The memory of that happy throng, stretching far up the south harbour at Ayr, all waiting in the summer sun to sail on *Waverley*, is a happy and vivid one (see photo no. 17). Such was the good weather, the public awareness of *Waverley* and the lure of Arran that we sailed with a full load of 819 on six consecutive Tuesdays that summer, and with 600 to 700 to Dunoon on most Wednesdays. I remember one of these sunny mornings, still alongside, the queue snaking from the single ticket window around the after deck shelter, and out into a strand from aft to forward funnel, as passengers still continued to board. The skipper stuck his head in through the open ticket office door, where Derek, Graham and I were pretty calmly selling faster than ever before. 'Well, you seem to be coping alright, eh!' We took it as a vote of confidence, the refrain of 'two to Brodick, please' not relenting for an instant on the other side of the ticket window.

After the passengers had all disembarked at Ayr on those balmy evenings in 1976, groups of officers and crew, WSN directors, PSPS stalwarts and volunteers, and enthusiast friends would often linger around the after funnel, which was still pleasantly warm. The blue polypropylene stacking chairs from the aft deck shelter were grouped in arcs as we mulled over the events of the day, the week, and inevitably general steamer and paddler stuff, past, present and future. It was a mutually supportive atmosphere, knowing that each week successfully completed was an achievement in itself. That the paddle wheels were the chief source of problems in 1976 is well known, but just how much running repairs were done during evenings and nights, especially during these mostly balmy ten weeks of weekday sailings from Ayr, I think is not widely appreciated and risks being forgotten entirely. Evening after evening after evening, and often right through the night, teams including not only the engineering department, but the skipper and first officer, deck hands and volunteers toiled on the wheels, replacing individual boards or whole floats, and running repairs on the metal frame itself. On more than just a few occasions, I left Ayr after 10 p.m. for the comfort of home and a good bed to return at 7 the next morning to find the same people working inside the paddle box. The successful constant tending of the paddle wheels was more than a small miracle. Despite many delays, bumps and thumps, only two sailings were missed in 1976, both from Ayr and both due to bad weather, not mechanical problems. I'm not embarrassed to admit I never spent a moment, let alone an overnighter, inside a *Waverley* paddle box. We all have our strengths, limits and comfort zones, and that was outside mine. A partial rationale was that the belief that pursers needed to be clean, smart, personable and presentable at all times, and that voracious interaction with the public led to a voracious appetite for sleep. Yet I have never forgotten the exceptional invisible effort, none of which was mine, that got *Waverley* through that idyllic summer. With important support from Fraser MacHaffie, from Alan Condie at weekends and hand-processing the paper wage bills, from Douglas and Terry, from George Train and Peter Reid, and with encouragement and tolerance from the skipper, officers and crew, Derek Peters, Graham McLeod and I – a purser's team with an average age of eighteen and not much life experience – were able to cope with almost 200,000 passenger journeys that summer. As we closed the traffic log on 19 September, the following season seemed to be as close to a certainty as could be imagined.

A floating classroom aboard training ship *Dolphin* at Leith Nautical College was the preparation for the 1977 pursering season for Derek and me. *Waverley*'s selection of deck crew had been limited by the need to carry a specified number with certificates of competence in handling a lifeboat. So it seemed an interesting and practical if unusual idea to gain this competence in areas other than the traditional deck hands. We commuted over from Glasgow each day of the last week of March, taking the training seriously, since a written and practical test had to be passed on the Friday to gain the certificate, and neither of us were used to failing exams. 1977 was the swansong of the former HMS *Dolphin*, and the gently moving and creaking hull certainly had a sense of history about her. Only in preparation for this article did I read that she was towed away and scrapped only three months later. Such was our focus on the paddler that we had little time for other historic ships. Launching the lifeboat from safety davits identical to those on *Waverley* but twice as high from the water's surface was learned by rote, and we had a few entertaining afternoons sailing an old clinker-built version around Leith harbour. We passed, let WSN know of this, and thought no more about it.

Waverley meanwhile was at Scotts of Greenock, and undergoing probably the most extensive set of renovations of what seemed then her long life. High among these was the almost complete rebuilding of the paddle wheels, and full replacement of all the boards with the most suitable timber available. Removal of the cast-iron galley range, deep cleaning of the bilges and removal of the accumulated superfluous objects of decades left her sitting an inch or more higher in the water. We joked that we had to fight to keep the heavy safe in the ticket office, but it too was removed in some later year. Sea trials went ahead on Monday 18 April, and the 23rd was the first passenger sailing of the year. The ship seemed transformed. Any vestiges of the benign neglect of former years seemed finally to have been banished, exorcised, rubbed, scrubbed or otherwise lifted out.

The 1976 purser team was reunited that weekend, but to my frustration I could not join the adventure to Liverpool because of unavoidable exams. Fraser and Derek would be the team. Without mobiles, SMS or e-mails, let alone Facebook or Instagram, following the ship's progress was achieved by simple phone calls and word of mouth between enthusiasts, the network radiating out from a few reliable sources and a few other 'chief nutters'. I was glad to hear she had arrived back safely at Ayr in the early hours of Tuesday 10 May, and we sailed on the Thursday from Ayr at 8 a.m. for Largs and Inveraray for a Clan gathering. The weather was grey and wet as only the west of Scotland can offer. Only twenty-two passengers joined at Ayr and eighty-five at Largs. Memorably described by Terry in one of his earliest fliers as 'remote and peaceful', Loch Fyne remained on that day exactly so. It was a full blown washout, and a painful reminder of the vagaries of both weather and weekday passenger footfall on the Clyde outside the main season. Numbers were back to a more healthy 624 from Glasgow on Saturday 14th, boosted by a large British Rail party who had travelled up from Sheffield. The month continued in a more or less routine fashion, although beneath the more tranquil exterior, there was still much unseen effort. A wedged log broke a paddle float as the engines were being warmed through, ready for departure on an evening cruise for invited guests and the public from Anderston Quay on Friday 20 May, and an 'all-nighter' reminiscent of 1976 replaced the float after return from the evening cruise in time for a 9.30 departure to Ayr next morning. Reliability was incomparably better than in the two previous years, but events still happened.

The pursers were reminded every day of the Queen's Silver Jubilee of 1977, since large adhesive jubilee decals were fixed to the glass of both ticket windows. When I mention 'both', this is also to recall that a second ticket window was cut during the 1977 refit, symmetrically to the starboard side of the original port side window. It was certainly a boon on the busy days and allowed for a more easily shared workload, and occasionally for different activities from each window. The view into the aft deck shelter and down the aft companionway to the dining saloon was more complete. Two windows and the door open created quite a through draught, so we often preferred to keep only the original window and the door open outside peak times.

Most of us by now had visited our former boss on the palatial turbine, and could still be forgiven for feeling like the poor north-bank relative. *Queen Mary*'s classic wood panelled main ticket office had a formal yet futuristic glass front, which I believe dated directly from 1933, and a side window and a separate cancellation office to boot! Relations with *Queen Mary* continued to be very correct. Few were in any doubt that 1977 would be her last season with CalMac. Despite her undoubted maritime significance, and even if the Clyde or the wider British coastline might in time find enough reliable passenger trade to support two day cruise ships, there seemed simply no real possibility of a *Waverley*-like future. Perhaps for that reason, and perhaps because *Waverley* felt so smartly and reliably turned out as to no longer be the underdog, there seemed ever more affectionate glances from the revamped paddler to the grand old survivor Queen.

As May drew to a close, our mentor and supporter, talented purser and polymath Fraser MacHaffie flew off to a permanent new life in the United States. He had always been there, in body or close spirit, since Harold's departure. We were of a younger generation, but had all grown to like his very calm, highly competent, gently interrogating and mildly intimidating style. It was one of the models on which we tried to base ourselves in the office. Fraser had gathered a variety of timetables, phone numbers and much other useful reference and emergency material, which was known to us as the 'Repository of Truth'. When things occasionally still got sticky in the ticket office, a good question remained, 'What would Fraser do?'

Friday 16 June marked the thirtieth anniversary of *Waverley*'s maiden voyage, and she was carrying schools parties to Millport, with 580 from Glasgow and a further 240 from Greenock. *Queen Mary* too was on an educational trip with schoolchildren to Millport, and between the two deposited in excess of 1,500 children and their teachers on Millport Old Pier in the space of an hour. *Waverley* had arrived at 1.15 p.m., and left the pier to lie in Millport Bay beyond the outer Eilean while the *Mary* came in. It had been previously agreed, at least by some, that the paddle boxes would be repainted in black that day to correspond more fully to her 1947 appearance. The contrary view prevailed in restoring the white rim at Glasgow on Sunday 4 September, but for a few high profile weeks of

1977, *Waverley* looked more the period piece than ever. Reloading the right children on the right steamer was quite a performance, and with *Waverley* departing first we were keen to forestall any turbine crossover traffic. The high amplitude electric loudhailer procured by the purser's department a few weeks earlier came into its own. Its piercing shriek was sufficient even to get the attention of a crowd on Rothesay pier on a Saturday afternoon, and the device was remarkably successful in helping restore a semblance of order on a number of occasions.

An unusual piece of cargo was aboard on Sunday 19 June, namely, the purser's car. Clyde paddlers carried the occasional motor vehicle, and there was nothing too unusual about this in the days before the purpose-built car ferries. I remember that as a child in Millport in the early 1960s one or two cars being driven off *Talisman* across two stout planks onto the Old Pier was an unexceptional but always interesting event. No one could remember with any certainty the last time *Waverley* had taken a car on board. In this case the vehicle was my distinctive and diminutive 1969 Fiat 500, known familiarly as 'Caesar', or more pejoratively, 'the Clockwork Orange', due to its vivid paintwork. Driven aboard the forward sponson using paddle boards, and parked behind the after funnel, the sight caused some astonishment to passengers boarding for the 9.30 departure. A falling tide meant the promenade deck was now far below the quayside, and it was far from obvious how the loading had been accomplished. The small size of the car allowed it to be driven in a full circle around the after funnel, and it was sited in various locations, and visited Dunoon twice and Millport three times during the day before being driven ashore at Ayr late that evening. The Glasgow to Ayr carriage of the car was repeated the following Sunday, conveniently for the beginning of scheduled summer sailings from Ayr. The late June and early July weather was rather mixed, and while the ship was running more smoothly and reliably than previously, passenger loadings were a little disappointing.

WSN brought the catering operation in-house for 1977, and chief steward Bill MacFarlane was raising standards, helped by an energetic team and the fitting of a modern Calor gas range to replace the astonishing coal-fired cast-iron behemoth that had been cannibalised from *Duchess of Hamilton* and fitted in *Waverley* in 1971. The dining saloon looked rather magnificent, with full-length dark blue Wilton carpet runners on the dark stained timber decking. The panelling had also been sanded and re-stained, and the visual and olfactory appeal was at a new high. The pursers made a concerted effort to maximise the numbers purchasing meals, and to be sure that every passenger knew what was being offered. Not only was the catering operation a potential source of much-needed income, but in 1977 there was no doubt that traditional sittings of luncheon and high tea significantly enhanced the on-board experience of the many who enjoyed them. I recall that Calum Bryce, who had joined the pursers for 1977, was particularly charming and successful at raising the sales of meal tickets. Indeed, such were Calum's interpersonal skills that we often pushed him into the fray when there was a particularly challenging passenger to deal with. Today, Calum has the rare distinction of being the only master mariner in the Caledonian MacBrayne fleet with ticket office experience on a paddler.

The engine telegraph on *Waverley*'s control platform lies approximately underfoot the ticket office, and the signal bell sounding up through the deck has the effect of keeping the office aware of the communication between bridge and engine room. Hearing a half or slow ahead will signal the approach to a pier, and if no pier is close, natural curiosity will often lead one of us to step out of the office or peer through the aft deck shelter, just to ascertain what is going on. So although in a sea-going sort of office, the daily life of *Waverley* pursers is punctuated by the ding of the telegraph and the resulting hisses, wheezes or clunk of the reversing engine as an engineer quickly responds to the command from the bridge.

And so the triple peal of an emergency full astern was instantly understood by us as it rang up through our soles on the afternoon of Friday 15 July 1977. The ticket door was open, and having announced our return arrival at Dunoon a little earlier, we could see we were turning to the north of the Gantocks, just as we had done a few hours earlier. The braking power and change of momentum was intense, and *Waverley* began to bounce. Not violently or alarmingly, just very unusually. Bolting out of the door and around the corner of the office to stand aft of the funnel, the nature of the unfolding event needed no discussion. The moment of grounding felt a bit like the joggling between carriages sometimes felt on an older train, not alarming, but disorienting to the sense of balance for a moment. I was more alarmed by seeing the funnels rock and some of the funnel stays drop, and in the first few moments instinctively and without any clear plan we asked passengers to move away from the area around the funnels and above the boiler. The 'streaker' *Juno* was first on the scene, and I remember being impressed that although other ships came to aid, she stood by until every passenger had left *Waverley*. The majority of passengers were transferred to *Sound of Shuna*, which had come alongside our starboard side, and the proceedings were calm, orderly and rapid. At one point, some wag did shout out 'women and children first', more as courtesy than concern, and as if to signal that Glasgow humour was alive and well.

After all the passengers were ashore, and the attempt by tugs to pull *Waverley* free had failed, the pursers joined the effort to move buoyant apparatus and anything else moveable towards the bow, to minimise weight on the stern, where she was aground. In late afternoon, close to low tide, *Queen Mary* passed by us as she arrived at Dunoon, and we could only imagine what a tragic sight we looked. As the tide came in, so did the water level in the lower dining saloon. Pumps brought by the US Navy from USS *Holland* in the Holy Loch, with whom gifts had been exchanged at Dunoon on 4 July the previous year, almost certainly saved the day. Lined up along the covered section to the side of the after deck shelter, wide-diameter hoses ran from the pumps down the aft companionway and from there into the lower dining saloon. I remember reminding myself as I winced at the sodden Wilton carpet and grime in the dining saloon that anything could be replaced if only we made it to shore, which of course we did. With five or six high-capacity pumps running flat out and spewing water over the side, *Waverley* floated off and paddled briskly and very noisily to the Coal Pier. I called Douglas from a payphone in the Argyll Hotel just after midnight. I was convinced she would be repaired and return to service, but whether it would be in that same summer remained to be seen.

I look back at that moment as the end of the beginning for the Waverley Steam Navigation Company, for having survived that misadventure, the ship was in fact already quite well prepared for the 1978 season. In a personal sense, it was also the end of my time on board. The pursers transferred to *Queen of Scots* and became part of her valiant and worthy effort to maintain some cash flow and to keep the spirit alive. Derek Peters took over as purser on *Waverley*'s reintroduction on 31 August, and served during university vacation for several more years, and in a relief capacity.

Almost forty years later, seeing *Waverley* looking better than ever is one of life's greatest pleasures. Hearing the paddle beat in the distance before she comes into view, spotting basking sharks and Portuguese men o'war in the lower firth from her decks, admiring a frequent glorious sunset over Bute or Holy Isle on an evening cruise, being cheered and jeered by children on the banks of the river at Clydebank or Govan, these are only a few of the thousands of timeless shared images and experiences which unite those who have sailed and worked on *Waverley* over these decades. To these I add my own astonishment, having been far from Scotland for so long, that these images are not just memories but can still be experienced. Imagine, for a moment, what it felt like in 1974 when she did not sail. Imagine, if you can, what it felt like in 1975, when *Waverley*'s reintroduction had yet happened. In many aspects of our lives, in the anticipation of loss, or in the reaction to loss, we can do little or nothing to change the outcome. *Waverley* differs from this, for we can continue to help determine the future. Sail on her, contribute funds to her, speak up for her. Remember it could still be lost, and do not let it happen!

Another winter is over, green is returning to the banks and braes, and steam is being raised in *Waverley*'s boiler. What could be more perfect?

With many thanks to Derek Peters for helping create these memories and bring them back to life, and for the use of parts of his PSPS Scottish Branch talk, 'Waverley Steam Navigation Company, celebrating forty years'.

Cameron Marshall

Waverley Connections

When asked which ship was their favourite, most seafarers would probably reply that it was their previous one, but, having now reached the age when I can definitely say that it was my final one, I must also consider another – *Waverley*. It may be indelicate to say so, but the 'Lady' is almost a year older than I am and while I cannot recall our first meeting, as a child of a steamer-oriented family I fancy that it was at an early age.

Born quite literally a stone's throw from Gourock pier head, I do not know how often *Waverley* would have called there during the summer of 1948, but I feel sure that at some point my infant gaze must have glimpsed that first coat of buff paint to adorn her funnels.

Be that as it may, my parents soon relocated to Port Glasgow and houses with panoramic views across the river that always enabled us to see *Waverley* and other vessels coming and going from Craigendoran, or passing upriver to Glasgow. The steamers remained a focus and there was now the added attraction of a trip on a steam train to join them, as was the family's habit during the summers of the 1950s.

Many are the memories of such journeys and the great excitement when catching sight of one of the splendid turbine vessels, *Duchess of Montrose* or *Duchess of Hamilton*, from the train as it drew into the bustling hub which Gourock was in those days. Throngs of expectant passengers bound for an assortment of locations; hard pressed pier staff patiently trying to marshal them into the appropriate queue; the excitement of boarding; freshly hosed down decks, beads of water on the varnish work; the evocative aroma of warm oil seeping from engine room vents; and of course the brisk salty tang carried on the breeze. All of this under clear blue skies because the summers were like that in those days, were they not?

We may have regularly sailed on the turbine ships but the paddlers were a great fascination – even the diesel electric powered *Talisman* – but the magical sight of those magnificent triple expansion steam reciprocating engines of *Jeanie Deans*, *Caledonia* and *Waverley* was wonderful. Paddlers are quite addictive.

It is also a fact that along with many of my contemporaries, I soon acquired the ability to distinguish at long range the identity of various steamers by the rake of their bow, type of stern, cross trees (or not) and number of windows etc. I suspect that my children, despite being properly brought up in a *Waverley* culture, would regard this as quite sad.

While on a hike during a Scout camp on Bute, one of the leaders asked if any of our group could identify the distant silhouette of a steamer passing the north coast of Arran. '*Waverley*,' came the instant reply from several of us.

By 1960 I was in Port Glasgow High School and deemed responsible enough by my parents (big mistake!) to have an eight-day ticket allowing complete access to the entire Caledonian Steam Packet Co.'s fleet (including Loch Lomond), all for the princely sum of 24s 9d. Armed only with a steamer timetable, a Kodak Instamatic camera and some tomato sandwiches, I gleefully set off each day to enjoy the steamers and hitherto unrivalled freedom.

For four seasons I enjoyed this generosity, shared with some of my equally fortunate and like minded friends, and during this time I became better acquainted with *Waverley*. She carried me to and from Scout camp, did the Friday upriver sail to Glasgow – a great favourite – and there was the Arrochar sailing, which allowed sufficient time to walk to Tarbert, from where *Maid of the Loch* made the connection to Balloch and a train back to *Waverley* at Craigendoran.

School ends, then real life begins and at a time when least equipped to do so, we all have to make decisions which will affect the rest of our lives. I opted for a career as a deck officer in the Merchant Navy and even today would struggle to explain the thought process leading to such a choice, but I do not blame *Waverley*!

After a year at the Glasgow Nautical College, I joined my first ship in October 1965 and for the next thirteen years, life revolved around lengthy spells at sea, college and the Board of Trade exams, but also generous amounts of leave during which, if in the season, I always included a voyage on one of the now declining number of steamers. What else would you do after eight months at sea?

Eventually only *Queen Mary* and *Waverley* remained and while away at sea news came to me that the paddler was to be withdrawn but had become the object of a preservation attempt by an upstart organisation calling itself the Paddle Steamer Preservation Society! Whoever heard of such a thing?

The summer of 1975 was, as I recall, a glorious one and I came home to days of sunshine and the ability to savour it from the decks of a paddle steamer brought back from the brink against all the odds. Before that, and prior to actually seeing *Waverley* in her splendid new livery, it was the sound of her paddle beat that alerted me to her as she passed our house on the way up river.

The following year, when I came home on study leave, I discovered that some of my seagoing contemporaries had been at various times been helping out as chief officer and through them I soon found myself doing the same.

The transition from casual passenger to being professionally engaged in the day to day running of *Waverley* was quite stark and immediate. What had previously been pure pleasure was now work but not really 'work' as I had come to know it. Long hours and demanding situations were standard throughout the British Merchant Navy but many aspects of *Waverley*'s navigation and watch keeping were a world away from what any deep sea officer would consider normal. Sailing close to land; piers in quick succession; the need for slick gangway handling; passengers in all their infinite variety; and cramped, poorly ventilated and very basic living accommodation which no self respecting penal colony would tolerate. (I think that I had been rather spoilt up until then.)

Apart from condensation and whatever occasionally dripped through the timbers of the deck above, there was no running water in the accommodation and the nearest shower was located one deck up, in the forward end of the starboard sponson. Here it was never a good idea to assume that the supply of hot water, or indeed cold water, would be available for as long as you needed it. We all soon learned to fill the wash hand basin as a precaution against being left covered in soap suds. In regard to other domestic considerations, with no onboard laundry facilities, I was not alone in relying heavily on family support for a regular supply of clean white shirts.

The relative informality was also strange but as part of a mainly young team filled with a 'can-do' pioneering spirit buoyed up by good will and good fun, all of the above was, against the odds, still a pleasure.

A typical day would start with a call at 0700, then after breakfast there would be a chat with the bosun to discuss issues of the day. Meanwhile the crew would 'turn to' and begin the wash down, clean the brass, put up flags and generally prepare to take on passengers. The fresh water tanks would be topped up, fuel might be taken, stores manhandled down the gangway, toilets cleaned and so on.

Many have asked why the ship was always wet from the wash down when passengers were boarded in the morning. In those days, the old boiler would require to be flashed up from time to time overnight in order to maintain steam pressure and this could leave soot particles on the seats and deck. It was always felt best to hose away such deposits first thing in the morning in order to best protect the passengers.

In any week the timetable was different every day and factors such as weather, tides, traffic and passengers made for infinite variety.

At the end of a long day, once the ship was secured for the night and the initial clean up complete, bed was often the preferred option, but from time to time the opportunity was taken to convene an 'interdepartmental meeting' in a local hostelry. Many were the issues discussed and problems solved. Nowadays it would be called 'networking' or some such business-speak!

It wasn't all beer and skittles, however, and there were dark times too.

The Gantocks incident of 15 July 1977 is well documented and was traumatic for all concerned.

Having agreed to return as mate after completing the main part of my master's exams, I was newly part of the crew suddenly faced with this event.

Not a situation imagined by any of us, it quickly focused the minds of all and with the passengers quickly and safely evacuated, attention turned to doing what we could for the ship. With the stern stuck fast, the bow buoyant and the tide falling I had as much weight as possible transferred forward to minimise the stresses on the mid-section of the hull. At the same time steps were taken to shore up one of the watertight bulkheads, which was under severe stress.

Never could I have imagined that these and other measures so recently the preserve of my college lectures and books of theory would be happening in a manner that was all too real.

In a life of seagoing, it is sometimes difficult to comprehend just how some incidents fit into the bigger picture or how they influence your later decisions and actions. One thing I can say is that awful as this situation unquestionably was, I still count it as an honour and privilege to have been part of such a superb team, who when challenged by a great and sudden emergency rose to the occasion and were not found wanting.

Having survived the Gantocks and docked for examination, *Waverley* had another threat to surmount, and it was only after she had narrowly avoided being declared a constructive total loss by the insurers that repairs could be put in hand.

With the ship out of action and the revenue stream cut off, things were very serious; indeed, it was far from certain that the company would survive. However, to the rescue came McAlpine & Co.'s small passenger vessel *Queen of Scots*, which was made available, and this unlikely lifeline in the form of a onetime Scarborough pleasure craft dating from the 1930s tipped the balance.

Hastily given a red, white and black funnel, *Queen of Scots* began operating on an amended timetable, carrying fewer passengers at slower speed to fewer destinations, but crucially she did provide cash flow.

On one arrival at Glasgow, the starting of a generator blasted an accumulation of soot and oily deposits from the funnel, with the resulting filthy cloud descending indiscriminately upon decks and passengers alike and prompting claims running into many hundreds of pounds, including one for a new wig.

On another occasion, after suffering mechanical problems it was necessary for *Queen of Scots* to return to Glasgow from Millport on one engine in order to allow repairs on the other. In Clyde terms this was an epic voyage, taking in excess of six hours, and on the way upriver we had the unusual experience of being overtaken by vessels of the dredging fleet. I suspect that it was a fairly unusual situation for them as well!

To be brutally honest I did not like the *Queen of Scots* in any shape or form and have little in the way of happy memories of my time on her. She was a far cry from the comparative luxury of *Waverley*, having no crew accommodation (not even a faulty shower!), no proper feeding and none of the daily buzz. I was not alone in being glad to see the day when the 'flagship' returned.

After her time off service and spells in dry-dock at Greenock, then Govan, *Waverley*'s repairs were eventually completed and she returned to her Glasgow berth with a view to getting back into service with minimal delay. There was much to be done to make the ship ready for passengers, not least a thorough clean up, and it was quite heart-warming to find a small army of willing volunteers comprising some crew family members, various supporters and assorted others who beavered away for hours in order to augment the efforts of the crew.

I remained with *Waverley* until the season ended in the latter part of September, then went back to college to complete (I hoped) the final part of my master's Foreign Going Certificate. With that outcome still unknown, it was back to the real world and my real employers, Denholm's of Glasgow, who soon arranged for me to fly out to Tampa in Florida, where I would join the bulk carrier *Caledonian Forest* as chief officer.

As for that bunch of upstarts, the PSPS? Well, I had by this time joined them and was now a fully paid up 'nutter'.

Due to some sort of mix-up, I had arrived in Tampa five days before the ship and as I languished in the local Hilton Hotel, the agent was most attentive to my needs and furnished me with the means to travel around the area. In the course of this short-lived idyll I discovered that a nearby Disney theme park had paddle steamers of a sort and duly took the opportunity to sample them. Interesting, though I doubt that either would have coped with a stiff southerly breeze at Kilcreggan; however, it is a good example of what you do if smitten. That addiction again!

I was soon back at sea and while in the Panama Canal on New Year's Eve, word came that my studies had not been in vain.

We sailed north to Los Angeles, where we took on bunkers before setting out for Japan. On paper this should have taken us around sixteen days, but due to some of the worst and most consistently bad weather I have ever experienced the passage took almost twice as long. For the entire crossing our average speed was little more than eight knots and in those days before the Global Positioning System, when the sextant was our only means of mid-ocean position fixing, the generally overcast conditions regularly denied us the two essentials for obtaining accurate celestial observations: a firm horizon and the ability to see the sun or stars. So much for the calm, blue Pacific!

Oh to be back in the Kyles of Bute on a pouring wet day – even on the *Queen of Scots*!

We were only about a day and a half from the Japanese coast when, after several days of getting no observations, I finally got a decent set of star sights from which we could then plot an accurate course to our intended landfall.

No chief officer lacks for things to do and there are generally not enough hours in the day; however, during this long and unpleasant voyage I did take time to ponder what I might do now that I had the Holy Grail of a Master's Foreign Going Certificate, if not in my possession then waiting for me.

From Japan we proceeded to Canada, where we were due to load timber in a variety of ports around British Columbia, where some of the densely forested inlets are reminiscent of Loch Goil, albeit on a slightly grander scale.

By that time I had decided to seek pastures new but without really much idea as to where they might be.

My resignation would be winging its way to Glasgow soon after we docked in Vancouver and once there was time to distribute the incoming mail brought onboard by the ship's agent, I found that among mine was a letter from the Waverley office asking if I would be interested in returning as mate for the 1978 season.

Such timing!

Why not?

Laden with timber, including 9,000 tons on deck, *Caledonian Forest* made its way back to LA then down to the Panama Canal, through the Caribbean, across the Atlantic to Liverpool, where we anchored off the Bar Light vessel on St George's Day. We went up the Mersey in the early hours of 24 April and squeezed through Langton Locks to berth in Brocklebank Dock to await discharge.

I left my last deep sea ship next day to drive home with my father, who had come down to meet me.

After an enjoyable spell of leave, during which I made sure to collect my new 'Ticket' from the Glasgow marine office, I rejoined *Waverley* on Saturday 27 May.

Before the main season began at the end of June, a varied programme of charters and special sailings was scheduled, during which a wide spectrum of groups would be carried.

Because of the post-Gantocks docking to repair damage caused by the grounding, *Waverley* was not required to dry-dock ahead of the 1978 season and while that was good in terms of the company's hard-pressed finances, it left the ship bereft of a good overall paint job, the normal legacy of refit.

There was much to be done and we entered service not looking our best, but hopefully the initial passengers overlooked this and hats off to the deck crew and pursers, who all pitched in to redress the situation with great enthusiasm.

One of the early charters was by the National Trust and with them came two special guests, both familiar to listeners and viewers of the BBC, who were to provide commentary throughout the day. The first of these was Jack House, who had written many books about the Clyde and its major city and was known as 'Mr Glasgow'. These commentaries could only be done from the wheelhouse and we had not long departed from Anderston Quay before it became apparent that Mr House was struggling to make sense of the river he once knew. Such was the pace of change and the sad decline of shipyards, docks and other long-established landmarks that he was rather perplexed. In the end he managed to fulfil his remit, though much of what was heard by his attentive audience was owed to prompts and guidance from various members of the bridge team.

The wider reaches of the firth was covered by the urbane Maurice Lindsay in his trademark spotted bow tie. He was more at home in these less changed areas but I do recall the caravan sites at Cloch Point and Wemyss Bay being referred to as 'a form of pollution'.

On other days there were some public sailings, but also charters for various groups, including school parties. In respect of the latter, we marvelled at the level of noise they could produce and the fact that this was exceeded only by the litter they generated. But they all did seem to enjoy themselves.

On 24 June *Waverley* sought to retrace the steps of the veteran MacBrayne paddle steamer *Columba* and accordingly set off from Glasgow at precisely 0711 hrs. During the cruise, it was hoped to capture the 'Blue Riband' of Loch Fyne by beating the old paddler's best time between Ardrishaig and Tarbet.

With the cranks and connecting rods a blur (a reported 52 rpm!) in the dimmed lights of the engine room and the bow wave up to the anchor, the ship thundered along at goodness knows what speed and was pronounced to have taken the record by the smallest of margins.

At Tarbet it was discovered that the port bow line was missing. Between piers this rope is normally led through a fairlead on the fo'c'sle and has its eye held by a hook on the outside of the rails below the bridge wing. We will never know, but perhaps someone was careless in all the rush and the eye not properly attached. If so, and we can only speculate, with the eye falling unseen into the water, when the ship was at full speed might it pull the rest of the coil overboard as well? At the speed we were doing it could have been catastrophic had it wrapped itself around the paddle wheel. A lucky escape!

Such exertions are not good for the elderly and on 6 July, while off Kilchattan Bay, word came from the chief engineer that the boiler had developed a serious leak. We immediately diverted to Largs, where all passengers were landed before the ship made for Glasgow. This was a devastating and demoralising blow and while repairs were being put in hand some staff went on leave, and with those remaining as much maintenance as possible was prioritised.

Since returning to the ship, I had been studying with a view to being examined for a Clyde Pilotage Exemption Certificate, so the time off service was an ill wind giving me much more time to prepare.

Repairs were scheduled to be completed on 12 July, at which point steam would be raised with a view to returning to service the following day.

On the morning of the 13th I walked along to the Clyde Port Authority office in Robertson Street to keep my appointment with Captain George Stronnach GC, the pilot master. In addition to being a holder of the George Cross after heroically distinguishing himself during the war, Captain Stronnach was a gentleman of the old school who would occasionally come for a sail on *Waverley* and enjoyed seeing parts of the river rarely visited by the regular pilots. More importantly for me on the day, he passed me out with a full Clyde Exception Licence.

Back onboard, expectations were high for the return to service, but shortly before the scheduled sailing time we were astounded to learn that a new leak had developed, this time in the opposite end of the boiler, below the centre furnace. A day of highs and lows if ever there was!

Having missed the Glasgow Fair for a second year, we finally returned to service on 19 July.

As far as I recall, the remainder of the season passed off more or less as planned, with some of the highlights being a visit to Irvine, landing passengers by ferry at Lamlash, a very well patronised Millport Illuminations evening and a successful end of season sailing on 25 September.

Earlier, during July, a seagoing friend of mine casually informed me that the Clyde Port Authority was advertising a vacant position of assistant harbour master, for which he had applied. Having no plans (or income) beyond the end of the season, I thought that I would toss my hat into the ring as well. To my utter surprise I was offered the job. Flattered beyond belief, I none the less felt like a dog that had chased a car and caught it. What now?

As *Waverley* cast off and made her way to the Govan dry-docks on 26 September, I let her ropes go and watched from the quay as she canted and proceeded down river, passing on the way an old, laid-up ore carrier which in a previous day as *Dunkyle* had been my first ship as third officer.

I made my way to the Clyde Port Authority office in Robertson Street and the start of a new chapter.

My time with the CPA was to be brief – less than two years – but it was a wonderful experience and I would not have missed it for the world.

From the outset I was made very welcome, treated with great courtesy and shown every consideration as I settled in to my new duties and began to find my way around. It was wonderful to have access to so many areas of interest and so much detail relating to the river I had grown up beside.

Essentially it was a desk job but I was encouraged to get out and about to all areas of the port and its various component parts. Transferring from seagoing to harbour responsibilities is akin to being poacher turned gamekeeper and I was and am deeply indebted to many really fine people who took the time and trouble to give me an insight into such departments as dredging, hydrography, stevedoring, port control and much more. Later in life I was to be very grateful for these experiences and the understanding the information enabled me to have.

With regard to *Waverley*, my new employers seemed quite relaxed about me continuing to work on her at weekends and during holidays and I did so as a relief mate as and when required.

Having previously been in touch with Sealink at Stranraer, I was offered a position as second officer with them in March 1980 and at the end of the following month, with some sadness, left CPA and returned to seagoing. I would then spend the rest of my working life, around thirty-two years, with Sealink and their successors, British Ferries and Stena Line.

Here too there was no objection to me doing voluntary work as a relief deck officer on *Waverley* and on Friday 18 September 1981, this stepped up a gear as I did my first day as master.

My father decided at the last minute to come for a sail that day and as we drove to Glasgow together he did not know that I would be in command.

It is stating the blindingly obvious to say that you can only ever have one first day at anything and if there is ever a day when you don't want to foul up, this is it.

All went well and the piers at Kilcreggan, Dunoon and Rothesay all came and went, outwards and on the return, with little to remark upon except for my increasing sense of relief. A day to remember and I did enjoy it – I think. My father later told me that unexpectedly sharing my first day in command had made his day. Just getting him and everyone else back safely made mine!

From now on, my connection with *Waverley* would be confined to generally short spells as mate or, occasionally, as master. I had been offered full time employment but, now married, and in deference to my family and the long term, I felt that my future lay elsewhere. I do not regret that decision.

In years to come, my wife and I introduced our sons to the joys of paddle steamers at age three weeks and five weeks respectively.

Over the years I was able to take part in some of *Waverley*'s more exotic excursions, occasionally as relief or just as an extra watch keeper on the long positioning runs.

Of particular note was an Ayr to Southampton trip, taking around thirty-six hours and just about the entire amount of fuel onboard. I was quite familiar with the area around Land's End, at the extreme south-west tip of England, but as we rolled our way onwards with the intermittent beam of the Longships Lighthouse regularly illuminating the wheelhouse, I nearly had to pinch myself to be sure that I was where I was on what I was on.

At Southampton we berthed astern of a large supertanker and we could not help but notice that the top of her rudder was the same height as *Waverley*'s funnels. Further along the quay lay the P&O liner *Canberra* and in those innocent and less security conscious days, some of us later had little trouble in being allowed access to have a look around this iconic ship.

At other times I was able to experience south coast ports such as Poole, Bournemouth, Torquay and Plymouth, then back round Land's End for a stint in the Bristol Channel with its fearsome tides before returning up the Irish Sea.

During a spell on the Thames there was a rare opportunity to sail under Tower Bridge into the heart of the nation's capital, a great experience, but it was also quite an intense area to work and the need to move to a refuelling jetty in the evenings meant there was little respite.

On yet another occasion there was a positioning trip from the Thames up the English Channel, into the southern North Sea and along the coasts of Suffolk and Norfolk, bound for Hull and Goole. This passage includes an area off East Anglia where an unhappy combination of strong tides and numerous sandbanks keeps navigators on their toes. While serving on the aforementioned *Dunkyle*, I had traversed this area often.

From the Humber, we headed north to Scarborough and Middlesbrough in thick fog. I went home from the latter.

Interesting and enjoyable as these longer trips were, I must admit that for entirely selfish reasons I generally preferred the convenience of being on the Clyde and one of my final outings in local waters was to help not *Waverley* but the motor vessel *Balmoral*.

In 1997 *Balmoral* had been tasked to come north and fulfil a programme of sailings from Glasgow over the September holiday weekend. As neither the ship's master nor mate held local Pilotage Exemption Certificates, I was asked if I could assist as the holder of a still valid licence.

Uncannily, everything fell into place perfectly and on a Wednesday, when I was due home from my own ship, I altered my usual route in favour of a train to Largs. After a coffee and checking on local taxi availability, I simply walked down the pier and stepped aboard when *Balmoral* glided in.

It was a beautiful sunny day and the trip to Glasgow was a real pleasure. Between Friday and Monday I was pilot while the ship did all the scheduled sailings.

Once back in Glasgow after the final sailing, *Balmoral* took on fuel and fresh water, then with the purser's signature tune, 'New York, New York', blaring over the tannoy, off we went back down the channel.

They could go to New York if they wanted to, but my job was to pilot the ship back to Largs. It was a lovely, crystal-clear evening/early morning with not a cloud in the sky and maximum visibility, and soon after departure from Glasgow the master and mate went below to get some sleep ahead of their long passage to Wales – despite what the purser might think! It was a rare joy to be doing such a late night run in near perfect conditions and apart from the fact that a few of the buoys and the Cloch light were extinguished, other lights cast long reflections on the mirror calm waters and nothing troubled us as we made good speed towards Largs.

Nearing destination, the master was called and as he lined the ship up for Largs pier I phoned the local taxi number to discover that contrary to previous assurances there weren't any at this time. When the ship touched the pier I quickly stepped ashore and after watching the stern light disappear into the night I turned around to face my next problem – how to get off the pier. Unknown to me, there was now a tall security gate, closed at night, to deny access to the pier, or in my case bar exit. Obviously designed to deter only the more arthritic of terrorists, I did manage to climb over it after pushing my bag under. Now, how to get home?

A few minutes later on the dark streets of Largs, I encountered two police officers in their patrol car and asked them about taxis while explaining my plight. Noting that I was in uniform and exchanging glances with each other, they told me to get in and gave me a lift to Wemyss Bay station, from where I could phone for a Greenock cab. Quite soon a taxi duly appeared and responded to my raised arm. I wearily got in and when about half way home, my conversation with the driver revealed that his was not the taxi I had phoned for. By then, I was well beyond caring. I should have known better and stuck to the paddler!

Not everything about *Waverley* was fun or easy, and like everything in life there are two sides to the coin. That said, through the ship I have been fortunate to have enjoyed many good times, professionally interesting and fulfilling experiences and a lot of friendship.

I still have a view over the Clyde and we all still have the ship. As a family we have regularly enjoyed sailing on *Waverley* and our sons have grown up with it as part of their lives. They became quite enthusiastic about the paddler and looked forward to every opportunity for a trip during the Clyde season.

I hope that the 'Lady' will go on to enchant us all for many years to come. As for the 'addiction', it is incurable – just accept it!

Captain Murray Paterson
Retired Senior Mater
Stena Line, Stranraer,
March 2014

Prince Ivanhoe Memories

Notes by Jim Buchanan on the year 1980

A very busy and exciting year for me. During the earlier part of the year, I was involved with Waverley Excursions, buying for and setting up the proposed tills from our very highly valued shop on *Waverley*, which involved me, in conjunction with the co-operation and input of valued members of Waverley Excursions and PSPS, with tiring trips involved outwith Scotland, for instance to Tilbury, where I and my wife became white van man and woman stocking *Waverley*'s shop after an overnight drive to the south of England. During the course of my happy involvement with *Waverley*, Terry Sylvester contacted me by telephone and advised me of his close involvement with the proposal to buy in the *Shanklin* and set up a new company, to be known as the Firth of Clyde Steam Packet Company.

He asked me if I would represent Waverley Excursions on the board as nominated chairman of this new operation, in conjunction with Bill Lind, Alan Hamilton, Jim Alexander and of course David Neill. What a challenge that was!

The *Prince Ivanhoe* story which follows, ably researched and coordinated by Iain Quinn, brought back to life for me this most challenging time, culminating in the enormous tragedy of her sinking in Port Eynon Bay. I was happy to co-ordinate as much as I was able to and to create a common purpose among our unpaid board of management for *Prince Ivanhoe*. It was a very intensive time and the year 1980 is certainly brought back into great clarity by Iain's research which follows.

I will very briefly give great tribute to David Neill's involvement, combined with Bill Lind's assistance during her short life and the subsequent sad loss on that sandy bay in South Wales. It was an enterprise which I had hoped would have succeeded and certainly showed great expense of purpose.

*****

A precognition from Jim Buchanan with his involvement with the Firth Clyde Steam Packet Company and *Prince Ivanhoe* in 1980.

My involvement with *Prince Ivanhoe* commenced with a telephone call from Terry Sylvester, the ultimate enthusiast, in collaboration/partnership with Douglas McGowan, both of whom brought their driving enthusiasm and competence by resurrecting the *Waverley* from the time of her purchase from Caledonian MacBrayne to her ongoing story, which in 2014 is still marching on.

I was asked by Terry Sylvester to join the board of the *Waverley* and to look after the shop after Douglas considered that he had every right to expect to be able to retire from the very intensive requirements of managing the shop/buying/stocking/staffing. My business life, which at that time involved running three estate agencies/property manager businesses, was somewhat stressful and I was happy to contribute what I could to setting up and continuing Douglas's activities on the *Waverley*. I received a call from Terry Sylvester advising me that he was looking for subscribers to fund the purchase of *Shanklin* and would I be interested in becoming one of the subscribers of a limited board which would be formed to manage and run the ship in conjunction with the *Waverley*? This followed under Terry's enthusiastic direction and culminated with me being contacted by Terry, asking for thoughts on the naming of *Shanklin*, which we agreed to suggest would be suitably renamed *Prince Ivanhoe*, having an attractive sound to it with the *Ivanhoe* connection being paramount. Terry asked me to become the nominee chairman for the Firth of Clyde Steam Packet Company and set up a board of management which included, of course, Captain David Neill; Ian Hamilton, who had become involved with me in the setting up of *Waverley Times*, produced for circulation for sailings from Glasgow or Ayr in two editions; Bill Lind, who was well known for his helpful enthusiastic involvement in all problems which had been encountered by the *Waverley*; Jim Alexander, with his electrical background and *Waverley* enthusiasm; and Kenneth Mackenzie, whose input in shop management was already established being part of a successful pharmacy business.

Board meetings were set up in the WSN offices and a hectic period thereafter followed, in which the technical aspects of repairing *Ivanhoe*'s port engine were discussed and set up, and with David Neill's technical input *Ivanhoe* was brought to Glasgow, and thence work commenced on the rebuilding of the port engine together with the development of vacant space on the main deck of *Ivanhoe* for a shop. Additionally, and concerning me, was the provision of cabin accommodation to be built, in conjunction with Bill Lind's participation on the lower deck aft of the engine room and the provision of galley and catering facilities forward of the bridge, on the lower main deck, which involved the employment of sub-contractors to work on *Prince Ivanhoe*. A hectic period of meetings involved discussions with the captain, Mike Harkness and subsequently Jimmy Addison as master. The company's offices in Glasgow provided us with accommodation for the considerable board meetings which followed to coordinate the various activities which were required to bring the *Ivanhoe* up to a full complying standard. Bill Lind was a tower of strength in these early days; in fact, he was with the organisation in a major contributory basis right up to the time of eventually attending the enquiry into her unfortunate stranding in Port Eynon Bay. A quiet man, Bill was always there when required and with his considerable involvement in the building trade, he was also very helpful in obtaining answers to the many questions which resulted. Our board was very proud of the standards we achieved with *Prince Ivanhoe* in such a short period of time and I would take this opportunity to say to all those in Waverley Excursions congratulations on rescuing *Prince Ivanhoe* following her demise with British Railways and bringing such colour into what was a dead maritime shell, a living illustration of what can be done when enthusiasts can really turn their hand to achievement.

Jim Buchanan
Former chairman of the Firth of Clyde Steam Packet Co.
Shareholder, WSN Co. Ltd

Waverley Shop

My father, Jim Brackenridge, was born in Glasgow in 1914 and he and his twin brother spent a good deal of time aboard the Clyde steamers, both on the Firth and on the Belfast run, up until the outbreak of the Second World War.

My mother, Betty, was an English Midlander who, apart from trips from Scarborough, had little experience of ships until after the second war and marriage, when they lived on Merseyside and regularly sailed aboard the Steam Packet and the North Wales steamers. My mother, though, was a frustrated shopkeeper, which perhaps explains what was to come!

In my case, I had an early interest in shipping of all kinds and spent a deal of time by the Mersey, river and docks, together with time aboard tugs of the Rea Towing Company.

In practical terms, my father's interests and mine came together at Whitsun 1963, when he decided that a few days R&R might benefit me before my A Levels. We travelled to the Clyde and sailed aboard PS *Jeanie Deans* on the Saturday afternoon from Craigendoran to Tighnabruaich, passing PS *Waverley* in the Kyles, possibly on a round Bute sailing. That was my introduction to Scottish paddle steamers (I had already sailed aboard PS *Ryde* and PS *Whippingham*). The following day was spent aboard PS *Maid of the Loch*. Memory tells me that the weather (and lunch) was magnificent.

My father retired in 1977 and I think it was in 1978 that I spoke to Terry Sylvester at my father's request, to offer his services as a volunteer. Terry asked about his occupation (chartered accountant) and replied that he thought there were enough of them about (!) but that he would bear my father in mind. In the event, it was not until June 1980 that my parents joined the ship as shopkeepers. I believe the catalyst was the non-availability, due to illness, of Bunty Collinson, the long-serving shopkeeper. Thus started seven consecutive years of shop keeping.

My mother kept very limited records of her time aboard and fortunately my sister has kept them. As I can, I have extrapolated from those diaries where my parents got to on *Waverley*'s programmes. They started off at Fleetwood on 9 June 1980 and left after nineteen days on 28 June. This turned out to be their shortest spell. 1981 saw a round Britain journey, starting at Glasgow on 20 April and finishing at Ayr on 5 June, a spell of forty-six days.

1982 was another round Britain trip, lasting forty-nine days, having joined on 19 April at Glasgow and departing at Bristol on 7 June.

1983 was a monster, sixty-four days, joining at Ayr on 12 April and leaving on 15 June at Avonmouth. 1984, 1985 and 1986 followed similar patterns, with times spent aboard amounting to forty-three, twenty-one and thirty-seven days. There were also various spells on the Clyde in September some years but unfortunately the records are not available for those periods.

Turning to life aboard, as everyone with experience of *Waverley* in those days knows, conditions were pretty spartan. She was hardly built with cruising around Britain in mind! In those days, the shop was split in two lengthways by a bulkhead. Behind the bulkhead was a *Porridge*-style double metal bunk and nothing else. No washing facilities or wardrobe, etc. For two pensioners, spending lengthy periods aboard would have required some constitution. Conditions improved after a few years and a double cabin was made available to them. This would, though, have been before the rebuild at Great Yarmouth so it would still have been fairly basic.

As far as life aboard was concerned, my mother was very happy and she made many friends aboard, friendships which continued well after she ceased shop keeping. It was the shop she never had. My father was different. It is fair to say that he lacked the patience to be customer-friendly and I think only really enjoyed the vessel when she was light ship. One diary entry stands out. It may be an exaggeration but on 16 June 1980 there were 1,000 children aboard between Rothesay and Tighnabruich. I would imagine he took to his bunk as refuge that day.

All in all, however, they must have enjoyed their time aboard as they completed seven years and I think they had much satisfaction from helping the ship in a small way.

During their spells aboard, my family would help them in the shop (against the rules nowadays), so it was not totally strange to me when I did a short, sixteen-day spell on the Clyde in July 2012. I can confirm that keeping the shop is hard work and I have admiration for those who do a lot more than I did. All in all, it emphasises just how much my parents contributed in time and effort.

Peter Brackenridge

The *Waverley* Triple Expansion Engine Model

The *Waverley* paddle steamer engine model was a long term project, which I started in August 1973. The *Waverley* at that time was still under the ownership of Caledonian MacBrayne and this would be her final year with Cal Mac.

I was only sixteen years old at the time and had never built an engineering model before, although I had built a few model boats. I was really keen and thought that the engine model would be an interesting challenge. My first sailing on the *Waverley* was in 1970 and I was always fascinated by the 2,100 horse power engine driving the paddle wheels.

Contact was made with the chief superintendent engineer, R. G. Brand, at Caledonian MacBrayne's headquarters at Gourock and I travelled through to see if I could borrow some of the main engine drawings. The engineering team there were very helpful and allowed me to borrow six of the massive drawing sheets. These were far too big for me to photocopy but I could study and record the necessary dimensions to let me start the project. I also had a tour of the company's bakery and was fascinated by the pie making machine. When I returned the drawings to them after a couple of weeks, I was surprised to find that they had photocopied all of the remaining engine drawings for me.

So a start was made in 1973 and a decision was made to build the model to a large scale of 1:8, which works out at 1½ inches to the foot. This would give model cylinder dimensions of a 3-inch diameter for the high pressure, 4⅞ inches for the middle pressure and a very big 7¾-inch diameter for the low pressure piston. Together with a stroke of 8¼ inches, this was going to be a very large model indeed and I would need to use substantial pieces of metal in its construction. To give you an idea of what was required, the crank webs would need to be machined from 1 inch thick steel.

I will not go into any detail about the construction of the model as there is just too much to cover. It was an ambitious project to tackle with very little engineering experience, but I had just passed my Higher Metalwork Exam and had a small workshop but also had access to larger machinery. I do not think I realised what I had taken on and as work progressed it was doubtful if the project would ever be completed. I did lose interest on more than one occasion, but usually a trip on the *Waverley* would rekindle my enthusiasm.

The time scale was in years and although I started in 1973 it was, after a struggle, almost complete in 1989. One stumbling block was the three large steam pipes between the cylinders and the main exhaust from the LP to the condenser. Luckily, CalMac had followed my progress with interest and I received a visit from Mr R. Brand, who had come to view the nearly completed model. On informing him that I had difficulty with shaping and bending these four pipes, he came up with a solution. He very kindly organised for these to be manufactured by James Lamont's shipyard in Port Glasgow/Greenock. In due course, the pipes were made by Lamont's and delivered to me by Willie Carmichael, who was a member of CalMac's mobile repair unit. Previously, he worked for the company as second and chief engineer. An interesting fact about the pipes is that as far as I know, Lamont's also made the real ones for the *Waverley*.

After a period of seventeen years the model was complete and in steam, working as a fully operational triple expansion model with condenser and air pump. It steamed up beautifully and all worked well with all valve timing correctly set. I was also able to go forward or reverse with the use of the steam operated reversing engine, adjusting the radius links and motion. To see this model running under its own steam was a joy. The sound of it working and the smell of the hot oil were just superb. I finally had completed a 1:8 scale model of the *Waverley*'s engine and just as fascinating to watch.

Now that the engine was complete and working, there wasn't anything to show the scale of the model. Another decision was made, to construct the engine room around three sides of the model, also adding the hull and companionway on one side. This again was a mammoth task, due to the fact that hull frames have to be bent to shape and all of the hull plates would need to be riveted in place. To assist with this procedure, aluminium angle was used with aluminium sheet metal and all of this was assembled using hundreds of rivets. Once this was completed and fitted to the model, it gave the model 'scale' and produced a good background for close up photographs.

I thought at this stage that the model was finally complete. Family, friends, Scouts and other groups would visit the house to see the model in action. Then one visitor commented, 'But what does it do?' He could see a crankshaft running across a model engine room but not driving anything. So guess what? Yes, I decided to add to the model and construct one paddle wheel and connect it to the crankshaft. This would make the model self-explanatory. However, I did not stop there and kept going by adding one complete paddle box with paddle sponson. This, of course, was another challenge, with a fully working feathering paddle wheel.

So at last, after a total of twenty years, the model is finished. It has been an interesting experience and I have learned a great deal in the process. I really appreciate the engineers of the Clyde shipyards: true pioneers of engineering.

The main engine performed well over the years and has been in steam many times. At the moment it has suffered a condenser failure and this was due to my inexperience of metals and their properties. I did notice that the drawings stated that the condenser tubes should be manufactured from Admiralty grade brass as this has low zinc content. I just used normal brass pipes, which have high zinc content. At that time, I did not know that water and steam would remove all of the zinc from the pipes, a process known as dezincification. The result of this is that all of the condenser tubes have become porous and the only solution will be to re-tube. The main engine is fine and will be able to steam again after repairs have been completed to the condenser.

What next? Well, the engine model is trapped in the attic and it is a great shame that it cannot be viewed by more people. Perhaps I will need to plan ahead and arrange for the model to go on loan to a suitable museum. It will not be possible to remove the model in one piece due to its size and weight. It would need to be partially dismantled into three main sections and then reassembled again, so another challenge lies ahead.

My thanks go to Caledonian MacBrayne and especially Mr R. G. Brand, without whose help and advice this model would not have been possible.

Robert McLuckie
20 April 2014

The model engine, showing the crankshaft and the valve gear.

The model feathering paddle wheel and paddle box.

Waverley's Preservation: An Enthusiast's View

Like many of the post-war generation, those who would later be known as the Baby Boomers, I grew up with an abundance of Clyde steamers. From an early age, a steamer trip was an essential part of summer, with the Saturday afternoon sailing by *Jeanie Deans* from Gourock to Tighnabruaich being a favourite family trip. Great was the disappointment when *Waverley* replaced *Jeanie* on the run. *Waverley* was in her youth then, and did not have the appeal of the pre-war steamers. But the steamer fleet was diminishing in these days. The turbine *Marchioness of Graham*, on which I was told I had sailed to Arran in 1954, although I have no memory of so doing, was withdrawn after the 1957 season and was sold to Greece in early 1959 and the paddle steamer *Jupiter* did not sail after the 1957 season, being laid up until she was sold for scrapping in April 1961. I remember meeting family friends, who had been on holiday in Islay, at Gourock off MacBrayne's *Saint Columba* in 1958. She had the distinction of being the final pre-1914 steamer to be in service on the Clyde.

In 1963, at the age of thirteen, I was allowed by my parents to purchase a seven-day runabout ticket for the Clyde sailings and connecting train services. A meticulous study of the timetables ensured that I could sail on as many steamers as possible and call at as many piers as possible in the time allowed, although this was six days rather than seven, Sunday being most definitely devoted to going to church.

The steamers then in operation were the two turbine Duchesses; the paddle steamers *Jeanie Deans*, *Waverley* and the Ayr-based *Caledonia*; the all-the-way turbine *Queen Mary II*, which with a starting time of 11 a.m. was difficult to fit into the itinerary; the diesel-electric paddler *Talisman*, on the Wemyss Bay–Largs–Millport service; the four diesel Maids on shorter trips, including the 'Forenoon café cruises', which included a free cup of coffee and chocolate biscuit; and the car ferries, *Arran*, *Bute* and *Cowal* serving Dunoon and Rothesay, and the larger *Glen Sannox* on the Arran run, not forgetting the smaller craft *Ashton* and *Leven* on the Largs to Millport route and *Countess of Breadalbane*, appearing here and there on various odd services, not always on timetabled services, e.g. she ran an evening Rothesay to Tighnabruaich service on Mondays and Wednesdays in connection with the Arran via the Kyles service, and a Dunoon to Largs run on Tuesdays and Thursdays in connection with the Loch Eck Tour.

In 1964, I again had a Runabout ticket. That was the final year in service of *Jeanie Deans* and *Duchess of Montrose* and I managed to fit in some parts of the Firth that I had missed in the previous summer. By 1965, my father had opened a camera shop in Paisley and I stared working there in the summer months, only able to catch the odd day trip here and there on the Firth. *Talisman* was withdrawn at the end of 1966, *Caledonia* and MacBrayne's diesel-electric *Lochfyne* after the 1969 season and *Duchess of Hamilton* after the 1970 season. From the beginning of 1969 ownership of the steamer-operating company Caledonian Steam Packet passed from British Railways to the Scottish Transport Group. 1973 saw the merger of the Caledonian Steam Packet and David MacBrayne Ltd to form Caledonian MacBrayne. By now there were only two Clyde steamers left, *Queen Mary II* and *Waverley*, plus the turbine *King George V* at Oban and the paddle steamer *Maid of the Loch* on Loch Lomond.

The number of piers and destinations had decreased alarmingly as well as the network changed from one with long routes based at the Victorian railheads to one of short routes geared to car ferry traffic. The Ayr-based steamer service had ceased after 1964, the 'doon-the-watter' sailings from Glasgow (Bridge Wharf) in 1969, calls at Millport (Keppel) Pier in 1971 although this reopened just as this book went to press in summer 2014, due to the closure of Millport (Old) Pier, sailings from the north bank terminal of Craigendoran in 1972, and sailings to Arrochar and Inveraray and calls at Lochranza in 1972.

There had been some promotion of *Waverley* by the Paddle Steamer Preservation Society (PSPS), and her paddle boxes had been painted black with a white surround in 1972. The announcement of her withdrawal from service after the end of the 1973 season came as no surprise, just another act in the ongoing decline of the much-loved Clyde steamer services.

The news the following May that she had been sold to the PSPS came as a pleasant surprise, although I little suspected that they would be able to get the steamer in service again, but I surmised that she would lie somewhere on the Clyde as a floating museum or a pub, like *Caledonia* on the Thames. It was wonderful news when I heard, early in 1975, that she would be operating that summer. When the timetable was published, it was exciting to see a variety of sailings from Glasgow, where for my lifetime they had been purely to Tighnabruaich, and the revival of day sailings from Ayr after a gap of ten years since *Caledonia* had stopped running from there.

By this time I was married and other matters took priority over my free time, but I managed a trip on *Waverley* on her second weekend in service at the end of May. More trips followed in that and the next season, including a long day trip up Loch Fyne to Inveraray, a special sailing to Cairnryan, followed by a cruise to off Portpatrick and regular sailings to Tighnabruaich, Rothesay and Brodick. I grew to recognise and get to know those of the enthusiast fraternity who were involved with the running of the steamer and who were approachable, unlike the professional seafarers of CalMac. The beginnings of lifelong friendships emerged in those early years of *Waverley*'s preservation.

In May 1977, my wife and I went down to Liverpool in early May to sail on *Waverley* on her first sailing outwith the Clyde, from Liverpool to Llandudno and a cruise to Puffin Island. It was an interesting trip, but the long passage over open water out past the Bar, and the distance of the scenery for the majority of the trip, meant that it was not a patch on sailing on the Clyde with its lochs and mountains.

The birth of our daughter Melanie in June of that year brought new challenges. She was taken on her first trip on *Waverley* when she was three weeks old and the sails on the paddler continued. She was made welcome in the shop by Bunty, who, sadly, became seriously ill in 1980 and died in early 1981.

Occasional business trips to the south over the following few years were combined with trips on the steamer, once from London to Southend, once from Bournemouth to Swanage and off Lulworth Cove, and once round from Ryde round the Isle of Wight. Twice in the years that she was on the Firth of Forth, I sailed on her. I have memories of very choppy weather on one of those occasions, when we were attempting to berth at Burntisland.

In 1978 a holiday in Switzerland introduced me to the delights of paddle steamers on the Swiss lakes and holidays over the next thirty-five years were spent, in the main, visiting and sailing on preserved paddle and screw steamers across Europe and North America. But my first love was the Clyde steamers and I managed a sail on *Waverley* on several occasions each year.

In 1981 my marriage broke up and my children and I moved back to live with my parents. Sailings on *Waverley* continued, including an annual visit to the West Highlands, normally for a single day with a bus connection from Glasgow and a sail to Iona or up past Ardnamurchan Point and the Small Isles to Armadale. These trips have continued, with sailings to Inverie on Loch Nevis and to the island of Rum to land. In 2013 stormy weather conditions meant that a cruise to Loch Sunart and time ashore at Tobermory had to be substituted for a trip to Inverie.

It has given me enormous pleasure to sail aboard *Waverley* over the past thirty-nine years under the WSN flag, to enjoy the sight and smell of the steam machinery, and to visits parts of the British coastline that I would otherwise never have visited.

Alistair Deayton

Crew Photos

The crew and directors at Rothesay Pier, 1975, including George Train, Douglas McGowan and Peter Reid (all below forward funnel) and the external contractor's catering staff.

Officers, 1975. From left: Alan Condie, Ian Muir, the captain, Angus McLean, Murray Paterson and Alistair Goldsmith.

Chief engineer Keith Blacklock and mate Robin Barr on the bridge, 1977.

Sharing chat on the *Prince Ivanhoe*, 1981.

The Fortieth Anniversary celebration, 1987, in the Jeanie Deans Lounge. From left: J. Terry Sylvester, David K. Duncanson, Lord Provost of Glasgow David Hodge, James M. Moore, Douglas McGowan and Peter Reid.

From left: Comedian Ronnie Barker, Craig Peacock, catering manager, and Jim McFadzean, purser. The date was 19 October 2003.

The captain with Captain Jimmy Addison, a valuable contributor to WSN's success.

Bosun Roddy McIsaac with his dog at home at Howmore, South Uist. A lovely, genuine and loyal character. Roddy's contribution was huge and his humour essential.

Timetables and Publicity

The first leaflet to promote *Waverley*, produced by Terry Sylvester in 1971. The reverse side included a list of *Waverley*'s sailings for the 1971 season and the membership form for the Paddle Steamer Preservation Society. The photograph of *Waverley* was taken by a young Andrew Clark.

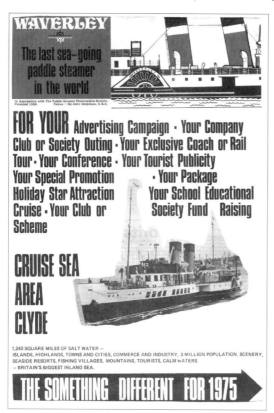

The first publicity brochure to obtain bookings, distributed in autumn 1974. Note the funnel and paddle box logo showing the differently raked funnels.

The 1975 timetable from Ayr and Troon. Note the Tuesday cruise to Tarbet, which survives in the timetable to this day, now on a Wednesday. Similar timetables were issued from each Clyde departure point, with the header in different colours for each place.

Timetables and Publicity

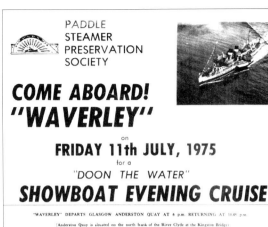

A flyer for a PSPS evening cruise 'Doon the Watter' in the first season under preservation, on 11 July 1975.

The timetable for the spell in 1977 when *Queen of Scots* deputised for *Waverley* following the Gantocks grounding.

```
PADDLE STEAMER PRESERVATION SOCIETY

PROVISIONAL ARRANGEMENTS FOR
WAVERLEY'S SPRING VISIT TO THE SOUTH COAST

It is hoped that WAVERLEY will be able to visit the South Coast this spring
and the cruise information given below is the very latest provided by the
Waverley office. YOUR SUPPORT FOR THIS VENTURE IS VITAL so please contact
the agents shown for further details and make your bookings for these unique
sailings as soon as possible. If applying to Stobcross Quay, please state
if you are a P.S.P.S. member.


SAT. 22 APRIL  - Newhaven 10.00, for day cruise passing Shanklin and Ventnor.
SUN. 23 APRIL  - Newhaven 10.00, Worthing 11.45 for day cruise to Ryde.
MON. 24 APRIL  - Schools cruises from Newhaven.
WED. 26 APRIL
THU. 27 APRIL  - Schools cruises from Deal and Clacton.
SAT. 29 APRIL  - Tower Pier 10.00 for day trip to Southend and sea cruise from
                 Southend 13.45 (not calling at Greenwich)
SUN. 30 APRIL  - Tower Pier 10.00, Greenwich 10.30 for day trip to Southend
                 and sea cruise from Southend 13.45
MON.  1 MAY    - Greenwich 9.30, Southend 12.30, Clacton 15.00 and afternoon
                 cruise from Clacton.
TUE.  2 MAY
WED.  3 MAY    - Schools cruises from Greenwich.
THU.  4 MAY    - Schools cruises from Tilbury, Southend and Clacton.
FRI.  5 MAY    - Schools cruises from Tilbury, Southend and Deal.
SUN.  7 MAY    - Clacton 09.30 for day cruise to Deal.
TUE.  9 MAY
WED. 10 MAY    - Schools cruises from Newhaven.
THU. 11 MAY    - Schools cruises from Portsmouth and Ryde.
FRI. 12 MAY    - Senior Citizens and Senior Schools cruise from Southampton
                 11.00.
SAT. 13 MAY    - Southampton 10.00 for cruise around Isle of Wight, calling
                 at Bournemouth with afternoon cruise from there at 15.00.
SUN. 14 MAY    - Southampton 10.00 for day cruise to Ryde and Worthing.
MON. 15 MAY    - Senior schools cruise from Southampton to Bournemouth.
                 Return trip from Bournemouth 14.00 to Southampton.
                 Evening cruise from Bournemouth 20.00 to Poole.
TUE. 16 MAY    - Schools cruises from Poole and Bournemouth.
                 Evening cruise from Poole 19.00, Bournemouth 20.00

                                                              P.T.O.
```

A provisional list of *Waverley*'s first south coast sailings in 1978. Note the number of schools cruises, a revenue earning stream that is now defunct.

The 1978 Clyde timetable, the first in a newspaper style.

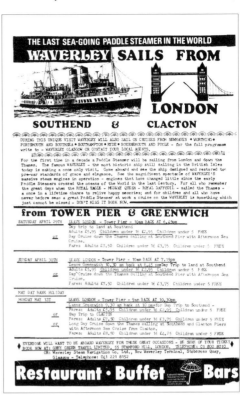

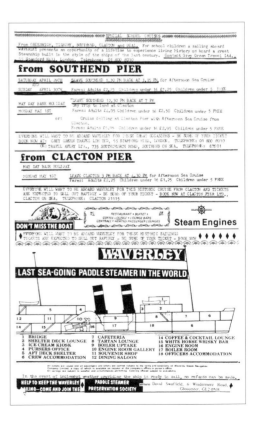

This page: The handbill for the first cruises from London, Southend and Clacton, spring 1978.

The spring 1981 timetable 'Steaming round Britain', with cruises from the south coast, the Thames, Humber, Tees, Tyne and Forth, and a couple of days in the West Highlands on the homeward leg.

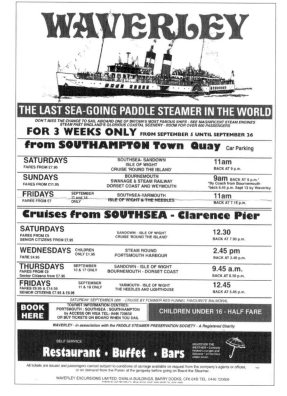

An example, dating from 1992, of the many advertising cards produced for all departure points on the Clyde, Bristol Channel and Solent and in North Wales. Thousands of these were sent to, or personally delivered to, and displayed in hotels, guest houses, steam railways, museums and tourist information centres. Later versions were produced in full colour.

Inclusive Cruising Holidays in North Wales

from **£159** per person

See North Wales glorious coast & islands

You will enjoy some of the World's finest scenery on our unique Cruising Holiday. The spectacular Menai Straits the excitement of sailing under Telford's beautiful Suspension Bridge - a glorious cruise 'Round the Island of Anglesey' & be aboard the first sailings to Blackpool since pre-war days. These are pleasures that you can only experience aboard Balmoral - don't miss the opportunity- book now!

Ffestiniog Steam Railway & Portmerion Village

... &, as an extra delight to the magnificent cruising programme, you'll enjoy 1 day of your holiday taking a memorable journey through the Snowdonia National Park on the famous Ffestiniog Steam Railway. Your historic steam locomotive will take you through remote areas, magnificent forests, past lakes & waterfalls- the journey of a lifetime- & you will then enjoy a visit to the fairy-tale village of Portmerion -created by Sir Clough Williams-Ellis & the famous setting of many television programmes

Stay at the Lynwood Hotel - off the Promenade - a lovely Victorian 'Upstairs Downstairs' property, privately owned & under the personal supervision of the owners - just a stroll along the promenade to the Victorian Pier, to join your cruise ship.

Beautifully restored, in association with the Paddle Steamer Preservation Society- a Registered Charity- your cruise ship Balmoral is 200 feet long, with room aboard for almost 700 passengers. Centrally heated lounges-traditional promenade decks-self service restaurant & snack buffet-even a souvenir shop & post-box-& the lounge bars will be open throughout your cruises

A 1990 leaflet for two inclusive cruising holidays organised and led by Sue Koops. The reverse side included the full six-day programme.

Further Reading

Birth of a Legend, Paddle Steamer Preservation Society (Scottish Branch), 1987.
Brown, Alan, *Craigendoran Steamers*, Humber Paddle Steamer Group, 1975.
Brown, Alan, *Craigendoran Steamers*, Aggregate Publications Ltd, Johnstone, Renfrewshire, 1979 (second edition).
Brown, Alan, *Shanklin: Ill Fated Prince*, Waverley Excursions Ltd, 1985.
Brown, Alan, *Craigendoran Steamers*, Waverley Excursions Ltd, 2007 (third edition).
Cameron, Stuart and Joe McKendrick, *Waverley: A Legend Reborn, The Completed Heritage Rebuild*, Waverley Excursions Ltd, 2003 (second edition)
Clyde River Steamer Club, Special Excursion booklet, 23 May 1970 (Photographic history of *Waverley*).
Clyde River Steamer Club, Special Excursion booklet, 4 September 1971 (With history of *Waverley*).
Clyde River Steamer Club Review, 1971–2012. (Annual publication. *Waverley* is covered season by season.)
Clyde Steamers Vol. 2 (1966) (Ardrishaig visit, 1966); Vol. 14 (1978) (Irvine visit, 22 August 1978); Vol. 23 (1987) (Photos); Vol. 29 (1993). (Annual magazine of the Clyde River Steamer Club)
Deayton, Alistair and Iain Quinn, *PS Waverley: The First Sixty Years*, Tempus Publishing/The History Press, Stroud, Gloucestershire, 2007. (Photographs of *Waverley* at places she has called at and in various conditions.)
Down to see the Engines, Waverley Excursions Ltd, 1985.
Coton, Richard H., *PS Waverley: Last in the World*, Paddle Steamer Preservation Society, 1973.
Henderson, K. J. and R. J. Ramsay, *Paddle Steamer Machinery: A Layman's Guide* (Second edition), Paddle Steamer Preservation Society, 2001. (Covers machinery post-rebuild.)
McGowan, Douglas, *Waverley: The World's Last sea-going paddle steamer*, Clyde & Bonnie (Publishers) Ltd, Kilchattan Bay, Isle of Bute, 1984.
McGowan, Douglas, *Waverley: Paddler for a Pound*, Tempus Publishing/The History Press, Stroud, Gloucestershire, 2000.

Muir, Ian W., *Dinosaur Down Below: The Adventures of a Foreign-Going Paddle-Boat Man*, Peveril Publications, Neilston, Glasgow, 1980.

Nicholson, John, *Waverley and other Paddle Steamers*, Waverley Steam Navigation Co. Ltd, 1975. (A children's colouring book.)

Paddle Steamer Preservation Society (Scottish Branch), *Paddle Steamer "Waverley" charters 1972: Ormidale 21st May, Inveraray 23rd September*.

Paddle Steamer Preservation Society, *Paddle Steamer Waverley, 1992 Onwards* (Scottish Branch). (Daily diary.)

Paddle Wheels 1974–99. (Quarterly magazine of the Paddle Steamer Preservation Society.)

Ramsay, R. J., *Paddle Steamer Machinery: A Layman's Guide*, Waverley Excursions Ltd, 1995.

Shirres, David, *A Simple Guide to the PS Waverley's Machinery*, 2013. (Sold on board.)

Waverley: The Story of the World's Last Sea-Going Paddle Steamer, Waverley Steam Navigation Co. Ltd (eleven editions 1976–2011). (Souvenir booklet sold on board.)

Waverley: The Golden Jubilee, Allan T. Condie Publications, Nuneaton, and Waverley Excursions Ltd, 1997.

Whittle, John, *Speed Bonnie Boat*, Saltire Publications Ltd, Edinburgh, 1990.

Final Thoughts

As you will have read, the preservation of *Waverley* was far from easy. These men took very brave decisions, from John Whittle and Caledonian MacBrayne/the Scottish Transport Group, who decided to withdraw from service the last real Clyde paddle steamer, through to their gift to the nation for just a token gesture.

Western Ferries, a new company themselves in 1974, made very commendable gestures to Waverley Steam Navigation Co. Ltd by way of crew for *Waverley*. We pay a real tribute to Andrew Wilson, managing director of the company, for his loyalty and to Iain Harrison for his invaluable commitment for many years, and to those men from Western Ferries who made the *Waverley* sail again.

To the founding fathers of Waverley Steam Navigation, well done for the determination and will to succeed in the face of adversity. You all deserve tribute.

To George Train, whose timetables and love for the *Waverley* from 1975 until his death in 2006 were well-known. His legacy lives on with the Wednesday schedule on the Firth of Clyde form Ayr to Tarbert. Many thousands of passengers, and money to keep *Waverley* sailing, have and will be earned from that day alone. It was George Train who planned the cruise schedule, many of the sailings remaining as such.

To those directors sadly no longer with us and the crew members gone before, we record their contribution collectively.

John Innes, who designed the WSN house flag in 1974, based on the LNER house flag, deserves acknowledgement.

The volunteers who served in the shop: Bunty and Reg Collinson, Jim and Betty Brackenridge and the shop managers, Douglas McGowan, Jim Buchanan and the late Dr Joe McKendrick. The contribution from them is huge.

In among the vast array of others whose commitment to the company has been of value, we single out J. Terry Sylvester and his family for never failing to stand by their firm beliefs that *Waverley* should continue and the strong message that the last paddle steamer should not be destroyed. To his family, we must say you have tolerated all this so well over so many years.

One thing is for certain: passengers are *Waverley*'s future. Take them away and she fails. At every pier possible the gangway must go out and take 6 or 600 passengers aboard.

Everyone counts for success and all involved in this book recognise this vital task in *Waverley*'s life.

I firmly believe *Waverley* will go on for many more years, as do my companions in this book. We have all taken part in what has been one of the finest examples of heritage preservation of maritime interest in the UK. We did it for you, and to all who have supported *Waverley* we owe our debt for backing us all the way. We hope you have enjoyed our story of how Waverley Steam Navigation Company Limited got through it all. Somehow, it tells me that in today's climate it may not have started at all. *Waverley* most definitely has had a valuable and committed team.

The final tribute goes to *Waverley* herself, the true personality of this book. We all hope the last true burst of colour on the Clyde, and elsewhere, continues for many seasons to come.

Iain Quinn

For timetables and information contact:
http://www.waverleyexcursions.co.uk/
Waverley Excursions Ltd.
36 Lancefield Quay
Glasgow
G3 8HA
Tel: 0141 221 8152

For information on the Paddle Steamer Preservation Society go to:
http://www.paddlesteamers.org/
and the information leaflet available on board

This publication marks the span of forty years of WSN Co. Ltd. It is our collective wish that you continue to support *Waverley*, the last sea-going paddle steamer in the world, now and way into the future – keep sailing and enjoy the last ever opportunities to cruise our coast, islands and lochs and the Firth of Clyde.

Photographic Credits and Acknowledgments

We wish to thank the following for the use of photographs and assistance with text: Mrs Sue Koops, Ashley Gill, Edward and Iain Quinn, Derek Peters, Harry Hay, Robert McLuckie, Peter Brackenridge, the many, many contributors to the captain's collection, J. Terry Sylvester, D. W. McGowan, Chris Jones, I. A. Somerville, Alistair Deayton, Captain J. Murray Paterson, who gave us free access to his vast archive, the local history department of South Ayrshire Council and Keith Robertson for the WSN house flag. Thanks also to Alistair Deayton for editing.

Can we thank all the contributors for their efforts, research and unique contributions.

If we have forgotten anybody please accept our apologies. This publication would not be possible without them all.

Who Owns *Waverley* and *Balmoral*?

The ships are owned by Waverley Steam Navigation Company Limited, a charity. Waverley Excursions Limited operates the ships and is wholly owned by Waverley Steam Navigation. The Paddle Steamer Preservation Society, also a charity, is the major shareholder, and therefore has the controlling interest in Waverley Steam Navigation.

You can support the future of *Waverley* and *Balmoral* by joining the Paddle Steamer Preservation Society. Annual membership costs only £23 with reductions for senior citizens, junior members (under eighteen), couples and senior couples. There is also life membership for £450. Membership application forms are available from PSPS, 17 Stockfield Close, Hazlemere, High Wycombe, HP15 7LA or you can pick up a membership form on board Waverley.

Members receive four copies every year of the society's magazine, *Paddle Wheels*, which contains free tickets for children, 20 per cent off tickets to sail aboard PS *Kingswear Castle* on the River Dart, and other benefits. The society will welcome you aboard.

By the time of publication of this book, ownership of *Balmoral* may have been transferred to a separate charity of which the Paddle Steamer Preservation Society will remain the major, and controlling, shareholder.

Business Principles

Although *Waverley* and *Balmoral* are charity owned, the principal income to continue to maintain the ships and sail them has to be earned by running the business. The following quotes, from professionals, provide essential reminders to everyone running any business.

'Publicity is a most important function of any organisation relying for the bulk of its funds on public participation'.

'Marketing either controls or influences decisions. We must be a marketing-led organisation'.

'Money is made from marketing, not manufacture'.

'Marketing is the way in which a firm identifies and adapts to changes in its environment and exploits them for the purpose of profitable survival'.

'Only some 14 per cent of all households comprise the "classic" family of two adults and two children. Over two-thirds of all households do not contain children'.

'Some 73 per cent of marketing budgets are spent in newspapers with 19 per cent spent on TV advertising'.

'We serve mainly pensioners during the week – they are the ones with the money to spend today'.

'Heritage is about using history for marketing purposes'.

'Management is doing things right, whereas leadership is doing the right thing'.

'As chief executive you've fot to play a number of roles: you've got to be a figurehead at times, involved in all aspects of the business, supportive and motivational. You've also got to build external relationships, whether it's with suppliers or advisors, and you've got to coordinate across the business functions'.

'Those who wish to destroy only have to win once; those who wish to preserve have to win every time'.